PUBLIC ADMINISTRATION IN THE MIDDLE EAST AND NORTH AFRICA

This book examines the status of public administration in eight countries—the United Arab Emirates (UAE), Turkey, Lebanon, Jordan, Morocco, Tunisia, Sudan, and Libya—in the Middle East and North Africa (MENA). This volume explores the issues, perspectives, traditions, and cultures that shape the operation of public administration in the region. This book also offers critical narratives on how the region's governments manage the state and statecrafts regarding their governance design. It reflects on the multiplicity of public administration structures, functions, processes, and procedures, as well as reform schemes, which are critical in achieving good governance to continuously improve the human condition in the MENA region. *Public Administration in the Middle East and North Africa* will be of interest to scholars, practitioners, and students concerned with the ways in which technological change, knowledge accumulation, and dissemination can increase a state's effective governance capacity.

Shahjahan Bhuiyan is an Associate Professor of Public Administration at The American University in Cairo (AUC), Egypt. Currently, he is the Associate Dean for Undergraduate Studies and Administration in the School of Global Affairs and Public Policy at AUC. He has published a number of books, book chapters, and journal articles.

"*Public Administration in the Middle East and North Africa* is a welcome addition to the comparative public administration cannon. This edited volume increases the field's knowledge about public administration about an underexplored region."

Trevor Brown, *Dean at John Glenn College of Public Affairs, The Ohio State University & President of Network of Schools of Public Policy, Affairs, and Administration (NASPAA)*

"This book is a valuable addition to the small but growing literature on public administration and governance in the Middle East and North Africa. The wide variety of topics covered in the book would be of great benefit to scholars as well as practitioners of public administration, public policy, and development studies."

M Ramesh, *Professor & UNESCO Chair of Social Policy Design in Asia, Lee Kuan Yew School of Public Policy, National University of Singapore & President of International Public Policy Association (IPPA)*

PUBLIC ADMINISTRATION IN THE MIDDLE EAST AND NORTH AFRICA

Edited by Shahjahan Bhuiyan

NEW YORK AND LONDON

First published 2023
by Routledge
605 Third Avenue, New York, NY 10158

and by Routledge
4 Park Square, Milton Park, Abingdon, Oxon, OX14 4RN

Routledge is an imprint of the Taylor & Francis Group, an informa business

© 2023 Taylor & Francis

The right of Shahjahan Bhuiyan to be identified as the author of the editorial material, and of the authors for their individual chapters, has been asserted in accordance with sections 77 and 78 of the Copyright, Designs and Patents Act 1988.

All rights reserved. No part of this book may be reprinted or reproduced or utilised in any form or by any electronic, mechanical, or other means, now known or hereafter invented, including photocopying and recording, or in any information storage or retrieval system, without permission in writing from the publishers.

Trademark notice: Product or corporate names may be trademarks or registered trademarks, and are used only for identification and explanation without intent to infringe.

Library of Congress Cataloging-in-Publication Data
Names: Bhuiyan, Shahjahan, editor.
Title: Public administration in the Middle East and North Africa / edited by Shahjahan Bhuiyan.
Description: New York, NY : Routledge, 2023. | Includes bibliographical references and index. |
Identifiers: LCCN 2022061873 (print) | LCCN 2022061874 (ebook) | ISBN 9781032486215 (hardback) | ISBN 9781032485348 (paperback) | ISBN 9781003389941 (ebook)
Subjects: LCSH: Public administration--Middle East. | Public administration--Africa, North. | Middle East--Politics and government. | Africa, North--Politics and government.
Classification: LCC JQ1758.A58 P85 2023 (print) | LCC JQ1758.A58 (ebook) | DDC 351.56--dc23/eng/20230310
LC record available at https://lccn.loc.gov/2022061873
LC ebook record available at https://lccn.loc.gov/2022061874

ISBN: 978-1-032-48621-5 (hbk)
ISBN: 978-1-032-48534-8 (pbk)
ISBN: 978-1-003-38994-1 (ebk)

DOI: 10.4324/9781003389941

Typeset in Bembo
by KnowledgeWorks Global Ltd.

My mother passed away while I was working on this project. Unfortunately, I was unable to even bade her goodbye as she embarked on her eternal journey. This has torn a deep hole in my heart, one that perhaps will not be mended until we meet again. This book is dedicated in her loving memory.

CONTENTS

List of figures	*ix*
List of tables	*x*
List of contributors	*xi*
Foreword B. Guy Peters	*xiv*
List of acronyms	*xvii*
Acknowledgments	*xix*
Introduction	*xxi*

PART I
Public administration in the Middle East countries   1

1. Theory and practice of public administration reforms: The case of the United Arab Emirates   3
   Abu Elias Sarker and Mohammad Habibur Rahman

2. Reconstruction of Turkish public administration under the new presidential government system   20
   Yılmaz Üstüner

3. Public administration in the republic of Lebanon: Recent reforms, current constraints, and future prospects   34
   Thomas W. Haase

4. Public administration and development in Jordan   62
   Jamil E. Jreisat

PART II
Public administration in North African countries   81

5 Governance and public administration reform in
   Morocco: A "glocal" perspective   83
   Rabia Naguib

6 Institutional and economic reforms challenges during a
   democratic transition: A case study from Tunisia   105
   Nizar Jouini and Taoufik Rajhi

7 The erosion of public administration in Sudan   123
   Ibrahim Elnur

8 Libya's public administration: Burdens of the
   past and challenges of transition   134
   Youssef Mohammad Sawani

Index   *175*

FIGURES

1.1	From DGEP to Fourth-Generation Excellence—Shift toward Vision and Innovation	10
2.1	Organizational Layout of the Turkish Presidency	23
2.2	Attached Institutions of the Turkish Presidency	25
6.1	Number of Yearly Legalized Reforms within the Parliament	106
6.2	Reform Project Cycle	110
6.3	Evaluation and Follow-up System Graph	117

TABLES

1.1 Governance Indicators in the UAE   14
1.2 E-Government Development Index   14

CONTRIBUTORS

Shahjahan Bhuiyan is an Associate Professor of Public Administration at The American University in Cairo's School of Global Affairs and Public Policy (GAPP). Currently, he is the Associate Dean for Undergraduate Studies and Administration at GAPP. He has published books, book chapters, journal symposia, and articles in refereed journals such as *Public Administration and Development, Government Information Quarterly, Habitat International, Information Development, International Journal of Public Administration, Politics & Policy,* City, *Culture and Society, Journal of Asian and African Studies, Public Organization Review,* and the *International Journal of Public Sector Management.*

Ibrahim Elnur was the Chair of the Political Science Department at The American University in Cairo (AUC) from 2013 to 2016. He was previously the Director of the Middle East Research Awards at the Population Council in Cairo and Co-founder and Coordinator of the Group for Alternative Policies for Sudan (GAPS). He is a member of the editorial board of the European Training Foundation (ETF) in Turin, Italy, and was an elected member of the Internal Conflicts Sub-Committee of the International Peace Research Association (IPRA) Conference: Building Sustainable Futures, Enacting Peace and Development, Leuven. He is the author *of Contested Sudan: The Political Economy of War and Reconstruction* (2009).

Thomas W. Hasse is an Associate Professor at Sam Houston State University's Political Science Department. Prior to joining Sam Houston, he served as an Assistant Professor in the Department of Political Science and Public Administration at the American University of Beirut. Dr. Hasse has published several articles in refereed journals.

Nizer Jouini is an Associate Professor of Public Policy at the Doha Institute for Graduate Studies' School of Public Administration and Development Economics. Dr. Jouini has more than 15 years of experience in program evaluation, cost-benefit analysis, and econometric modeling. He served as an economics consultant in the African Development Bank for over ten years. He is a research associate in the CEQ Institute, one of the leading institutes, working to reduce poverty and inequality and increase active engagement with the policy community. Dr. Jouini speaks and frequently writes on policy analysis and evidence-based policy analysis issues in Arab countries. His articles have appeared in journals such as *Politics & Policy*, the *Canadian Journal of Development Studies* and the *Journal of Development Economics*.

Jamil E. Jreisat (deceased) served as a Professor of Public Administration at South Florida University. He was a globally renowned scholar in the field of public administration. He published numerous books, book chapters and journal articles.

Rabia Naguib is an Associate Professor of Public Policy at the Doha Institute for Graduate Studies' School of Public Administration and Development Economics. Her publications have appeared in *Gender in Management: An International Journal*, *International Journal of Business Strategy*, *Journal of Business Ethics*, and the *International Journal of Productivity and Performance Management*.

Mohammed Habibur Rahman received his PhD in Public Administration from the University of Wales, UK. He is currently a Non-Resident Research Fellow at the Mohammed Bin Rashid School of Government in Dubai and a Research Affiliate with the Centre on Governance, University of Ottawa in Canada. Professor Rahman was a Senior Fulbright Scholar at the Maxwell School at Syracuse University in the United States and a Visiting Fellow at the York Centre for Asian Research at York University in Canada. His current research interests include public sector reform, digital governance, and agile policy implementation. Professor Rahman contributed consulting and advisory support to government, as well as international organizations and industries.

Taoufik Rajhi is the former Minister of Reforms for the Government of Tunisia (2014–2019). He is an international expert in development economics and a ranked professor for universities in France. In 2000, he graduated in economics from the University of Paris 1 Panthéon-La Sorbonne, where he then taught Economics for several years. He has published several articles in the field of macroeconomics and endogenous growth. Since 2004, he worked at the African Development Bank, where he held several positions in the field of economic development. Dr. Rajhi is also the president and founder of the Circle of Economists in Tunisia.

Abu Elias Sarker is an Associate Professor of Public Administration at the University of Sharjah's Department of Management. He has a PhD in Public Administration from the University of Liverpool, UK. Dr. Sarker's articles have been published in journals such as the *International Review of Administrative Sciences*, *International Journal of Public Sector Management*, *Public Administration Quarterly*, *Public Organization Review*, *International Journal of Public Administration*, *Asian Journal of Political Science*, and the *Journal of Asian and African Studies*.

Youssef Sawani is a Professor of Politics and International Relations at the University of Tripoli. He has published books and articles which have appeared in the *Contemporary Arab Affairs*, the *Journal of North African Studies*, and the *International Journal of Public Administration*.

FOREWORD

I am very pleased to see that this collection of studies on public administration in the MENA countries will be published soon. Far too little is known about public administration in these countries, and what is thought to be known is often composed of stereotypes and poorly supported assumptions. Further, although the countries studied in this book are often lumped together as one entity, the authors in this book demonstrate that there are important differences among the countries. Some of those differences have to do with degrees of relative affluence and of poverty, and perhaps especially between some of the wealthier countries of the Middle East and some much less affluent countries of North Africa. But the social and political differences appear at least as important as wealth in explaining differences among the cases.

The selection of countries in this volume provides some sense of the variation of governments within this region. The coverage of the Middle East includes Turkey with its aspirations to join the European Union, as well as three smaller countries with varying degrees of wealth and varying degrees of internal political conflict. Similarly, the North African countries range from largely stable Morocco to Sudan and Libya also with varying degrees of internal unrest. These countries also have different colonial experiences, with Turkey having escaped external control, while France and the United Kingdom controlled the others at some point in their histories. I could continue to list the differences in background characteristics of the eight countries, but the important point is that there is variation, and that variation can be used to understand the differences in public administration that the authors observe.

The intellectual approaches taken within this volume also make important contributions to understanding government in these countries. First, the editor is emphasizing governance as the fundamental role for public administration. Too often studies of public administration emphasize the formal, mechanical aspects of the bureaucracy, but it is crucial to consider the role that the public bureaucracy plays in the more general, and more important, tasks of governance. Governance involves all the efforts of governments and their partners to steer the economy and society and provides a means of understanding the complex relationships that exist between State and society.

The public bureaucracy plays a central role in governance. The role usually assigned to the bureaucracy – implementing public policies – is important, but it is only one part of the governance role of public administrators. Public administrators advise political leaders – whether elected or not – and play a role in shaping policy as well as making it work within society. The bureaucracy also can play a role in reform and in modernizing society and has its own linkages with donor organizations and other international organizations promoting improved governance.

Finally, the public bureaucracy is the face of government for most members of the society; Citizens rarely encounter political leaders in their daily lives, but they do frequently come into contact with members of public administration, whether it is in the post office, or seeing the police on patrol, or talking with their children's teachers. These street-level bureaucrats not only shape the services that citizens receive but also they provide images of what the State is and what the members of the State apparatus think about its citizens. Those images are important for the legitimacy, or lack thereof, of the State, perhaps especially when the legitimacy of the State is not firmly established.

The role of the public bureaucracy in governance may be especially important in developing and transitional regimes. As already noted, in these regimes, the State is often facing numerous challenges to its legitimacy, and one way to build that legitimacy is thorough effective public services. In addition, the public bureaucracy is often the most modernized aspect of government, having greater professional contacts and training than other actors. Thus, although constrained by important conventions about being apolitical and the obedient public servants, the bureaucracy also has a capacity for leadership for change.

While bureaucracies may be agents of change within government and within society, they also often need to be reformed themselves. The chapters in this book contain a number of discussions of reform of the bureaucracy. Reform is a continuing challenge for public administration almost everywhere, and the MENA countries are certainly no different. In some cases, the reforms may be fine-tuning, but, as the chapters in this book illustrate, reform can also be fundamental. Reform may have to address basic issues such as eliminating (or at least reducing) corruption and establishing fair and effective personnel practices within government itself. These reforms are often difficult for the public administrators involved, but they may pay dividends for government and the society.

This volume represents a very important contribution to the literature on public administration. It advances our knowledge of administration in this diverse and important set of countries. The book also tells us a good deal about public administration more generally and helps the reader understand the challenges faced when attempting to govern in often trying circumstances. These countries may all have some of the characteristics of MENA countries described in the introduction, but each manifests those characteristics to differing degrees and in different ways. A thorough reading of this book will enrich the reader's comprehension of this portion of the world, as well as of public administration more generally.

B. Guy Peters
University of Pittsburgh

ACRONYMS

AI	Artificial Intelligence
AHDR	Arab Human Development Report
AKP	Adalet Ye Kalkinma Partisi
BTI	Bertelsmann Transformation Index
CDA	Constitution Drafting Authority
CICP	Central Instance for Corruption Prevention
CPF	Country Partnership Framework
CSO	Civil Society Organization
DEG	Digital-era Governance
DGEP	Dubai Government Excellence Program
DQA	Dubai Quality Award
DNA	Deoxyribonucleic Acid
EBRD	European Bank for Reconstruction and Development
EFQM	European Foundation for Quality Management
ESCWA	Economic and Social Commission for West Asia
ESRP	Economic and Social Reform Program
GDP	Gross Domestic Product
GIS	Geographical Information System
GNI	Gross National Income
GNPOC	Greater Nile Petroleum Operating Company
GTZ	German Technical Cooperation
HCS	Higher Council State
HDI	Human Development Index
HoR	House of Representatives
HR	Human Resources
HRM	Human Resources Management

IBRD	International Bank for Reconstruction and Development
ICT	Information and Communication Technology
IMF	International Monetary Fund
IoT	Internet of Things
IRA	Independent Regulatory Authority
LGL	Local Government Law
LNA	Libyan National Army
LPDF	Libyan Political Dialogue Forum
MCA	Moroccan Courts of Accounts
MENA	Middle East and North Africa
MHP	National Movement Party
MMPS	Ministry for the Modernization of the Public Service
MoE	Ministry of Energy
NGO	Non-governmental Organization
NIF	National Islamic Front
NPM	New Public Management
NSEP	National Salvation Economic Program
NTC	National Transitional Council
OECD	Organisation for Economic Co-operation and Development
OMSAR	Office of the Minister of State for Administrative Reform
OPEC	Organization of the Petroleum Exporting Countries
PARP	Public Administration Reform Program
PDIA	Problem-driven Interactive Adaptation
PGS	Presidency Government System
PPP	Public-Private Partnership
QMS	Quality Management Systems
RSF	Rapid Support Forces
RTI	Roads and Transport Authority
SKEA	Sheikh Khalifa Excellence Award
SLDC	Solution- and Leader-driven Change
SoE	State-owned Enterprises
SPP	State Personnel Presidency
SSA	Sub-Saharan Africa
TCRPSE	Technical Committee for the Release of Public Sector Entities
TT	Turkish Posts
UAE	United Arab Emirates
UNDESA	United Nations Department of Economic and Social Affairs
UNESCO	United Nations Educational, Scientific and Cultural Organization
UNESCWA	United Nations Economic and Social Commission for West Asia
UNHCR	United Nations High Commissioner for Refugees
UNSGSR	United Nations Secretary General's Special Representative
UNSMIL	United Nations Support Mission in Libya
VRP	Voluntary Retirement Program

ACKNOWLEDGMENTS

John Dixon, Yilmaz Üstüner, and I edited a special issue on Public Administration in the MENA region for the *International Journal of Public Administration* (Vol. 41, Issue 10, 2018). The special issue was a great success. As a result, the journal's then Editor-in-Chief, Ali Farazmand, inspired me to convert it into a book. He put me in contact with Laura Stearns Varley, the Senior Publisher at Routledge, during the 2018 NASPAA (the Network of Schools of Public Policy, Affairs, and Administration) Conference held in Atlanta, GE. Laura quickly recognized the importance of publishing a book on public administration in the MENA region and advised that I submit a proposal. I am grateful to both Ali and Laura for their gestures of goodwill. John and Yilmaz, two coeditors of the special issue, enthusiastically endorsed the idea of this book and encouraged me to advance the project as its Editor. To them, I extend my sincerest gratitude.

After many rounds of reviews, the proposal was accepted. Apart from the new contributors, I invited the authors of the special issue to contribute to this book, most of whom warm-heartedly accepted the offer. In doing so, they had to write their chapters afresh, with new materials and analyses, a painstaking job indeed. A well-known public administration scholar, Jamil Jreisat, published an article on Jordan in the special issue, but also expressed his keen interest to rewrite the piece for this book. While working on the chapter, he sadly passed away. Hence, honoring Professor Jreisat, and with the permission of Routledge/Taylor & Francis, his special issue article is included in this book with minor editorial changes.

This book includes chapters on Lebanon and Libya which were previously published in the aforementioned special issue of the *International Journal of Public*

Administration. Although both chapters were substantially revised and updated, I thank Routledge/Taylor & Francis for granting copyright clearance to publish them in this volume.

I must note that the publication of this book has been delayed for various reasons, including the onslaught of the COVID-19 pandemic, which affected all of us in one way or another. I am deeply grateful to the distinguished authors, as well as the Editorial Team at Routledge, Laura Varley and Elizabeth Hart, for their excellent support throughout the process.

I am also grateful to my wife, Umme Kulsum Zamena, and our children, Nawaal and Safwan, for their love, support, and understanding. Many thanks to Routledge for giving me the opportunity to publish this book with them.

Shahjahan Bhuiyan

INTRODUCTION

Shahjahan Bhuiyan[1]

Many salient features of public administration resemble a chameleon that changes its color based on its surrounding environment, as Hustedt et al. (2020) have noted. Public administration structures must take on different shapes to cope with the ever-increasing local, regional, and global challenges that arise from the interplay of complex, country-specific governance challenges and ever-changing global conditions. As a result, public administration as an academic discipline remains indeterminate. It must encompass complex concepts that take on different meanings in different contexts. This ambiguity impacts the practice of public administration as a state function (Bouckert & Jaan, 2020).

While there is no agreed-upon definition of public administration, scholars have defined the concept from various strategic perspectives. Henry (2001, p. 1) argues that the purpose of public administration "… is to promote a superior understanding of government and its relationship with the society it governs, as well as to encourage public policies more responsive to social needs and to institute managerial practices attuned to effectiveness, efficiency, and the deeper human requisites of the citizenry." Harader (1977, p. 98) labeled Henry's definition "a classic" as it identifies the issues and problems associated with the actual functioning of public administration.

Berkley (1975, p. 3) characterizes public administration as "a process involving human beings jointly engaged in working towards a common goal." Corson and Harris (1963) characterized public administration as the active part of government, an instrument to achieve the purpose and goals of government. Analyzing these definitions reveals that the core function of public administration is to achieve the goals of government in an efficient and timely fashion for the benefit of citizens. The goal of any government is to deliver public services, irrespective of the nature of that government, be it democratic or not (Fukuyama, 2013).

The role public administration plays in support of governance institutions is critical to guide society along human-centered development pathways for the betterment of the human condition (Puppim de Oliveira et al., 2015). Over the years, there has been a gradual shift in understanding of the role public administration plays in making development a reality. Puppim de Oliveira et al. (p. 66) have identified several global trends: (1) the movement of the focus of analysis from organizations and processes (for example, the Weberian model or internal organizational design) to broader discussions and analyses on governance design and frameworks, (2) the shift of focus from the improvement of public administration quality so as to achieve greater efficiency in the public sector for delivery of public services to incorporating accountability and responsiveness, and (3) the emergence of new global issues such as the COVID-19 pandemic, climate change, artificial intelligence, human rights, and migration. Together, these trends have ushered in new challenges to the effective operation of public administration. These global issues are large-scale forces, making it nearly impossible to fully understand the administrative apparatus of government without closely studying the impact of such forces and the conditions under which they emerged (Roberts, 2014).

Referring to Kettl (2015), Stillman (2015) rightly points out that if effective public administration, in the United States context, had prevailed during many of the tragic events that took place in the twenty-first century, such as 9/11, the torture and cruelty that Abu Ghraib prisoners experienced, the devastating impact of Hurricane Katrina, and many such governance failures could have been avoided. This is perhaps equally true for other countries, developed and developing alike: they could have circumvented or at least reduced the impact of many of their most dreadful events if they had been able to improve the quality of public administration.

In an attempt to support the gradual improvement of public administration, Guy and Rubin (2015) have identified ten emerging trends in public administration: from intergovernmental to intersectoral, from trust to doubt, from local to global, from silos to networks, from administration to management, from outputs to outcomes, from paper to cloud, from sameness to differences, from equality to social equity, and from ethical expectation to professional standards. If public administration gradually absorbs and internalizes the trends in congruence with each country's culture and local context, it may successfully transform "public administration" to "Good Public Administration" to achieve good governance for the greater benefit of their citizenry (see Aoki, 2015). This assertion further emphasizes public administration's reflective role in nation building, governance, and promotion of broad political values, including transparency, representation, participation, and human rights (Rosenbloom & Abdel-Moneim, 2020).

Haque (1996) argues that the nature, scope, structure, and functions of public administration in a country are largely shaped by numerous factors in its sociohistoric context. This observation clearly holds true for the formation and growth of public administration in the Middle East and North Africa (MENA). In this context, understanding the meaning of the state, Anderson (1986, p. 1) highlights how "the roles of tribalism, sectarianism, regionalism, primordial sentiments, and ascriptive identities in Middle Eastern politics contributed to the view that the state is little more than an arena of socially engendered conflict or an instrument of family, sect, or class domination." Consequently, the features of public governance systems are a reflection of how a state in the MENA is formed and functions, which Schomaker and Bauer (2020, pp. 379–380) succinctly summarized as having:

1 High levels of centralization of public authority;
2 Religious and cultural elements of governance;
3 Cronyism, nepotism, and corruption (and *wasta*);
4 Autocratic leadership and unclear or unstable succession modes;
5 Gridlock of administrative reform; and
6 Mistrust within the politico-administrative system.

Evidence suggests that there is comparatively sparse public administration scholarship on MENA and the Arab[2] world. Drawing on Dedoussis (2004) and Iles et al. (2012), Rosenbloom and Abdel-Moneim (2020) noted that there is lack of theory of administration in the Arab world. This observation was further strengthened by a 2015 United Nations Development Program (UNDP) report, which emphasized that public administration scholarship from the MENA region following the Arab Spring failed to address "the needs to transition, and presenting insights into the values' conflicts that generally accompany such periods" (Rosenbloom & Abdel-Moneim, 2020, p. 5). Despite the 2015 UNDP report that identified the failure of policy reform as one of the push factors of the Arab Spring, the Arab countries in transition have received financial assistance and technical support from donors and international development agencies for building electoral institutions, writing constitution, settling conflicts, and reforming security sectors, but this assistance has generally failed to address public administration and policy issues (Abdel-Moneim, 2015; Rosenbloom & Abdel-Moneim, 2020; UNDP, 2015). Schomaker and Huck (2022) found that public administration research in MENA is largely fragmented as well as isolated from international debates and discussions as the number of scholarly works published in the English language is relatively insignificant. Dixon et al. (2018) also made a similar observation. In this critical milieu, research on MENA public administration can make an essential contribution to the meager literature that exists in this area of inquiry.

Structure of the book

The book is divided into two parts. Part I deals with public administration in four Middle East countries: the United Arab Emirates (UAE), Turkey (the Republic of Türkiye), Lebanon, and Jordan. Part II addresses public administration in four North African countries: the Kingdom of Morocco, Tunisia, Sudan, and Libya.

Chapter 1 critically discusses the UAE's public sector reform dynamics. Sarker and Rahman analyze the UAE's path toward public sector reform since the 1990s and the progress they have made thus far, exploring the contextual factors, the trends, and the results of reform undertaken in the UAE. The findings of the study demonstrate that the UAE government not only successfully implemented selected public sector reforms, which contributed to several tangible outcomes, but also encountered challenges that constrain the reform initiatives.

Chapter 2 reviews the reconstruction of Turkey's public administration in the context of its new presidential government system. Üstüner argues that the reform was an outcome of an overcentralized bureaucratic structure that connected the executive power with the presidency and the President himself, thus undermining democratic governance and inclusive participation. The chapter further argues that the rationale offered for this structural transformation becomes clearer when the tensions between new public management and the precepts of democratic governance and participation are put into context.

In Chapter 3, Haase provided a compelling account of public administration in Lebanon. The chapter presents Lebanon's public bureaucratic challenges and reforms undertaken between the end of the Lebanese Civil War (1975–1990) and 2015. During this period, the government of Lebanon and international donor agencies attempted to improve the quality of public administration by improving transparency, promoting modern management techniques, and encouraging the use of information and communication technology (ICT) across the public sector. Haase argues that, in spite of the reform efforts, Lebanon's public administration remains centralized, corrupt, tied to outdated bureaucratic structures, and deficient in modern administrative knowledge.

Chapter 4 deals with public administration development in Jordan, particularly its transformation from a British colony to an independent state. Jreisat examined how the transition contributes to contextual attributes and influences that have affected the administrative system and its processes up to the present. Consequently, Jordan has experienced many challenges such as overcentralization, demographic explosion, low economic growth, and excessive reliance on patronage in recruitment for public positions. Jreisat further argues that these factors along with others constrained administrative reform efforts, blocked the application of the merit system, and hindered the improvement of the accountability and professionalism of the public service.

Naguib, in Chapter 5, provides an overarching discussion on Morocco's governance and public administration reforms. She shows that public administration in the global governance context is largely affected by domestic, regional, and international actors and is subordinated to certain intrinsic and extrinsic factors. Naguib observes that Morocco offers an interesting case of this duality in governance and public administration, resulting in an unresolved tension between tradition and modernity in a monarchical regime.

Chapter 6 focuses on policy reforms in post-revolution Tunisia. Jouini and Rajhi conclude that a mixed approach combining political economy (positive) and economic rationales (normative) is needed to implement an effective public policy reform agenda in Tunisia. They further examine how the new post-revolution environment underlines the importance of a progressive consensual reform strategy to preserve the interests of different groups and overcome counterproductive legislative polarization. The finding of the study shows that building an effective reform system in Tunisia requires improving institutional public administration capacity, enriching political leadership, and developing an effective system of coordination, evaluation, and feedback.

Chapter 7 paints a canvass describing how three decades of authoritarian rule have effectively undermined public administration in Sudan. Elnur presents an alternative conceptual framework for understanding processes that accelerated the erosion of the structural foundation of post-colonial Sudan and the emergence of a new political and socio-economic landscape. The chapter emphasizes the challenges of regaining state control over the economy and especially the "deep state."

Finally, Chapter 8 analyzes the growth and development of public administration in Libya since its independence in 1951. Sawani describes the major changes that have taken place and underscores the issues that have continued to impede effective governance despite radical political changes. The chapter presents an analysis of the key characteristics of Libya's public administration, including legislative frameworks, as well as public sector recruitment, compensation, corruption, and accountability. Sawani outlines the key future challenges Libya faces, including the immediate need for effective public administration and civil service reform.

Notes

1 The American University in Cairo, Egypt.
2 Several Middle Eastern countries are part of the Arab world.

References

Abdel-Moneim, M. A. (2015). *A political economy of Arab education: Politics and comparative perspectives.* Routledge.

Anderson, L. (1986). The state in the Middle East and North Africa. *Comparative Politics*, 20(1), 1–18. https://doi.org/10.2307/421917

Aoki, N. (2015). Let's get public administration right, but in what sequence?: Lessons from Japan and Singapore. *Public Administration and Development*, 35(3), 206–218. https://doi.org/10.1002/pad.1714

Berkley, G. E. (1975). *The craft of public administration.* Allyn and Bacon.

Bouckert, G., & Jaan, W. (2020). The EPPA Project. In G. Bouckert & W. Jaan (Eds.), *European perspectives for public administration: The way forward* (pp. 21–42). Leuven University Press. https://www.jstor.org/stable/j.ctvv417th.6

Corson, J. J., & Harris, J. P. (1963). *Public administration in modern society.* McGraw-Hill.

Dedoussis, E. (2004). A cross-cultural comparison of organizational culture: Evidence from universities in the Arab world and Japan. *Cross Cultural Management: An International Journal*, 11(1), 15–34. https://doi.org/10.1108/13527600410797729

Dixon, J., Bhuiyan, S., & Üstüner, Y. (2018). Public administration in the Middle East and North Africa. *International Journal of Public Administration*, 41(10), 759–764. https://doi.org/10.1080/01900692.2018.1433207

Fukuyama, F. (2013). What is governance? *Governance*, 26(3), 347–368. https://doi.org/10.1111/gove.12035

Guy, M. E., & Rubin, M. M. (Eds.). (2015). *Public administration evolving: From foundations to the future.* Routledge.

Haque, M. S. (1996). The contextless nature of public administration in Third World countries. *International Review of Administrative Sciences*, 62(3), 315–329. https://doi.org/10.1177/002085239606200303

Harader, W. H. (1977). Whither public administration? *Public Administration Review*, 37(1), 97–102.

Henry, N. (2001). *Public administration and public affairs* (8th ed.). Prentice-Hall.

Hustedt, T., Randma-Liiv, T., & Savi, R. (2020). Public administration and disciplines. In G. Bouckert & W. Jaan (Eds.), *European perspectives for public administration: The way forward* (pp. 129–146). Leuven University Press. https://www.jstor.org/stable/j.ctvv417th.11

Iles, P., Almhedie, A., & Baruch, Y. (2012). Managing HR in the Middle East: Challenges in the public sector. *Public Personnel Management*, 41(3), 465–492. https://doi.org/10.1177/009102601204100305

Kettl, D. F. (2015). From intergovernmental to intersectoral. In M. E. Guy & M. M. Rubin (Eds.), *Public administration evolving: From foundations to the future* (pp. 18–37). Routledge.

Puppim de Oliveira, J. A., Jing, Y., & Collins, P. (2015). Public administration and development: Trends and the way forward. *Public Administration and Development*, 35(2), 65–72. https://doi.org/10.1002/pad.1716

Roberts, A. (2014). *Large forces: What's missing in public administration.* CreateSpace.

Rosenbloom, D., & Abdel-Moneim, M. A. (2020). Don't forget Law and Politics! What can Arab Public Administration scholars learn from the fluidity of the field in the US experience? *AlMuntaqa*, 3(2), 35–49. https://www.jstor.org/stable/10.31430/almuntaqa.3.2.0035

Schomaker, R. M., & Bauer, M. W. (2020). Public governance in the MENA region: Reforms trends and patterns. *International Journal of Public Administration*, *43*(5), 378–391. https://doi.org/10.1080/01900692.2019.1669179

Schomaker, R. M., & Huck, V. (2022). Public administration research in and about the MENA region – Taking stock, looking ahead. *Administrative Theory & Praxis*, *44*(4), 321–339. https://doi.org/10.1080/10841806.2022.21244744

Stillman, R. (2015). Foreword. In M. E. Guy & M. M. Rubin (Eds.), *Public administration evolving: From foundations to the future* (pp. x–xxii). Routledge.

United Nations Development Program. (2015). *Defining the challenge, making the change: A study of public administration reform in Arab transitions*. UNDP.

PART I
Public Administration in the Middle East Countries

1
THEORY AND PRACTICE OF PUBLIC ADMINISTRATION REFORMS

The Case of the United Arab Emirates

Abu Elias Sarker and Mohammad Habibur Rahman

Introduction

Since the end of World War II, public administration reforms in the non-Western world have been systematic. In most parts, the contours of such reforms began with the implantation of the Weberian model of bureaucracy in evolving and paradoxical environments. The development of the strong state was contemplated as the foremost tool for nation building and socio-economic transformations. Institution building and capacity development appeared as an essential focus of administrative reforms. The post-World War II era was a mixed bag of successes and failures. While some countries succeeded in reforming the administrative system and enhancing bureaucratic capacity, many also failed (McCourt, 2018). Nevertheless, further reforms became inevitable on account of over-burdened states, administrative inefficiency, corruption, lack of accountability, and so forth (Zafarullah & Sarker, 2016). The response was the adoption of the neo-liberal market ideology which advocated small government and instilled managerial principles in public services. Popularly known as new public management (NPM), this emerged as a global model. In spite of heavy criticisms of NPM in both Western and non-Western countries, the model is still prevalent in many countries in varying degrees (Aoki, 2015, 2019). Over the past two decades, the literature on public administration reforms has been inundated with newer concepts and models. Presumably, the digital model has impacted public services most on account of easing the service delivery system, ensuring service quality, disseminating information, and so forth.

This chapter focuses on public administration reforms in the United Arab Emirates (UAE). Like most other countries, the UAE commenced public administration reform programs in the 1990s. But unlike many countries, the UAE concentrated on the selected aspects of reform options that yielded better results globally. Keeping state reform at bay, it introduced a few key elements of NPM and the digitalization of public services. In this chapter, the key aspects of this reform journey are presented. The fifth and sixth sections discuss managerial reforms and digital governance. The seventh section reflects on the results and policy implications. The eighth section draws conclusion.

Public administration reforms: Concepts and models

Reforms are inevitable in public administration. Since the emergence of modern nation-states, change has become a common lexicon in administrative systems throughout the world. However, the rubric, pattern, and *modus operandi* of administrative reforms have exhibited different shapes at different periods of history. Particularly, the discourse of administrative reforms in the post-colonial era took diverse forms having been galvanized by both internal and external factors. As public administration as an important organ of the government cannot remain static, its structure, functions, processes, and behavioral patterns need overhauling periodically to ensure efficiency, effectiveness, the upholding of democratic norms, consensus building, and equity in core public service institutions (Zafarullah & Sarker, 2021). Reform implies grappling with uncertainties and rapid changes in the organizational environment (Caiden & Sundaram, 2004).

Borrowing Western models for administrative reforms has been the most dominant feature of the developing world. After decolonization, the states in post-colonial societies had uphill tasks of nation building and socio-economic development. Consequently, there was a need for transforming the administrative system. All post-colonial states adopted the Weberian impersonal bureaucracy in order to put governments on an orderly and efficient footing. In spite of many shortcomings such as rigidity, risk-aversion tendencies, and corruption, the model remained dominant. Amid the shortcomings, some developing countries succeeded in enhancing bureaucratic efficiency (McCourt, 2018).

Public bureaucracy came under severe attack in the late 1970s following perpetual dismal performance as well as fiscal crisis, which eventually paved the way for the emergence of the neo-liberal market ideology and triggered the clamor for market-oriented reforms (Knafo, 2020). NPM, a brain child of the neo-liberal market model, emerged "to become an approach in public administration that employs knowledge and experiences acquired in business management and other disciplines to improve efficiency, effectiveness, and general performance of public services in modern bureaucracies" (Kisner & Vigoda-Gadot, 2017, p. 534). NPM first became popular in the Anglo-Saxon administrative systems. Eventually, it was adopted by the rest of the world in different forms. It truly became a global model of public administration reforms with varying degrees of effects. More importantly, its label as a best practice model begged questions regarding its efficiency in the context of the poor and transitional economies (Zafarullah & Sarker, 2016).

Three decades later, this paradigm was challenged as for many, the NPM model lost its appeal in the beginning of the new millennium (Dunleavy et al., 2006; Pollitt & Bouckaert, 2011). The post-NPM reforms generated a good number of trends, rather than any one dominant model. Most of these trends such as new public governance, networked governance, co-production, collaboration and partnerships, and so forth are found in various degrees mostly in the European context (Cavalcante, 2019). However, there are strong arguments regarding the diversity of trajectories of reform as well as an overlapping of different doctrines and trends across the globe (Aoki, 2015, 2019; Goldfinch & Yamamoto, 2019; Klenk & Reiter, 2019).

In the post-NPM era, the digital government model has made a forceful inroad into the public administration reform discourse. Dunleavy et al. (2006, p. 478) in their influential article emphasized the role of information and communication technology (ICT), which is "the most general, pervasive, and structurally distinctive influence on how governance arrangements are changing in advanced industrial states." In the digital-era governance (DEG) model, they have identified three key themes: reintegration, needs-based holism, and digitalization changes. Reintegration includes, *inter alia*, rollback of agencification, joined-up governance (JUG), the reinstating of central processes, network simplification, and so forth. Needs-based holism centers on an integrated approach involving needs-based reorganization, one-stop provision, end-to-end service reengineering, and so on. The digitalization processes facilitate electronic service delivery. It goes without saying that the digital government model has rendered a huge leap for public service delivery and made the system more citizen-centric (Criado & Gil-Garcia, 2019).

Amid an aura of failures in the public administration reform regime, "islands of success" or "positive deviance" has opened new horizons for achieving success. The positive deviance theory entails two components: "solution- and leader-driven change" (SLDC) and "problem-driven iterative adaptation" (PDIA) (Andrews, 2015). According to SLDC, the success of reforms is fostered by a well-articulated reform plan. However, the PDIA is a micro-level approach that adopts the adage, "find a problem and fix it" (Grindle, 2017). Reforms are introduced through an iterative process that includes identifying a particular problem in a specific context, nurturing continuous dialogues and brainstorming to generate new ideas, having an authorizing environment, and engaging broad sets of agents (Andrews, 2018).

The recent discourse about agile government is also in the offing in academic literature. In the current context of increased engagement between states and citizens, technological advancement, and a complex globalized world presenting multiple challenges in international trade, climate change, and global health, "agile government" proponents are pressing for an adaptive change in government. The discourse is provoking the rise of a new form of government that can address the complex issues of the future with adaptive leadership and flexible policies (McPherson, 2016; Stephens et al., 2019).

The context of government in the UAE

A review of the context of public administration in the UAE is necessary to reflect upon its fallout on public administration reforms. The UAE political system combines tradition and modernity. The seven emirates, popularly known as "local governments," comprise the federal government. Constitutionally, the Supreme Council of Rulers, comprising the rulers of seven emirates, is the highest policy-making body. The office of the president, the Council of Ministers, the judiciary, and the Federal National Council are the vital institutions of the federal government. The Federal National Council is the legislature comprising indirectly elected and nominated members. Though it does not have law-making authority, its role is confined to discussion and making suggestions on draft laws and vital policy matters. By and large, the UAE is an executive-dominated state. The president is elected by the members of the Supreme Council of Rulers. The constitution clearly demarcates the operational jurisdictions between the federal government and the local governments. Local governments enjoy a substantial amount of autonomy. Rulers are the highest political authority of the respective emirates (Sarker & Al Athmay, 2019).

While political structure is dominated by the members of the royal family, the administrative system is modeled on the Western precepts of administration. The civil service system of the federal government is governed by the outward-looking Human Resource law. The law provides articulated guidelines regarding all human resource management practices in order to instill the ethos of professionalism in civil service (Sarker & Al Athmay, 2019).

Socio-economic dynamics

The UAE is an oil-rich country with around 9.5 million people of which around 11% are indigenous Emiratis and the rest are the expatriates. Tribal societies under the reign of the Sheikh Kingdoms with collectivist social features formed the federal state and have undergone massive transformations over the last five decades. Vast oil resources and the prudent leadership catapulted the country into modernity (with all modern amenities). The per capita GNI is around $75,000 dollars (purchasing power parity (PPP), current international). Currently placed the 33rd globally, the country enjoys one of the highest Human Development Index (HDI) rankings in the world (UNDP, 2019).

While in the initial years after independence in 1971, the oil sector provided the needed revenues, the volatility of oil prices as well as widespread negative shocks, starting with the 2008–2009 global financial crisis and followed by the European sovereign debt crisis, propelled the government to embark on massive economic diversification focusing on a global, knowledge-based, and competitive economy (MoE, 2018). The contribution of the oil sector to GDP has declined considerably with the dramatic increase of the non-oil sectors (approximately 70%) (MoE, 2018).

The UAE has adopted the most liberal economic policy, with colossal incentives, in the Arab world, which has given meaningfulness to economic diversification. Foreign direct investment is allowed in all sectors except a few such as petro-chemical, telecommunications, armories, and so forth (Sarker & Al Athmay, 2019).

Global embeddedness

Globalization became an invincible force in the late 20th century and remains unabated till today. The impacts of globalization on society, economy, governance, and administration have been insurmountable in either positive or negative ways. According to Farazmand (1999, p. 514):

> … the globalization of capital, politics, administration, and culture has affected virtually every nation; no country has been left untouched.

The UAE is one of the few countries which prepared itself to embrace the global order by liberalizing the economy, rationalizing the business regulatory regime, and adopting the global best practices (Pelton, 2018). There is in fact a paradigm shift in terms of the government's response to globalization. While the government intends to reap the benefits by adopting best practices in diverse spheres and showing the nation's tradition of openness and peaceful coexistence, it is determined to repel the destructive effects of globalization. Jones (2017, p. 34) unequivocally states:

> With its broad-based efforts at social engineering—improving education; fostering creativity; encouraging tolerance, cosmopolitanism, and social responsibility; building an entrepreneurial spirit; taking on rentierism—the UAE …. is doing internally what many observers have long recommended for the Middle East as a whole for the purposes of adapting to globalization.

Public administration reforms in the UAE

In its post-independence period (since 1971), the UAE's leadership understood that people's needs had to be fulfilled, their concerns had to be addressed, and the state's vision had to be realized. The leadership's role became more momentous in the current era of globalization, technological innovation, and the call for responsive governance as enunciated by Sheikh Mohammed Bin Rashed Al Maktoum, the Vice President and the Prime Minister of the UAE, in his book *Flashes of Thought: Inspired by a Dialogue at the Government Summit 2013* as means to an end, ought to deliver on public promises: creating values that match people's hopes, outcomes that can instill common happiness among citizens (Al Maktoum, 2013).

The UAE has inordinately succeeded in making tangible progress with its managerial reforms in recent decades, which has helped establish effective government institutions at the federal and local levels. The UAE administration, known to be one of the most innovative and outstanding in the world (Sarker & Al Athmay, 2019), has remained persistent in implementing policies and strategies to achieve appreciable results in the six segments of its Vision 2021 (Government of the UAE, 2010). With a longer-term outlook, the country has even gone beyond its Vision 2021 to deliver a five-decade government plan called "UAE centennial 2071," whose aspiration is to make the UAE the best country in the world by 2071.

Widely known as an investing government, the UAE, over the past three decades, has implemented a range of transformational changes in its public sector that included numerous managerial reforms as well as digitization and smart government initiatives to improve public service quality and achieve customer happiness. These changes can be seen within the broader reform models adopted by a number of countries in the world. The UAE leadership has responded timely to both the NPM call (e.g. reforms in service excellence, corporatization, and public-private partnership (PPP) and post-NPM reform paradigms (e.g. digital governance, citizen-centric governance, and collaborative governance).

Managerial reforms

Service quality and excellence

The Quality Management System (QMS) was adopted in the UAE in the mid-1990s soon after the International Standard Organization started developing its standards in the late 1980s. The effort to transform the UAE into a knowledge-based economy necessitated quality and performance improvements and customer-centric service delivery (Rahman & Said, 2015). The Dubai Quality Award (DQA) and professional groups like the Dubai Quality Group were formed in 1994. Other emirates soon followed. The quality management models, once adopted in silos and at the lower ranks of agencies based on initiatives rather than commitments, were now driven comprehensively by public-sector leaders (Rahman & Said, 2015).

The next step taken was the adoption of excellence models. In September 1997, the Dubai Government Excellence Program (DGEP) was launched as the first integrated program of its kind in the world (Nuseirat, 2008, cited in Rahman & Said, 2015). Based on the European Foundation for Quality Management (EFQM) ideal and following a client-centric approach, DGEP was designed to be the catalyst in developing Dubai's public sector as a whole and service delivery in particular. It was used to organize quality competitions to assess "enablers" (i.e. policy and strategy, leadership, people, partnership and resources, and process) and "results" (in terms of customer results, people results, society results, and key performance results). The grand total of points determined an organization's overall excellence rank (Ahrens, 2014). The intent was to stimulate and achieve better performance, driven by the NPM reform (Rahman & Said, 2015).

Two years later, the Sheikh Khalifa Excellence Award (SKEA) was initiated in the Emirate of Abu Dhabi in 1999 (Abu Dhabi Chamber, 2020). During 2004–2006, more excellence initiatives were adopted in the Emirates of Ras Al Khaimah, Dubai, and Abu Dhabi. After the UAE saw a landmark reform in the excellence journey with Mohammed Bin Rashid Government Excellence Award in 2009, the year 2012 was marked by a unique "Global Star Rating System" to instill further values in customer-centric service improvements. Public organizations started receiving star ratings based on customer survey evaluations for service centers (Government of the UAE, 2020a). Following the launching of an m-Government strategy in 2013 and the UAE National Innovation Strategy the following year, the UAE continued its robust excellence reforms in 2013, 2014, and 2015 with the launching of Best m-Government Service Award, Hamdan Bin Mohammed Award for Smart Government, and the Fourth Generation of Government Excellence System consecutively.

Transition from the EFQM-based DGEP to fourth-generation model

In 2015, the DGEP excellence practices, which were based on the EFQM model, were replaced by a landmark shift to the fourth-generation model of government excellence with less focus on enablers (20%) and more on results in terms of promoting innovation (20%) and achieving vision (60%) (Government of the UAE, 2015). Lately, the model has been restructured with 25% assessment value of enablers, 15% for innovation, and 60% for vision achievement (Executive Council (Dubai), 2020). Along these motivations in the excellence model, the system of government tends to achieve vision and attain innovation

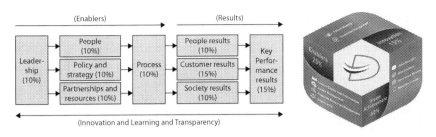

FIGURE 1.1 From DGEP to Fourth-Generation Excellence—Shift toward Vision and Innovation

Source: Adapted from Ahrens (2014) and the Executive Council (Dubai) (2020)

to increase people's happiness through improved services. Figure 1.1 exhibits the transformation from the old model to the new.

A study by Rahman and Sarker examines how the UAE leadership seizes the opportunity in blending a diffusion of technological advancement and institutional changes in spearheading an agile and citizen-centric public service delivery. Based on a case study on DGEP reforms toward the Elite Model of excellence, which is built on the success of the Fourth-Generation excellence framework, the researchers perceive how data science and artificial intelligence (AI), organizational agility and partnership inspire the public organizations to embrace the momentum of change in digital process. The study on this diffusion process concludes that digital transformation practices in the UAE could inspire the digital reform initiatives in the Arab region (Rahman & Sarker, 2021).

The quality and excellence reforms over the past three decades helped the UAE government and the private companies in striving to continuously improve their citizen-centric and customer-driven services in a competitive manner. Sheikh Mohammed Bin Rashid has inspired the public sector to conceive the government as one of achievements, not a government of lectures with a "team of accomplishers, not a team of preachers" (*Gulf News*, 2019, August 31). On the other side, the DQA has supported the private sector to strengthen their quality initiative as DQA they perceived as a useful approach to improve quality (Lasrado & Uzbeck, 2017).

The 2016 reform with happiness, citizen-centric governance, and future outlook

In 2016, the UAE leadership announced the largest-ever shake-up of its federal government in a bid to make it more flexible and future-oriented. The main direction, set out by the leadership, was toward a collaborative government with citizen-centric strategies to maximize people's happiness and well-being.

New ministry portfolios were created for Happiness, Tolerance, Food Security, and AI and in 2019, another ministry called the Ministry of Possibilities added a unique cadence to public policy and service delivery. To facilitate youth-focused inclusive governance, a Youth Council, comprising men and women serving as advisors to the government on youth issues, was formed. These steps were taken with an emphatic vision toward the Arab world and the UAE, as Sheikh Mohammed comprehends:

> …. there can be no bright future for the Middle East without an intellectual reconstruction that re-establishes the values of ideological openness, diversity, and acceptance of others' viewpoints, whether intellectual, cultural, or religious …. The happiness of individuals, families, and employees, their satisfaction with their lives and optimism for the future, are crucial to our work, which cuts across every sector of government.
>
> *Government of the UAE (2016)*

Collaborative governance and public-private partnerships

The UAE government's new cabinet formation in 2016 clearly signaled a shift from the traditional role of government and hierarchical construct to a more partnership format that could inspire the future government to what can be called "networked holacracy" (Oxford Analytica, 2015). The UAE public sector is now delving into new strategies, like focusing on national private sector employment (emiratization policies) in order to deflate its bloated structure so that it might reduce the financial burden on fiscal budgets, activate the private sectors role, and cope with changing production and manufacturing trends. One such example is the ratification of the PPP law in the country in 2015. The government is committing itself to developing a professional entity that is geared to partner with private sector through commissioning work and outsourcing services, albeit this has somewhat been limited until now. Nevertheless, the future of government lies in this reconstructed relationship (Mohammed Bin Rashid School of Government, 2017). In the transport sector, the Dubai Roads and Transport Authority (RTA) began the year by releasing the request for qualification for its first PPP to the market, the Union Oasis Project (DLA Piper, 2016).

The January 4, 2020 charter for Dubai

To ensure more professionalism and accountability in public-sector projects, Sheikh Mohammed announced on January 4, 2020 a major restructuring in Dubai's government. A new council was formed focusing on six development tracks. Major government departments have been regrouped. In addition to revitalizing the government, the changes aim to strengthen seamless collaboration between departments (and sectors) and enhance public policy (Government of the UAE, 2020b).

Digital governance

Just as the NPM reform paradigm enthused the UAE leadership to adopt numerous managerial reforms (as discussed in the preceding section) in the 1990s, the digital governance paradigm equally inspired the government to adopt an e-Government as early as 2001 with the e-Dirham project. Over the past 19 years, the country has established itself as a leading ICT-based society. The UAE, and Dubai in particular, has made concerted efforts to transform the economy to a knowledge-based one, with comprehensive digital infrastructure. The transformation from an e-Government strategy to m-Government in 2013 is a demonstration of the country's bold reform toward mobile-based 5G smart services (AlBalooshi & Rahman, 2019). The outlook is very clear: the leadership's vision, smart governance, and citizen engagement will together make the case for smart society a reality in future where five main forth-industrial revolution technologies, including the internet of things (IoT), AI, robotics, 3D printing, and wearables, will have an impact (Mohammed Bin Rashid School of Government, 2017). The next stage in the country's m-Government journey will entail linking all the services together, improving the quality of smart applications, and achieving a high satisfaction rate for smart services.

The ICT sector is a main economic pillar and is part of the UAE's ICT Strategy 2021, which is a federal national plan. IoT is already being used to drive driverless cars powered by solar energy in Masdar City, Abu Dhabi. In Dubai, for example, IoT has been used by the RTA to connect traffic lights in the city to a central command center. Surveys show that of all the emerging technologies, 3D printing in particular has the highest level of support by internet users in the Arab region. Dubai is pioneering the use of blockchain technology as part of its smart city initiatives, especially with the launch of the Dubai Blockchain Strategy (Mohammed Bin Rashid School of Government, 2017). The UAE is targeting 2020 to fully launch 5G technology and its industries are leading the way in adopting these technologies.

Dubai Data Law, 2015

The significant accomplishment is the enactment of Dubai Data Law,[1] which stipulates that all data which is not personal, sensitive, or confidential is to be made public. The law also requires strategic private companies to give open access to their data except those deemed sensitive and confidential. Salem (2016) summarizes the potential impact of the data law that is expected to contribute to economic growth and raise the standards of living as follows:

a Enabling the creation of new business and employment opportunities
b Facilitating a tripartite relationship between the government, the private sector, and individuals
c Improving the efficiency of managing and using data and creating new innovations and services in the city (Salem 2016, cited in Rahman et al., 2016)

Social media as a catalyst

Sheikh Mohammed also used social media as a catalyst to promote innovation in service delivery and encourage citizen engagement. This focus was institutionalized in government summits, convened in Dubai in 2013 and 2014. The clearest manifestation of a deeper public engagement for performance improvement was carried out in December 2013, when Sheikh Mohammed called for a national brainstorming campaign leveraging social media to generate creative ideas. The campaign was meant to overcome hindrances for the health and educational sectors. This citizen-centric approach in governance and performance improvement was not limited to that event, but rather started a chain reaction, where, since then, many public-sector entities adopted a similar public consultation approach for their planning purposes. Recently, Sheikh Mohammed's social media approach brought benefits, as with the case of Emirates Post, in terms of alerting public entities for professional and accountable services.

Reform results and policy implications

Like other governments, the UAE government commenced diverse administrative reform programs in order to achieve certain goals such as efficiency, effectiveness, public service quality, and so forth. Credible international comparative data and numerous case studies provide evidence in favor of discernible improvements in public service delivery. The UAE government's record on government effectiveness and service excellence has been impressive over the past three decades.

The World Bank's Worldwide Governance Indicators reveal that except for voice and accountability, other areas of governance have performed well. These include government effectiveness, rule of law, regulatory quality, and control of corruption, which are very much tied to reform measures. Table 1.1 shows that in all these areas, the percentile rank is very impressive.

In the Ease of Doing Business global rank, the country has moved from 21st position in 2018 to 11th in 2019 (World Bank, 2019). The UAE has been quite steady in maintaining its ranking in the global competitiveness index. It was

TABLE 1.1 Governance Indicators in the UAE

Indicators	Year				
	2014	2015	2016	2017	2018
Voice and Accountability	20.2	19.2	20.2	18.2	17.7
Political Stability and Absence of Violence/Terrorism	71.9	70.5	65.2	66.7	71.4
Government Effectiveness	89.4	91.3	90.9	90.9	90.4
Regulatory Quality	80.3	82.7	80.3	80.8	79.8
Rule of Law	75.0	73.1	78.4	77.4	77.4
Control of Corruption	83.2	82.7	84.1	82.7	83.7

Source: Prepared by the authors from https://databank.worldbank.org/reports.aspx?source=worldwide-governance-indicators

ranked 25th in 2019 compared to 27th in the previous year (World Economic Forum, 2019). As a result, the global happiness rank of the UAE has steadily climbed from 28th in 2016 to 21st in 2019 (Helliwell et al., 2019).

The Fragile States Index has been conducting evaluations globally on 12 parameters. Public service is one of these parameters. It measures basic state functions, including general provision of public services, health, education, shelter, infrastructure, water and sanitation, security, and so forth. Available data shows that the UAE public service delivery system is one of the highest performers in the world, ranking the 149th of 178 countries, while Finland occupies the top spot at 178 (The Fund for Peace, 2020).

The impact of ICT on public service delivery has been profound in the UAE. The UAE e-participation has increased from 32nd in ranking in 2016 to 17th in 2018 (United Nations, 2018). According to the United Nations' latest e-Government survey, the UAE is one of the emerging leaders in the sphere of e-Government, earning the 21st place, and has witnessed gradual progress over the years (see Table 1.2).

The success of the UAE in the domain of e-Government can be attributed to many factors. First, the government had political will, which was reflected in taking prompt decisions, conducting extensive research, bench marking, and

TABLE 1.2 E-Government Development Index

Year	Rank	EGDI	OSI	TII	HCI
2018	21	0.8295	0.9444	0.8564	06877
2016	29	0.7515	0.9444	0.8564	0.6877
2014	32	0.7136	0.8819	0.5932	0.6657
2012	28	0.7344	0.8627	0.5568	0.7837

Source: Prepared by the authors from https://publicadministration.un.org/Portals/1/Images/E-Government%20Survey%202018_FINAL%20for%20web.pdf

prompt implementation. Second, the government integrated citizens through various means and shifted e-Government from a supply centric to citizen-centric system, which has been made possible by building trust. According to AlSayegh et al. (2019, p. 62):

> Trust in technology was developed by using high security applications in e-governance inclusive of quality, usability, privacy, interactivity and the security of services and information provided to citizens and businesses …. The government effectively managed the process of transition by proving to its citizens the reasons for adopting the new order and dropping the old way of operations.

Third, e-Government readiness, massive investment in infrastructure development, openness, the development of the culture of innovation, and so forth have also contributed significantly to the success of the digitization of public service delivery (Ahimbisibwe et al., 2015; AlSayegh et al., 2019).

Yet, two major challenges still lie ahead in terms of improving performance management in the UAE: (a) a shift from a government-led development to a functioning collaborative governance model of development is needed to ensure the sustainability of results; and (b) people have to rally behind reform ideas as well as keep pace with technological advancements in terms of the types of platforms such as big data, IoT, smart cities, and cloud computing solutions in order to capitalize on the supply of advanced technologies and innovation.

Conclusion

This chapter reflects on the trajectory of public administration reforms in the UAE. Having remained as an isolated hinterland, the country came into prominence after the discovery of oil resources in the late 1960s followed by planned development intervention in the subsequent years that resulted in tremendous economic growth and social development. The system of public administration has played its due role. Evidently, UAE reformers have found some points of convergence and developed unique ways to implant some Western-bred administrative reform precepts in the UAE public administration system. It is quite interesting to see the coexistence of the precepts of different models being adapted to UAE governance.

The UAE's public administration reform regime reveals some significant trends. First, administrative reform never aimed at hollowing up the state as evident in many cases around the world. Rather, the foundations of the state structure were further strengthened by undertaking capability-enhancing reforms, which can be found in many East and South East European countries (Zafarullah & Sarker, 2016) resembling the characteristics of the neo-Weberian state (Pollitt & Bouckaert, 2011). Second, the UAE government focused on selected managerial reforms such as service quality, excellence, corporatization, collaborative governance, and PPPs that have manifested in the development of the institutional structure, the allocation of resources, and the enforcement of commitment. Third, the application of digitization and smart services has shown remarkable results in a short period.

Putting it all together, it is conceivable that the UAE has set an example for a successful triangular relationship between "leadership" as a chief catalyst for reforms, "technology and innovation" as tools for achieving those reforms, and "responsible governance" as an institution that has positively impacted service improvement and people's happiness. This connectivity in the UAE is a reality and a strong harbinger of where the country will move in the years to come with rapid changes in technology taking flight vis-à-vis human relations.

Note

1 Law No. (26) of 2015 Regulating Data Dissemination and Exchange in the Emirate of Dubai.

References

Abu Dhabi Chamber. (2020). *Sheikh Khalifa Excellence Award*. Retrieved March 28, 2020, from https://www.skea.ae/

Ahimbisibwe, A., Cavana, R. Y., & Daellenbach, U. (2015). A contingency fit model of critical success factors for software development projects: A comparison of agile and traditional plan-based methodologies. *Journal of Enterprise Information Management*, 28(1), 7–33.

Ahrens, T. (2014). Tracing the evolution of the Dubai Government Excellence Program. *Journal of Economic and Administrative Sciences*, 30(1), 2–15.

Al Maktoum, M. B. R. (2013). *Flashes of thought: Inspired by a dialogue at the government summit 2013*. Motivate Publishing.

AlBalooshi, S. A. Y. A., & Rahman, M. H. (2019, February 18–21). *Proactive approach to the deployment of 5G technology: Insights from the UAE* [Conference session]. Presented at the 2nd MENA Regional ITS Conference, Aswan, Egypt.

AlSayegh, A., Hossan, C., & Slade, B. (2019). Radical improvement of e-government services in Dubai. *International Journal of Services Technology and Management*, 25(1), 53–67.

Andrews, M. (2015). Explaining positive deviance in public sector reforms in development. *World Development*, 74, 197–208.

Andrews, M. (2018). Overcoming the limits of institutional reform in Uganda. *Development Policy Review*, 36(S1), O159–O182.

Aoki, N. (2015). Let's get public administration right, but in what sequence?: Lessons from Japan and Singapore. *Public Administration and Development*, 35(3), 206–218.

Aoki, N. (2019). After all these years, what has happened to the international prevalence of NPM-inspired managerial practices? *International Journal of Public Sector Management*, 32(4), 403–417. https://doi.org/10.1108/IJPSM-10-2018-0215.

Caiden, G. E., & Sundaram, P. (2004). The specificity of public service reform. *Public Administration and Development*, *24*(5), 373–383.

Cavalcante, P. L. (2019). Trends in public administration after hegemony of the new public management. *Revista do Serviço Público*, *70*(2), 195–218.

Criado, J. I., & Gil-Garcia, J. R. (2019). Creating public value through smart technologies and strategies. *International Journal of Public Sector Management*, *32*(5), 438–450.

DLA Piper. (2016). *GCC PPPs 2016*. Retrieved March 28, 2020, from https://www.google.com/search?q=DLA±Piper±(2016).±GCC±PPPs±2016&oq=DLA±Piper±(2016).±GCC±PPPs±2016&aqs=chrome.69i57.442j0j7&sourceid=chrome&ie=UTF-8

Dunleavy, P., Margetts, H., Bastow, S., & Tinkler, J. (2006). New public management is dead—Long live digital-era governance. *Journal of Public Administration Research and Theory*, *16*(*3*), 467–494.

Executive Council (Dubai). (2020). *Assessment Cycle Manual*. Retrieved December 11, 2022, from https://dgep.gov.ae/en/file/preview/assessment-cycle-manual-2020

Farazmand, A. (1999). Globalization and public administration. *Public Administration Review*, *59*(6), 509–522.

Goldfinch, S., & Yamamoto, K. (2019). Citizen perceptions of public management: Hybridization and post-new public management in Japan and New Zealand. *Australian Journal of Public Administration*, *78*(1), 79–94.

Government of the United Arab Emirates. (2010). *Vision 2021: United Arab Emirates*. Retrieved March 23, 2019, from https://www.vision2021.ae/docs/default-source/default-document-library/uae_vision-arabic.pdf?sfvrsn=b09a06a6_6

Government of the United Arab Emirates. (2015). *Mohammed bin Rashid launches the fourth generation of government excellence system*. Retrieved March 30, 2020, from https://www.mocaf.gov.ae/en/media/news/mohammed-bin-rashid-launches-the-fourth-generation-of-government-excellence-system

Government of the United Arab Emirates. (2016). *Why ministers for happiness, tolerance, youth and the future?* Retrieved March 30, 2020, from https://uaecabinet.ae/en/details/news/why-ministers-for-happiness-tolerance-youth-and-the-future

Government of the United Arab Emirates. (2020a). *Global star rating system for services*. Retrieved March 30, 2020, from https://u.ae/en/about-the-uae/the-uae-government/global-star-rating-system-for-services

Government of the United Arab Emirates. (2020b). *January 4, 2020 charter*. Retrieved March 30, 2020, from https://u.ae/en/about-the-uae/strategies-initiatives-and-awards/local-governments-strategies-and-plans/4-january-2020-charter

Grindle, M. S. (2017). Good governance, RIP: A critique and an alternative. *Governance*, *30*(1), 17–22.

Gulf News. (2019, 31 August). *Message from Sheikh Mohammed for UAE government officials, ministers, leaders*. Retrieved March 30, 2020, from https://gulfnews.com/uae/message-from-sheikh-mohammed-for-uae-government-officials-ministers-leaders-1.1567268923770

Helliwell, J., Layard, R., & Sachs, J. (2019). *World happiness report 2019*. Sustainable Development Solutions Network. https://worldhappiness.report/ed/2019/

Jones, C. W. (2017). *Bedouins into bourgeois: Remaking citizens for globalization*. Cambridge University Press.

Kisner, M., & Vigoda-Gadot, E. (2017). The provenance of public management and its future: Is public management here to stay? *International Journal of Public Sector Management*, *30*(6/7), 532–546.

Klenk, T., & Reiter, R. (2019). Post-new public management: Reform ideas and their application in the field of social services. *International Review of Administrative Sciences*, 85(1), 3–10.

Knafo, S. (2020). Neoliberalism and the origins of public management. *Review of International Political Economy*, 27(4), 780–801. https://doi.org/10.1080/09692290.2019.1625425

Lasrado, F., & Uzbeck, C. (2017). The excellence quest: A study of business excellence award-winning organizations in UAE. *Benchmarking: An International Journal*, 24(3), 716–734.

McCourt, W. (2018). New directions for public service reform in developing countries. *Public Administration and Development*, 38(3), 120–129.

McPherson, B. (2016). Agile, adaptive leaders. *Human Resource Management International Digest*, 24(2), 1–3.

MOE (Ministry of Economy). (2018). *The UAE and the world's leading economies: Managing challenges and opportunities amidst global change*. Ministry of Planning.

Mohammed Bin Rashid School of Government. (2017). *First look: The UAE and the future of work* [Working paper]. MBRSG.

Nuseirat, A. (2008). *Dubai Government Excellence Program: Achieving sustainable results*. The Executive Council-Dubai.

Oxford Analytica. (2015). *Networked government: The transition to citizen centricity* [in collaboration with the Government Summit 2015]. Retrieved March 30, 2020, from https://www.oxan.com/media/1315/networkedgovernment-oxfordanalytica.pdf

Pelton, V. J. (2018). Rule of law in the UAE: The peaceful path to nation-building in Abu Dhabi and the UAE through global best practices. *The International Lawyer*, 51(1), 87–107.

Pollitt, C., & Bouckaert, G. (2011). *Public management reform: A comparative analysis* (3rd ed.). Oxford University Press.

Rahman, M. H., AlBalooshi, S. A. Y. A., & Sarker, A. E. (2016). From e-governance to smart governance: Policy lessons for the UAE. In A. Farazmand (Ed.), *Global encyclopedia of public administration and public policy*. Springer.

Rahman, M. H., & Said, W. Y. (2015, February 12–13). *Public sector performance and leadership in the United Arab Emirates* [Conference session]. Presented in the 3rd International Conference on Management, Leadership and Governance – ICMLG 2015, Auckland, New Zealand.

Rahman, M. H., & Sarker, A. E. (2021, November 12–14). *Is agile government the New Panacea? Lessons learnt from the UAE* [Conference session]. Presented at the NASPAA South Asia Virtual Conference 2021 Preparing Public Leaders in South Asia for a Post Pandemic World.

Salem, F. (2016). *A Smart City for public value: Digital transformation through agile governance-the case of 'Smart Dubai'*. World Government Summit Publications. https://ssrn.com/abstract=2733632

Sarker, A. E., & Al Athmay, A. A. A. R. A. (2019). Public sector reforms in the United Arab Emirates: Antecedents and outcomes. *Public Administration Quarterly*, 43(3), 330–371.

Stephens, M., Spraggon, M., & Vammalle, C. (2019). *Agile government*. Policy Council Paper Session no 13 September 2019, Mohammed Bin Rashid School of Government, Dubai, UAE. Available at: https://mbrsgcdn.azureedge.net/cmsstorage/mbrsg/files/eb/eb10cc47-8ed3-4e8c-bb0e-69afe615cf90.pdf

The Fund for Peace. (2020). *Fragile States Index, 2019*. https://fragilestatesindex.org/country-data/

UNDP (United Nations Development Program). (2019). *Human Development Index: United Arab Emirates*. http://hdr.undp.org/sites/all/themes/hdr_theme/country-notes/ARE.pdf

United Nations (2018). *United Nations E Government Survey 2018*. https://publicadministration.un.org/Portals/1/Images/E-Government%20Survey%202018_FINAL%20for%20web.pdf

World Bank (2019). *Doing business*. https://www.doingbusiness.org/content/dam/doingBusiness/media/Annual-Reports/English/DB2019-report_web-version.pdf

World Economic Forum. (2019). *Global Competitive Report 2019*. http://www3.weforum.org/docs/WEF_TheGlobalCompetitivenessReport2019.pdf

Zafarullah, H., & Sarker, A. E. (2016). Public management reforms in developing countries: Toward a new synthesis. In N. Ahmed (Ed.), *Public policy and governance in Bangladesh: Forty years of experience* (pp. 62–72). Routledge.

Zafarullah, H., & Sarker, A. E. (2021). Contemporary issues in civil service management in South Asia: Principles and practice in India, Pakistan, and Bangladesh. In H. Sullivan, H. Dickinson, & H. Henderson (Eds.), *The Palgrave handbook of the public servant* (pp. 81–101). Palgrave Macmillan.

2
RECONSTRUCTION OF TURKISH PUBLIC ADMINISTRATION UNDER THE NEW PRESIDENTIAL GOVERNMENT SYSTEM

Yılmaz Üstüner

Introduction

This study is about the recent change in Turkey from the parliamentary system to the presidential system, focusing on its impact on its public administration system. First, the main pillars of this change are outlined. Public bureaucracy in Turkey now is excessively centralized; policy-making and executing functions are put under the direct control and authority of the president. This is basically maintained by equating the executive power with the presidency and limiting parliamentary and, up to a certain extent, judicial control. Second, only a few but pivotal potential complications are discussed such as the problems of overloading work at the central level, overlapping functions among different agencies and units, and work alienation of the employees. The final section attempts a theoretical discussion of the transformation centering around how to give meaning to this new system. I argue that such an analysis, above all, must focus on the inherent contradictions between neo-liberal (new) public management principles and practices and participatory democratic governance which is a universal problem that may not be specific to Turkey alone.

The transformation

The Grand National Assembly of Turkey enacted a law to amend the constitution on January 21, 2017. As votes fell below what was needed for the direct implementation of the law, a referendum was held on April 16, 2017. Out of an 85.10 percent voter turnout, 51.41 percent approved amending the constitution. This result marked a crucial milestone for Turkish society in general and its public administration system in particular.

Since the proclamation of the republic in 1923, Turkey had adopted three constitutions (1924, 1961, and 1982), with several amendments (1928, 1937, 1972, 1995, and 2001). However, the 2017 amendment differs from the others with respect to the fundamental, and also radical, novelties it brought both to Turkey's political and social life and to the structure of its bureaucracy. It should be noted that, despite the fact that this "amendment" law consisted of only 18 articles, it revised nearly half of the existing constitutional provisions either directly or indirectly.

Turkey had been ruled by a parliamentary system dating back to even before the proclamation of the modern republic. However, the parliamentary system was not exercised continuously or without flaws. From time to time, military interventions temporarily interrupted its functioning and many claimed that the separation of powers principle was consistently violated. However, the 2017 amendment (of which most provisions were effective by June 24, 2018) put an end to both the parliamentary system and the full implementation of the separation of powers principle.

In the past, voices in favor of abandoning the parliamentary system in Turkey were first heard from politicians in power. Following the 1980 military intervention, the elected Prime Minister Turgut Özal championed Turkey's transition to a neo-liberal market economy and opened itself up to globalization by adopting new-right ideologies and politics.[1] Özal was followed by President Süleyman Demirel, who also had always been a prominent center-right-wing politician. The main argument made was that the presidential system was typical of "mature democracies" in the world and the democratic political life of Turkey needed it (Kalaycıoğlu, 2005, p. 13). However, due to lack of popular support and dissident voices from various segments of the society, this system could not be put into effect. After the Justice and Development Party (Adalet ve Kalkınma Partisi or AKP in short) under the leadership of Recep Tayyip Erdoğan came into power in 2002, requests for a presidential system were revived. At that time, another reason was added as to why it was needed: Turkish bureaucracy and public administration were in a state of inertia and it supposedly turned into a "bureaucratic oligarchy" and a presidential system would put an end to that.

To illustrate, in a speech delivered in a meeting of Turkish industrialists and businessmen in April 2013, Erdoğan said: "the presidential system can easily break the back of bureaucratic oligarchy. Things get much different there; decision making becomes much faster" (Cumhuriyet, 2013). Eventually, the transition had been formally completed with a little help from the Nationalist Movement Party (MHP), a right-wing nationalist coalition partner of the AKP, when its leader Devlet Bahçeli openly declared his party's full support for amending the constitution and establishing the presidential system in Turkey.

These examples show us that the transition from parliamentary system to the presidential system was basically a right-wing and neo-liberal project essentially initiated by political leaders rather than by mass demand and support from society. Referendum acceptance votes, having only remained at 51.41 percent, are evidence to this.

There was an ongoing debate during the transition process on how to name the new system. For some, it was not appropriate to call it a presidential system. This was mainly because of the nature of the "unconventional" relations between powers, especially as the executive reigned supremely over other branches of government. Comparing the Turkish case to the most conventional example of a presidential system, the United States, Gözler points out differences in the appointment of higher members of judiciary, the controlling powers the senate has over the president, the preparation of the state budget, the political relationship between the president and his/her party, and others, as areas where the United States performs better (Gözler, 2017). Even supporters of the new system, including the leader and the speakers of AKP, refrained from calling it as a presidential system. The preferred name was a "presidency government system" (PGS). In fact, PGS is the official name used today in bureaucratic correspondences within public administration system.

Article 8 of the amended Turkish constitution states that "executive power and functions shall be exercised and carried out by the President of the Republic in conformity with the Constitution and laws." Before the amendment, executive power and functions were vested in the president and the Council of Ministers together, although the president's role was more ceremonial. When the prime minister and the Council of Ministers' positions were abolished, all powers of execution were passed onto the president himself/herself. The president can be nominated by political parties if he/she meets stipulated qualifications, and following elections, he/she does not need to sever relations with the party and can even continue to be its leader. The first elected person under this new system, Recep Tayyip Erdoğan, is both the president of the republic and the leader of AKP. This results in a leader of a political party getting full hierarchical control over Turkish bureaucracy and public administration system due to extreme centralization as discussed below.

Currently, around 4,612,000 persons are employed in the public sector in Turkey. This number includes officials and workers located in various public institutions all around the country at central and local units (Presidency of Turkey, Presidency of Strategy and Budget, 2019). The bureaucratic apparatus is strong with a deeply rooted bureaucratic culture inherited from Ottoman Empire before the establishment of the modern republic.[2] With the transformation into PGS, almost all public institutions, except local government units such as municipalities and village administrations, were put under the control of the president (Zengin, 2019). The existing organizational layout of Turkish presidency is shown in Figure 2.1. The organizational chart reveals that both policy-making and executive functions are centralized and placed under the

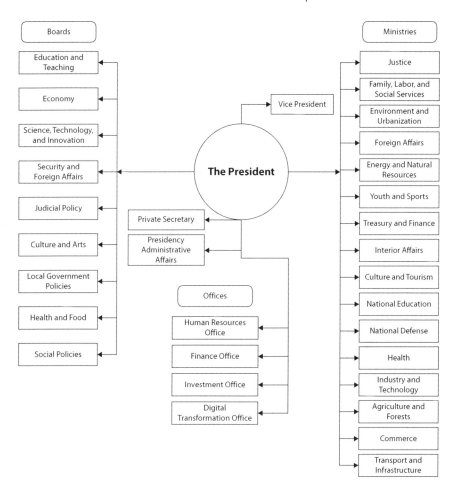

FIGURE 2.1 Organizational Layout of the Turkish Presidency

Source: The Author

authority of the president. Main units of the system are boards, president's offices, ministries, and attached institutions.

There are currently nine boards which specialize in important aspects of societal life, including economy, security, judicial affairs, social policy, and the like. Unlike the boards of independent regulatory authorities (IRAs) model (which also exist in Turkish public administration system although are less functional now), these boards are directly chaired by the president. Boards consist of a minimum of three members, all of whom are selected and appointed by the president. Article 22 of Presidential Decree Number 1,[3] dated July 10, 2018, about the duties and authorizations of these boards, states that, "these are in charge of bringing forward proposals about the decisions of the president and policies adopted" (Presidential Decree, 2018a).

Along with counseling policy boards, there are five presidential offices which have legal entities as well as administrative and financial autonomies. However, they are directly under the control of the president. This makes their administrative autonomy ambiguous. As to be mentioned in the next section, many of these boards' tasks and duties overlap with those of other units.

The third main group in the layout are the ministries. These are the conventional ministries, perhaps the most important components of the Turkish public administration system. They function as central institutions and most of them have field units all around the country, some even in foreign countries. With the new system, the president has the authority to appoint and remove the ministers. Their connection to the Turkish Grand Assembly has been minimized, almost totally putting an end to their control by the parliament, for instance, through interpellation as was the case before. As such, they are best described as "secretaries" to the president. In each ministry, there are "deputy ministers," who are usually persons with strong political ties with the party in power. Earlier, in each ministry, there were "undersecretaries," filling the highest rank public servants can fill and they played very crucial roles as the mediators between the ministerial bureaucracy and the minister being a political figure. These positions were totally abolished.

As there is neither a prime minister nor a Council of Ministers now, the "collective responsibilities" of ministers cease to exist; they are just responsible for their own actions and the actions of the ministries they are leading, and report only to the president himself/herself.

Finally, there are 11 attached institutions to the presidency. These also report to the president and their heads are directly appointed by her/him. Figure 2.2 shows the currently attached institutions. As can be seen, most of these are profound organizations shaping and regulating many aspects of the society ranging from religious affairs to national defense industries, and public finance and budget to national intelligence. In a sense, these units constitute the "backbone" of the Turkish public administration system. Among these units, two are worth mentioning separately. The first is the State Supervisory Council, which is in charge of auditing almost all public, non-profit, and professional institutions and organizations in Turkey except the judicial and the military ones. The audit is not automatic; it is realized upon the request by the president. The members of this board, who should serve at least 12 years in the public sector after their graduation from universities, are all appointed by the president. As this council does not act as a judicial body, there are no sanctions upon the results of the audit but their findings, if found illegal, are transferred to public prosecutors for legal action. The audit reports are submitted directly to the president.

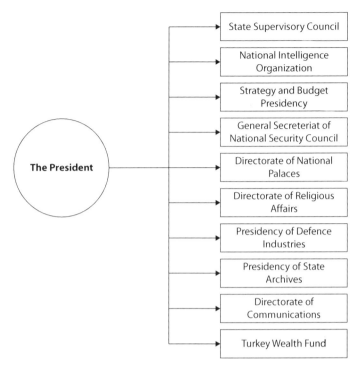

FIGURE 2.2 Attached Institutions of the Turkish Presidency

Source: The Author

The second attached institution worth mentioning is the Turkey Wealth Fund. It was established in 2016 with an incorporated company status. As such, it is subject to private law. The main goal of the fund is to manage the assets that belong to the public sector. To achieve that aim, since its establishment, highly strategic and profound assets that previously belonged to the Treasury were transferred and put under its control. Among these were one of the biggest public-sector-owned banks, the Bank of Agriculture (Ziraat Bankası), and other key organizations such as Turkish Petroleum Incorporated (Türkiye Petrolleri Anonim Ortaklığı), İstanbul Stock Exchange (Borsa İstanbul), National Lottery (Milli Piyango), and Turkish Posts (PTT). Further, the fund has partnerships in many public or semi-public companies, including Turkey's flag carrier airline company Turkish Airlines (THY).

As of 2019, the fund's total active size is more than 617 billion Turkish Liras, that is, approximately 80 billion dollars (Acabay, 2019). As mentioned, despite the fact that this fund is subject to private law and has a private corporation status, it is directly attached to the presidency, which chairs it, and moreover, members of its board of administrators are appointed by the president. The board is subject to private audit and is exempted from the Court of Accounts (the judicial institution in charge of auditing all public-sector institutions with respect to their financial and accounting affairs). Critics claim that the presence of this institution "defies the rule of law principle" in Turkey and should be "seen as a legitimate cover for the deepening partisan resource distribution" (Acabay, 2019, p. 92).

Within the presidential government system, the president holds another important executive authority. Article 104 of the amended constitution of Turkey on the duties and powers of the president states that "he/she shall appoint and dismiss the high ranking executives and shall regulate the procedure and principles governing the appointment thereof by presidential decree" (Turkish Constitution, Article 104). As the constitution does not define the details of this power, the list of these positions and the conditions for appointment are all determined by presidential decrees rather than, for example, by a law enacted by Turkish Grand National Assembly. Presidential Decree Number 3, issued in July 2018, enlists which higher positions are included and what should be the required qualifications for appointees. The decree makes the appointment of persons without any previous public service experience possible provided that they meet the stated qualifications. These positions include governors, the head prosecutor of the Court of Accounts, ambassadors, other chiefs of diplomatic missions, the board of administration members of the Higher Education Council, rectors of all the universities, and many other similar key posts in the Turkish bureaucracy. For these positions, incumbency is limited to the incumbency of the president, but their dismissal is possible any time before the termination of their duty (Presidential Decree, 2018b).

Finally, it should be noted that against all his/her substantial policy-making and execution powers, which can be realized through presidential decrees, the president's responsibilities and accountability are limited. It is a fact that the president is still subject to control by the legislative. However, this is only limited to criminal liability. Article 105 of the amended constitution states that an absolute majority (currently 301 members) of Turkish Grand National Assembly may request an investigation into the president for crime allegations. Three-fifths of the total number of deputies (currently 360 members) should accept the request through a secret ballot. Once accepted, a committee is formed and carries out the investigation and reports the result to the speaker of the parliament. With the plenary votes on the report following the debates on the report, and with two-thirds of all members' (currently 400 members) acceptance votes, the case is transferred to Turkish Constitutional Court for trial. But it should be noted that, according to Article 105 of the constitution, 12 out of 15 members of the assembly of the Constitutional Court, responsible for presiding over the president's case, are selected and appointed by him/her.

Some potential complications for public administration

Some of the major and most critical features of a presidential government system in Turkey as outlined above are that most of the decision making, spheres of action, and discretion capacity are stripped away from various levels of the bureaucracy and concentrated at the level of the presidency, if not the president herself/himself. Centralism had always been a typical characteristic of Turkish bureaucracy both at the micro (i.e., within units of administration) and macro levels (i.e., central government). However, the latest reform brings forth a radical change by equipping the president with unprecedented executive power. As the system is new, it is too early to comment on. Despite this, certain potential complications, which are already visible, may arise.

In general, it might be claimed that PGS will likely give way to a "closed" bureaucratic system with minimum democratic governance and undermine principles of participation and accountability. In particular, especially for the inner operation of the public administration system, other "less discussed" issues should not be disregarded. These are the overload problem, the overlapping problem, and the work alienation problem.

The overload problem

The overload problem is likely to happen when one considers the vast number of duties assigned to the president. As stated before, many of these tasks are assigned directly to the president's person and there are lots of matters which necessitate his/her revision, approval, and ratification. These would result in time-consuming personal workload of the president and paperwork. However, his/her ceremonial duties as the head of the state are equally dense, and what is more, the constitution allows him to be a political party leader concomitantly. The political arena in Turkey has always witnessed a very dynamic relationship and usually contentious struggles both between those holding power and opposition parties as well as inside the parties themselves. The president at the same time should try to fulfill his obligations to the voters and the party which possibly nominated him/her.

In fact, only considering the vast number of higher-level bureaucrats that the president should select and appoint without delays and follow up on their job performances, estimated to be nearly 1,500 employees, is enough to grasp the magnitude of his workload. As mentioned earlier, one of the most spoken justifications for the transition to the PGS was to increase the efficiency and productivity of public bureaucracy and eliminate inertia, but under these conditions, it seems that there are adequate reasons to be doubtful about realizing this aim. The problem might be alleviated to some extent if the president transfers some of her/his authorities to subordinates and potentially builds a strong inner presidential bureaucratic machinery. However, even if the president has the desire to do so, formal/legal arrangements have not been sufficiently made to enable that.

Task overlapping

The overlapping of tasks and duties exists especially in the offices of the presidency, attached institutions, and the ministries. Before the reform of the system, policy-making had basically been carried out by the conventional ministries and then settled and put into action through the decisions of the Council of Ministers. The role of the presidency was highly limited in that respect. With the new arrangements, although the function and power are vested at the presidency, there are still overlapping tasks with existing ministries. This is especially evident in the administration of the economy. To illustrate, Presidential Decree Number 3 stipulates the main tasks and duties of Ministry of Treasure and Finance. Article 217 states that this ministry is in charge of assisting the preparation of financial and economic policies; these include coordinating the drafting of the public revenues policy, preparing tax policies and policies on relations with the international financial institutions, and the like (Presidential Decree, 2018b). However, Decree Number 13 (Presidential Decree, 2018c) on the establishment of Strategy and Budget Presidency as a unit directly attached to the presidency assigns very similar tasks to this unit as well. It should be noted that alongside these units, there is also a policy board in charge of dealing with the affairs of economy within the presidency. In order to solve this potential overlapping problem, a provision had been added to Presidential Decree Number 13, allowing coordination meetings among these overlapping units to be held with the president as the chair or with a proxy delegated by her/him. Despite this, it is not clear now whether these meetings are done frequently and efficiently.

Work alienation

The third potential problem area is the alienation of public employees. Tummers et al. (2007, p. 4) define public employee alienation, especially toward the policies adopted, as "the mode of experience in which the public service worker, who on a regular basis interacts directly with clients, cannot identify himself with the public policies he has to implement." According to the authors, employee feelings such as powerlessness, meaninglessness, social isolation, and role conflicts result in public employee alienation. The alienation of public employees is likely to occur mainly because of the fact that during this restructuring process, many of the institutions, positions, and procedures of the bureaucracy have been shuffled, eroded, and abolished. These radical reform steps, unfortunately, were taken with the minimum participation and governance of the members of these institutions.

It is known that almost all the preparations leading up to the reform have been kept secret and only shared with a small number of bureaucrats, academics, and political advisers to the political authority. To illustrate the potential source of alienation among the employees, we should mention the "State Personnel Presidency" (SPP) case. Before the restructuring, SPP was one of the most crucial central units. Established back in 1960, first autonomous, then attached to prime ministry in 1984, it worked as a central policy-making body holding executive duties about personnel affairs of public employees. With PGS, it was abolished and all of its employees, most of whom were highly competent experts with a good knowledge accumulation and a strong established bureaucratic culture and experience, were transferred to the Ministry of Family, Labour, and Social Services. The job descriptions of most of these personnel now are unrelated to their expertise areas knowledge, and experience. SPP is not a unique and exceptional case in this respect, whose cadres were shuffled and repositioned. Although the state has carried out a mandatory job satisfaction survey among public employees, the results are not public. Due to the fact that the final words in both public policy-making and executive functions and procedures are determined at the highest level of the hierarchy, with minimum participation from the employees and minimum use of their technical bureaucratic expertise, it is no surprise that job dissatisfaction and work alienation could become widespread among public employees.

How to analyze the reconstruction?

The main question to be asked is: what factors and reasons forced Turkey to make the change to PGS? As mentioned earlier, this was a long-time project of right-wing parties since the adoption of neo-liberal economic, political, and social policies that aligned the system with neo-liberal ways of organizing and administering the bureaucratic apparatus. It is difficult to talk about massive popular support of this process. There is no doubt that this was a successful AKP project, especially with the initiation of Recep Tayyip Erdoğan who has been in power for nearly 20 years. AKP had sufficient experience on how to run the government and how to direct and lead the bureaucratic apparatus. Their awareness of the potential disadvantages of this system cannot be questioned as well. But can we still attribute the reasons for the system's introduction to personal attitudes, ambitions, and/or the subjective ideological choices of the party members and Erdoğan himself? I think this would be misleading and inadequate and does not provide a clear meaning to the rationale behind the making of the reform. It will be equally misleading to attribute this major reform only to administrative and technical reasons such as lack of efficiency and dynamism or the alleged dominance of a "bureaucratic oligarchy" over the elected politicians.

In recent years, many contributions on the topic of "neo-liberal authoritarianism" in political science literature have emerged (Bruff, 2014; Juego, 2018; Tansel, 2017). There are claims that some countries, including Turkey, that have been following neo-liberal policies are moving more toward authoritarian political and administrative ways of government.[4] Whether Turkey is one of these and whether PGS is a symptom of such a situation or not necessitates further in-depth analysis, which is beyond the scope and limitation of this work. Rather, this author prefers to focus on the discipline and theory of public administration.

Nearly 40 years have passed since the academic manifestations of a neoliberal public administration were formulated as a paradigm of public management. Two contributions, now classical theories, should be remembered: Perry and Kraemer's *Public Management: Public and Private Perspectives* (Perry & Kraemer, 1983) and Osborne and Gaebler's *Reinventing Government: How the Entrepreneurial Spirit Is Transforming the Public Sector* (Osborne & Gaebler, 1992). The former established the theoretical grounds for the forthcoming era of public administration following the "demise" of the welfare state and the rise of neo-liberalism. The latter, though not radically different from the former, established the necessary "corrections" to this paradigm by adjusting it to the emerging "regulatory state" phase starting in the middle of the 1990s and ripening in the 2000s. Osborne and Gaebler laid down the famous "ten commandments" for public administration. Through these, the state's role in market relations had been redefined from full liberalization and minimization to "steering" (but never rowing). These two classic contributions clearly defined the nature and shape of public administration even today. Regulatory state adjustments were necessary for the maintenance of the system against the emerging threats such as full liberalization, privatization, over-competition, and the rise of the oligopolistic and monopolistic tendencies of (international) big capital. New public management practice and theory made the necessary cybernetic correction by assigning a regulatory role to the state and adjusting public administration (management) accordingly.

Potential incompatibilities between new public management and democratic governance are a much-debated topic (Brint et al., 2016; Christensen & Lægreid, 2002; Cook, 2007; Haque, 2016). Aside from the theoretical debate, questions like how to maintain a "strong state" with "a less government" or how to "administer the state as if one is managing a private company" are still relevant questions after all these years.[5] "Strong state" and "entrepreneurial logic" are likely to necessitate more centralism and less barriers (such as popular participation, rule of the law, the separation of powers, and the de-centralization of the bureaucratic apparatus). To do that, the public should be "managed" and not "governed."

Turkey is one of the countries which strictly and unbrokenly adhered to (new) public management system. Transitioning to the free market economy in the 1980s has continued with AKP. However, the bureaucratic apparatus, despite many attempts of unsuccessful reform campaigns in the 1990s, could not be fully adjusted as desired. Despite this, until the introduction of the PGS, AKP was able to maintain a better equalization between neo-liberal policies and the bureaucratic apparatus.

But now, many real and potential problems are in sight such as an increasing unemployment rate of around 14.8 percent, a deepening income gap among social segments (the richest 40 percent of the population receive 76 percent of the total income with a Gini coefficient of 0.408), and the slowing down of construction as the "motor sector" of the economy especially after the 2018 crisis, to name a few. These problems are likely to be deepened following COVID-19 pandemic. Moreover, some of the major problems ahead include a trade deficit, foreign currency loans of the private sector, and the state being the warrantor for all public and private sector debt, including immense amount of public and private partnership projects. So is the continuous devaluation of the Turkish currency, putting more burden on national debt. Can PGS with its neglect of democracy and participatory governance respond to these problems? Naturally, only time will say.

Is Turkey unique and exceptional in this respect, with its own historical, political, and social dynamics? Or is centralization, and more disciplinarian governance and public administration systems, the inevitable outcome for at least some of the countries which adapted neo-liberal policies?

Whatever the answer, we should remember that 40 years ago, the popular "Blacksburg Manifesto" written in reaction to a newly emerging new-right-based neo-liberal bureaucracy and public administration in the United States and the "bureaucratic bashing" campaigns of the new-right ideology pinpointed this inherent contradiction:

> The problem then lies simply in a lack of organizing and managerial skills, though we still have plenty of room for improvement. Rather it goes beyond, to the problem of governing a modern republic with a commitment to freedom and justice on the one hand and commitment to a complex mixture of capitalism and state intervention on the other.
>
> *Wamsley et al. (1990, p. 32)*

It can be predicted that for global public administration practice and theory, this issue will likely continue as a challenge in the future.

Notes

1 For a detailed analysis of this transformation, see Yalman (2009).
2 For an overview and the main characteristics of Turkish public administration system and bureaucracy, see Üstüner and Yavuz (2018a) and Üstüner and Yavuz (2018b).

3 By the amendments, the president was authorized to enact "presidential decrees." Although this power existed in the previous constitution, it was seldom used. The abolished Council of Ministers held this power regarding limited topics, but with the amendments, this was transferred to the president under the only condition that decrees should be related to executive affairs and cover areas which are not subject to regulation by laws. Moreover, these decrees are not subject to the approval of the parliament and, as such, this is subject to criticism on the grounds that this would be violation of the separation of powers principle, giving the executive the rights of the legislative.

4 Many studies done with the aim of quantifying levels of democracy and authoritarianism by using indexes and scales claim that authoritarianism is on the rise in many countries. To illustrate, see https://www.eiu.com/topic/democracy-index, https://freedomhouse.org/countries/freedom-world/scores, https://www.bti-project.org/en/reports/country-report-TUR.html

5 For a detailed treatment of managing a private company and PGS in Turkey, see Güzelsarı (2019).

References

Acabay, S. (2019). *The political economy of Turkey Wealth Fund: A case study in the state-business relations in Turkey* [Unpublished MA thesis]. İhsan Doğramacı Bilkent University. http://repository.bilkent.edu.tr/bitstream/handle/11693/52412/10290250.PDF?sequence=1

Brint, M., Jensen, L., Roberts, A., Dussauge-Laguna, M. I., Junjan, V., Torenvlied, R., Boin, A., Colebatch, H. K., Kettl, D., & Durant, R. (2016). Is public management neglecting the state? *Governance*, *29*(3), 311–334.

Bruff, I. (2014). The rise of authoritarian liberalism. *Rethinking Marxism*, *26*(1), 113–129.

Christensen, T., & Lægreid, P. (2002). New public management: Puzzles of democracy and the influence of citizens. *The Journal of Political Philosophy*, *10*(3), 267–295.

Cook, B. (2007). *Democracy and administration: Woodrow Wilson's ideas and the challenges of public management*. Johns Hopkins University Press.

Cumhuriyet. (2013, April 7). Turkish Newspaper. www.cumhuriyet.com.tr/haber/erdogandan-baskanlik-sistemi-aciklamasi-414310

Gözler, K. (2017). *Cumhurbaşkanlığı sistemi mi, Başkanlık sistemi mi, yoksa neverland sistemi mi?* 16 Nisan'da Neyi Oylayacağız? http://www.anayasa.gen.tr/neverland.htm

Güzelsarı, S. (2019). Neoliberal Otoriterleşme, Devletin Şirketleşmesi ya da Şirket-Devlet: Cumhurbaşkanlığı Hükümet Sistemi. Ayrıntı Dergi, 29 (January). Ayrıntı Publishers.

Haque, S. (2016). Understanding democratic governance: Practical trends and theoretical puzzles. *Asian Journal of Political Science*, *24*(3), 340–347.

Juego, B. (2018). Authoritarian liberalism: Its ideological antecedents and policy manifestations from Carl Scmitts's political economy of governance. *Administrative Culture*, *19*(1), 105–136.

Kalaycıoğlu, E. (2005). *Başkanlık Sistemi: Türkiye'nin Diktatörlük Tehdidiyle Sınavı*. In T. Ergül (Ed.), *Başkanlık Sistemi*. Türkiye Barolar Birliği.

Osborne, D., & Gaebler, T. (1992). *Reinventing government: How the entrepreneurial spirit is transforming the public sector*. Plume.

Perry, J., & Kraemer, K. (1983). *Public management: Public and private perspectives*. Mayfield Pub.

Presidency of Turkey, Presidency of Strategy and Budget. (2019). *İşgücü Piyasasindaki Gelişmelerin Makro Analizi*. http://www.sbb.gov.tr/wp-content/uploads/2020/02/isgucu-Piyasasi-2019-iv-Ceyrek.pdf

Presidential Decree. (2018a). *Presidential Decree No 1*. July 10, 2018. https://www.mevzuat.gov.tr/MevzuatMetin/19.5.1.pdf

Presidential Decree. (2018b). *Presidential Decree No 3*. July 10, 2018. https://www.mevzuat.gov.tr/MevzuatMetin/19.5.3.pdf

Presidential Decree. (2018c). *Presidential Decree No 13*. July 24, 2018. https://www.mevzuat.gov.tr/MevzuatMetin/19.5.13.pdf

Tansel, C. B. (Ed.). (2017). *States of discipline: Authoritarian neoliberalism and the contested reproduction of capitalist order*. Rowman & Littlefield.

Tummers, L., Bekkers, V., & Steijn, B. (2007). *Public policy alienation of public service workers*. IRSPM XI. https://www.researchgate.net/publication/241861241_Public_policy_alienation_of_public_service_workers

Turkish Constitution. (1982). https://www.anayasa.gov.tr/en/legislation/turkish-constiution/

Üstüner, Y., & Yavuz, N. (2018a). Turkey's public administration today: An overview and appraisal. *International Journal of Public Administration*, 41(10), 820–831.

Üstüner, Y., & Yavuz, N. (2018b). Public administration in Turkey. In A. Farazmand (Ed.), *Global encyclopaedia of public administration, public policy, and governance*. Springer. http://springer.iq-technikum.de/referenceworkentry/10.1007/978-3-319-31816-5_3485-1#toc

Wamsley, G. L., Bacher, R. N., Goodsell, C. T., Kronenberg, P. S., Rohr, J. A., Stivers, C. M., White, O. F., & Wolf, J. F. (1990). *Refounding public administration*. Sage Publications.

Yalman, G. (2009). *Transition to neoliberalism: The case of Turkey in the 1980s*. İstanbul Bilgi University Press.

Zengin, O. (2019). Cumhurbaşkanlığı Hükümet Sistemi ve İdari Yapıya Etkisi. *Emek Araştırma Dergisi*, 10(15), 1–24.

3
PUBLIC ADMINISTRATION IN THE REPUBLIC OF LEBANON

Recent Reforms, Current Constraints, and Future Prospects[1]

Thomas W. Haase

Introduction

As the nineteenth century ended, Woodrow Wilson (1887, p. 200) wrote, "it is getting to be harder to run a constitution than to frame one." The sentiment behind Wilson's observation about the challenges of governance and public administration is especially relevant for Arab countries. According to Jamil Jreisat (2002, p. 129), this is because many Arab countries have adopted Western-style administrative institutions that interface with non-Western cultural patterns, social structures, and individual behaviors. Consequently, Arab countries face administrative challenges such as underproductive public organizations, a lack of skilled public managers, excessive centralization, widespread corruption, and outdated political and administrative structures (Jreisat, 2002, p. 132). Despite Jreisat's pessimism, efforts have been undertaken to strengthen the bureaucratic structures of countries throughout the Middle East (Antoun, 2007; OECD, 2010).

This chapter provides a general overview of the state of public administration in the Republic of Lebanon. While such a review is constrained by a lack of publicly available data, less-than-transparent government institutions, and a deficit of scholarly research, the goal is to highlight the primary themes and reforms that occurred between the end of the Lebanese Civil War (1975–1990) and 2015. The remainder of this chapter is organized into eight sections. Following an overview of Lebanon's socio-economic background, this chapter highlights the dynamic relationships that drive interactions between the state, civil society, and the economic markets. The focus then shifts to Lebanon's governmental institutions, particularly the country's legal structures, civil service

DOI: 10.4324/9781003389941-4

arrangements, budgeting processes, e-government strategies, and public-sector ethics. This chapter concludes with a discussion of the threats and opportunities that may affect Lebanon's bureaucratic institutions.

Socio-economic background

Lebanon is a country that has a diverse population, the size of which is unknown. The last official census was conducted by the French Mandate government in 1932 (Maktabi, 1999). World Bank and Central Intelligence Agency reports, however, provide some insight into Lebanon's demographic and economic situation. In 2014, for example, Lebanon's population was estimated to be 5.9 million (World Bank, 2016). This population is divided along religious lines, as approximately 54 percent are Muslim—Sunni (27 percent) and Shia (27 percent)—and 40.5 percent are Christian (CIA, 2015). These demographics have also been economically active. In 2014, Lebanon's Gross Domestic Product (GDP) totaled 45.7 billion dollars, an increase of 3.1 percent over the previous year. Although the GDP increased to 47.5 billion dollars in 2016, Lebanon's economic growth has been tempered by its public debt. According to the World Bank (2016), Lebanon's "public debt (as a ratio to GDP) continued to rise (157.5 percent of GDP at end-2016), due to low growth and a relatively high cost of debt financing."

In recent years, Lebanon has been impacted by the consequences of the Syrian Civil War. In 2016, the United Nations estimated that 13.5 million Syrians had been displaced by the conflict. According to the High Commission for Refugees (UNHCR, 2016), more than 1.03 million Syrians sought sanctuary in Lebanon, which put pressures on the country's political and economic institutions. The crisis has increased the incidence of poverty, widened income inequality, and raised questions about the long-term status of the Syrians who live in Lebanon. Indeed, by 2018, Lebanese politicians began to call for Syrians to return home and some Lebanese municipalities have begun to forcibly evict Syrians from their homes (Human Rights Watch, 2018). As the Syrian Civil War continues, Syrian refugees will continue to have long-term impacts on Lebanon's social, political, and economic situations.

Societal governance and public administration

Founded as a parliamentary democracy, Lebanon's political power is shared among the countries' religious communities (El-Zein & Holly Sims, 2004; Hasbani, 2011; Safa, 2010; Youngblood Coleman, 2015). This arrangement, known as confessionalism, has led to the establishment of political parties that reflect the Lebanese population's political ideologies and religious beliefs (Salamey, 2014; Youngblood Coleman, 2015). It is important to note, however, that Lebanon's political parties do not exist to encourage open and democratic political participation (Antoun, 2008). Rather, political parties are used by the sectarian elites to gain access to Lebanon's political institutions and to wield power over their constituents (Youngblood Coleman, 2015).

Scholars have described Lebanon's political system as dysfunctional (AbouAssi et al., 2013; Antoun, 2008; Makdisi et al., 2011; Salamey, 2014). The source of this dysfunction is the country's power-sharing scheme, which enables political parties to establish clientelistic relationships between the party leaders and their constituents (Makdisi et al., 2011). In this political system, citizens do not have the opportunity to participate in the decision-making process, as the interests of sectarian groups and their political parties supersede the interests of the people as a collective (Safa, 2010).

Similarly, Lebanon's bureaucratic system, influenced by deeply engrained political and cultural customs and a history of foreign domination by the Ottoman and French authorities (AbouAssi et al., 2013), has also been described as a sectarian establishment that represents specific religious and ethnic groups (Kisirwani & Parle, 1987). Lebanon's bureaucratic system suffers from three governance problems (AbouAssi et al., 2013; Kisirwani & Parle, 1987; OMSAR, 2011; Wickberg, 2015). First, the bureaucratic system is prone to sectarian influence and practices that encourage nepotism, patronage, and corruption (Antoun, 2007; Atzili, 2010; El-Saad, 2001; El-Zein & Holly Sims, 2004). Second, the system is highly centralized and unresponsive to the needs of citizens, especially those from lower socio-economic communities (AbouAssi et al., 2013; El-Saad, 2001). Third, the system suffers from deficiencies in strategic management, technology, policymaking, and planning (Office of the Minister of State for Administrative Reform (OMSAR), 2011).

Public-sector size and scope

Lebanon is considered to have a large public sector (Antoun, 2007; El-Saad, 2001; Habib, 2005; World Bank, 2005a, 2005b). Although the scope of Lebanon's public sector has varied (Salamey, 2014), the size of the public bureaucracy has expanded over the last 50 years. According to Antoun (2007), much of this growth occurred during the Lebanese Civil War, when Lebanon's public sector expanded to more than 180,000 employees. Since the end of the Civil War, the number of public employees seems to have further increased. Although reliable data are difficult to obtain, estimates suggest that the public bureaucracy employs between 220,000 and 230,000 people (Chaaban, 2013; World Bank, 2005b).

With respect to scope, Lebanon's public sector has the authority to address issues related to defense, telecommunications, agriculture, public works and transport, tourism, finance, social affairs, environment, youth and sports, labor, justice, economy and trade, and education. However, the public sector's capacity to adopt and implement policies that can address these issue areas is limited (Harb & Atallah, 2015). Moreover, public corruption and inefficiencies create public service delivery gaps, which are often filled by private and civil society organizations (Harb & Atallah, 2015; Leenders, 2012).

Informing values

The Lebanese Civil War had a tremendous impact on the country's public institutions. The conflict disrupted public services, destroyed critical infrastructure, and transformed public institutions into vessels for political parties and militias (Adwan, 2004; Antoun, 2008; El-Zein & Holly Sims, 2004; Mehanna, 1993). Although the violence has ceased, Ghosn and Khoury (2011) note that Lebanon's political situation remains tenuous. This is because the conflict enabled sectarianism to permeate Lebanese social and political life, which has undermined attempts to foster national unity. Furthermore, the conflict undermined the relationship between Lebanese citizens and their public institutions. In the simplest terms, many Lebanese are dissatisfied and mistrustful of their government's performance (Antoun, 2008; Hasbani, 2011). Although the reasons for these perceptions are complex, Lebanon's public institutions are considered non-responsive to the interests of the general public, and, more importantly, are not able to provide citizens with basic public goods and services (Atzili, 2010).

Lebanon's governments have long recognized the need for reform (AbuKhalil, 1989; D'Aspremont, 2011; Kingston, 2013). Early reform attempts were initiated following Lebanon's independence but were disrupted by the Civil War. After the Civil War, the government reinitiated reform efforts (Antoun, 2007). Most of the efforts focused on reforming Lebanon's public budgeting institutions and processes. For example, the Ministry of Finance was reorganized, and investments were made in information technology and human capital. With support from the United Nations, the government also established the OMSAR in 1994 (El-Zein & Holly Sims, 2004).

Charged with the responsibility to oversee the development of the bureaucracy, the OMSAR participated in an inter-ministerial committee that sought to identify areas of the bureaucracy in most need of reform. The committee identified five areas that needed attention such as employee compensation, job descriptions and classifications, the reorganization of administrative structures, the development of performance evaluation processes, and the simplification of laws and procedures (El-Zein & Holly Sims, 2004). Although OMSAR has spent decades working on these issues, Lebanon's public-sector reforms have been hindered by several problems, namely the lack of long-term planning, excessive centralization, ineffective program implementation, inadequate human resources, the lack of monitoring and accountability, the lack of information technology, inadequate facilities, and the lack of political support (OMSAR, 2011).

The state and civil society

The regulatory framework that governs Lebanese civil society was enacted by the Ottoman Empire as the 1909 Law on Associations (Elbayar, 2005; Joseph, 2010). This law continues to be one of the most liberal civil society frameworks in the Middle East (Abdel Samad, 2007). Consequently, Lebanon has experienced the emergence of a dynamic community of social activists and nongovernmental organizations (NGOs) known formally as associations.

Nongovernmental organizations

The relationship between the Lebanese government and civil society has vacillated between complacency and conflict (Haddad et al., 2018). During the Civil War, NGOs often replaced government institutions as providers of critical public services. In this capacity, NGOs gained social recognition and legitimacy. After the Civil War, and driven by Syria's involvement in Lebanon's internal affairs, the Lebanese government began to interfere in NGO affairs, which substantially constrained their civic activities. After Syria's withdrawal from Lebanon in 2005, NGOs obtained some freedom from government intervention. This enabled NGOs to initiate efforts designed to engage and pressure political institutions that had become paralyzed by domestic instability.

The precise number of domestic and international NGOs in Lebanon is unknown (El-Husseini et al., 2004; Gebara, 2007; Joseph, 2010). According to a study conducted by Bennet (1995), between 4,000 and 13,000 NGOs were active in Lebanon following the Civil War. Recent studies suggest that there are between 4,000 and 6,000 NGOs officially registered with the government (Altan-Olcay & Icduygu, 2012; Chaaban & Seyfert, 2012; Kingston, 2013; MOSA, 2009). At present, NGOs provide a variety of goods and services throughout Lebanon and work to protect family and communal interests, deliver essential public services, protect those displaced by domestic and regional conflicts, and organize social movements that pressure the government into undertaking political and institutional reforms.

Ombudsman

In an effort to improve public-sector accountability, the Lebanese government adopted an Ombudsman Law in 2005. Despite this legislative development, the Ombudsman Law has yet to be implemented (Safa, 2010). Prior to 2005, the Citizen's Complaint Office investigated and addressed matters of public concern. The office received public complaints, referred them to the appropriate office, and followed up on their resolution (President of the Republic of Lebanon, 2016). According to Safa (2010, p. 349), however, the activities of the

Citizen's Complaint Office have been the target of criticism. As a result, NGOs often operated as the informal interface between Lebanon's citizens and their governmental institutions.

Significant civil society reforms and developments

Lebanon's NGOs are well-positioned to facilitate social and political changes (Karam, 2008; Karam & Catusse, 2009; Kingston, 2013; UNESCWA, 2010). Nevertheless, NGOs encounter structural and organizational challenges that influence their mission and their ability to implement their social programs (Adjamian & Haase, 2018). These challenges exist because the 1909 Law on Associations is not adequate to regulate a civil society deserving of the twenty-first century (Traboulsi, 2000, p. 3). This regulatory inadequacy has enabled the government to exert its authority over associations (Makary, 2007, pp. 87–90). While systematic attempts to reform Lebanon's civil society regulatory framework have not occurred, the Minister of the Interior and Municipalities ended administrative practices that undermined the spirit of the 1909 Law on Associations. In taking these steps, the government reduced the extent to which it interfered with the establishment and operation of domestic civil society organizations. In recent years, the Lebanese government has started to use libel and defamation laws to constrain the freedom of social activists and NGOs that use social media to criticize public officials and their activities (Agence France-Presse, 2018).

The state and the marketplace

The Lebanese government has pursued a policy of minimal intervention in the country's economic markets. This policy has led to the development of a robust private sector. According to the Ministry of Finance (2014a, p. 22), Lebanon's private sector contributes "approximately 88 percent to national expenditures, and includes activities such as agriculture, manufacturing, construction, commercial trade and tourism, in addition to services such as financial services, hotels and restaurants, information and communication services, and consulting and professional services." While the private sector is driven by open competition, the economy remains constrained by nepotism, corruption, and critical infrastructure problems.

Marketization and privatization

Discussions about economic reform in Lebanon have typically focused on questions of privatization. These discussions have been driven by the need to improve the performance of state-owned enterprises (for example, see Blominvest Bank,

2015, p. 13). For instance, the government has adopted a regulatory framework for privatization (Law 228 of 2000). This legislation also established a ministerial-level committee—the Higher Council for Privatization—that would oversee the privatization of state-owned enterprises (Ministry of Finance, 2014a, p. 24). An additional step was taken in 2002, when the government established rules for the privatization of the state-owned mobile telecommunication enterprises with the adoption of the Telecommunications Law (Law 431 of 2002). That same year, the government also established the foundations for the transfer of the ownership and/or management of the state-owned electric utility enterprise to the private sector (Law 462 of 2002). These efforts were disrupted by the assassination of Prime Minister Rafik Hariri and the 2006 Lebanon War.

The government renewed its privatization efforts in 2007, under pressure from the international donor community during the Paris III Conference. According to Cynthia Abi Rached (2008), a Program Officer with the Arab NGO Network for Development (ANND), the Paris III Conference was designed to "provide support for the country's post-war reconstruction, secure cash for debt servicing, and cover the budgetary deficit." In exchange for 7.5 billion dollars in assistance, the Lebanese government agreed to adopt reforms that would promote economic stability and reduce the national debt (Youngblood Coleman, 2015, 184). The agreement led to the contracting out of two state-owned telecommunications networks to the private sector. Despite more than a decade of such initiatives, Lebanon's aspirations for privatization have yet to be fully realized.

Regulation

Lebanon has a complicated set of regulatory structures. The banking and financial service sector is the most regulated part of Lebanon's economy. This sector is managed by the Bank of Lebanon, under the supervision of the Banking Control Commission. Given the role of banking and finance in the Lebanese economy, these regulations are rigorously enforced to ensure that the sector adheres to global best practices. In contrast, while the government may have adopted regulations related to the environment, construction, water and food safety, and zoning, such regulations are often vague and weakly enforced. The lack of implementation and enforcement of such regulations is caused by limitations in Lebanon's bureaucratic capacity, as well as problems related to political tensions, corruption, patronage, and nepotism.

Significant market reforms and developments

The Higher Council for Privatization shifted its focus from privatization toward Public-Private Partnerships (PPPs) in recent years (Gavin, 2012, p. 34). Reflecting this shift, the Higher Council for Privatization drafted PPP legislation, which was sent to the Council of Ministers for consideration in 2010. The draft legislation gave the Higher Council for Privatization the authority to establish PPPs in the energy, transportation, education, and healthcare sectors. The draft legislation also defined the role that PPP institutions would play in the broader economy, as well as the processes that would be used to develop and implement PPP projects. While the Higher Council for Privatization argues that PPPs can help develop Lebanon's infrastructure and economy, the draft legislation remains unapproved.

The governance structures

Lebanon is governed by three institutional structures, according to its constitution (Republic of Lebanon, 1926). The most substantial of these structures is the national government, within which power and authority are highly centralized. The other two structures, the regional and municipal governments, have responsibilities related to the management of the territories within their jurisdictions.

National government

Lebanon's national government is divided into three branches: legislative, executive, and judicial.

Legislative branch

Lebanon's national legislative power is vested in a unicameral parliament, officially known as the Chamber of Deputies, to be referred to as the Chamber. The Chamber has 128 members, who are elected for four-year terms. Currently, the Chamber's seats are distributed equally between the Christians and Muslims. Within these communities, seats are further distributed proportionally among confessional groups and geographic regions (Constitution, Article 24). The Chamber of Deputies and the Council of Ministers can both initiate the legislative process by submitting draft legislation or other proposals to the Parliamentary Bureau (UNDESA, 2004b). The speaker of the Chamber then directs these submissions to the appropriate committee. After submissions are reviewed, the committee will then communicate an assessment report to the Chamber, where the issue is placed on the agenda. If the issue is not returned to the committee, the Chamber will vote on the proposed submission. If the Chamber ratifies the submission, it is then transferred to the President of Lebanon for consideration. If the law is signed, it becomes promulgated and is published in the *Official Gazette*. The president can effectively veto the legislation by returning it to the Chamber for further consideration. The Chamber can overturn the president's veto by reapproving the legislation by absolute majority vote.

Executive branch

Lebanon's executive officials are apportioned on a confessional basis and distributed among Lebanon's Christian and Muslim communities. According to Article 24 of the Lebanese constitution, the president must be Maronite Christian, the prime minister must be Sunni Muslim, and the speaker of parliament must be Shi'a Muslim. This legal structure was upheld by the Ta'if Accord, which ended the Civil War and shifted the confessional apportionment formula in favor of the growing Muslim population.

In terms of the separation of powers, Chapter 4 of the Lebanese Constitution divides executive authority among three actors. The head of the Lebanese state—the president—presides over the Council of Ministers and serves as the Commander-in-Chief of the Armed Forces. The prime minister is the head of the government. In this capacity, the prime minister executes policy directives that are promulgated by the Council of Ministers. The third actor is the Council of Ministers, which sets the government's general policy direction and supervises the execution of laws and regulations. Typically, decisions made by the Council of Ministers are based upon consensus.

Judicial branch

Article 20 of Lebanon's constitution states that the country's judicial power "shall be exercised by courts of various degrees and jurisdictions" (Republic of Lebanon, 1926). According to Mansour and Daoud (2010), Lebanon's civil court system is organized into three jurisdictional levels: the Courts of First Instance; the Courts of Appeal; and the Court of Cassation (the court of final appeals). The criminal court system is divided into two courts: those that adjudicate misdemeanors and those that adjudicate serious crimes. Finally, the State Consultative Council addresses administrative matters, provides the executive branch with opinions about administrative matters, and adjudicates disputes between "the State, legal persons of public law, and individuals" (Mansour & Daoud, 2010, p. 14).

Lebanon's judicial system also comprises religious courts. The Ecclesiastical Courts, while not a unified system, address matters related to Catholic or Orthodox rights, and handle issues related to marriage, divorce, and the custody of children. Likewise, the Shi'a Courts represent specific Muslim communities, particularly the Sunni, Shiite, and Druze sects, and are organized into Courts of First Instance and Courts of Appeal (Mansour & Daoud, 2010). The autonomy of the religious courts often comes into conflict with state sovereignty. This is because the judges that serve in these courts are religious officials who abide by religious doctrine. Additionally, religious courts have different relationships with the state. For instance, Ecclesiastical judges are paid their salaries by their respective communities (Mansour & Daoud, 2010, p. 15). In contrast, Shari'a Courts are considered to be part of the state.

Regional government

Lebanon is also organized into two politico-administrative structures. The first structure is called the *Muhafazah*, which operates at the provincial level. Lebanon is organized into eight *Muhafazahs*, which are all controlled by the central government (Antoun, 1995; Haase & Antoun, 2015). The *Muhafazah* resemble governorates that are overseen by a *Muhafiz*. Each *Muhafazah* is further subdivided into 24 *Qada'*, which are districts that are overseen by a *Qa'immaquam*. The responsibilities of the *Muhafazah* include protecting the health, welfare, and security of those within their jurisdiction and implementing the directives and laws of the central government. Each *Muhafiz* is assisted by a Council of the Muhafazah, an advisory body that comprises the *Muhafazat's* respective *Qa'immaquam* and various members of civil society. The *Qada'* possess responsibilities similar to the *Muhafazah*, but they also oversee the administration of the central government offices, supervise public servants, and implement local rules and regulations. Both *Muhafazah* and *Qada'* are directly subject to the authority of Lebanon's Minister of the Interior and Municipalities.

Municipal government

Lebanon's second politico-administrative structure is municipal. Lebanese municipalities, governed by the Municipal Act of 1977, are considered legal personalities with financial and administrative independence (Decree Law 118 of 1977, Articles 1 and 2). They are managed by Municipal Councils, which select a president and vice-president after local elections. The Municipal Act appears to provide municipalities with broad authority over police and fire services, transportation and other public programs, as well as over establishment of tax rates, budgets, and the salaries of municipal officials (Articles 49 and 89). Despite their perceived legal independence, the central government maintains the authority to review and authenticate municipal decisions (Articles 62–65).

Significant legal reforms and developments

The structure of Lebanon's legal system has remained unchanged since the end of the Civil War. Moreover, the foundations for the Lebanon's legal system were upheld with the May 2008 signing of the Doha Agreement, which ended 18 months of political instability. In recent years, attempts have been made to improve accountability within the central government and weaken its control over decision-making. Driven in part by civil society actors, the most substantial of these reform attempts have focused on elections and decentralization. Advocates for electoral reform have called for the use of a proportional system of representation with a quota for women, and a lowering of the voting age. Advocates for decentralization have sought to transform *Qada'* into independent entities that are governed by a publicly elected council, which could use national revenues to promote local and regional development (Haase et al., 2016). Although the Lebanese parliament has received draft legislation related to these proposed reforms, long-standing political disputes have delayed their consideration.

The civil service

Lebanon formally established its civil service system in 1953. Since then, the central government has undertaken reforms to strengthen its personnel management system.

The legal basis

According to Bashir (1977), Lebanon lacked a central personnel department when it acquired independence. At that time, civil service recruitment was characterized by nepotism and a lack of enforcement of personnel regulations (Bashir, 1977, p. 23). Recognizing the need for reform, steps were taken to formalize Lebanon's civil service system.

The initial step was taken with the passage of Legislative Decree No. 13 in 1953, which formally organized Lebanon's bureaucracy, created civil service grades, and established a competitive examination for the recruitment of high-grade civil servants (Bashir, 1977, p. 24). In 1959, the Council of Ministers issued three Legislative Decrees that reformed Lebanon's civil service system (Bashir, 1977, p. 31). The most substantial, Legislative Decree (No. 114 of 1959), established the Civil Service Board as the central personnel and training body for the Lebanese bureaucracy. Two additional Legislative Decrees (Nos. 112 and 113 of 1959) revised the procedures related to recruitment, training, retention, retirement and pension, and termination. Despite subsequent modifications, Legislative Decree 112 of 1959 remains the foundation for Lebanon's present-day civil service system (Bashir, 1977, pp. 91–92).

Structure and processes

Lebanon's Civil Service Board has two primary responsibilities: to oversee the implementation of the laws and regulations related to the recruitment and retention of public employees and to ensure that public employees are adequately trained (Bashir, 1977). Ultimate authority over civil service matters is made by the Council of the Civil Service Board, the members of which are appointed by the Council of Ministers.

Recruitment and promotion

Lebanon's civil service is divided into five grades. These grades are organized by rank, as opposed to administrative duties and responsibilities (Bashir, 1977). Senior ranking officials fall within Grades I and II (directorate generals, directors, and chiefs of services). Middle management positions are classified as Grade III (bureau and section chiefs), and clerical and manual positions are classified as Grades IV and V, respectively.

To qualify for employment in Lebanon's civil service, an individual must have held Lebanese citizenship for ten years, be 20 years of age or older, meet certain age requirements with respect to their retirement status, be in certified good health, have a clean security record, and as necessary, hold a required academic degree and pass the civil service examination. Additional qualifications may be created by authorized public agencies, especially for positions that require technical or administrative expertise (Bashir, 1977, p. 60).

Normally, public-sector vacancies are filled through a three-step process (Bashir, 1977). The first step is recruitment. To recruit an employee, an agency with a vacancy must submit a written request to the Civil Service Board. In its request, the agency should indicate that it would like to announce and fill the position. If approved, the Department of Personnel Administration issues a memorandum that announces that a position has opened. This memorandum, which is distributed through print and broadcast media, contains information about the application process, including the date, time, and location of the civil service examination. Currently, the government has frozen the normal recruitment process due to budgetary constraints.

The second step is the civil service examination. Only applicants approved by the Department of Personnel Administration can then take the civil service examination. The Examination Committee, which is independent from the Civil Service Board, manages the process (Bashir, 1977). Once the examination has been completed, the Department of Personnel Administration submits the results to the Civil Service Board, which may approve the results or cancel the examination. If approved, the list of eligible candidates is made public.

The third step is the selection process. Agencies with approved vacancies must select from the published list of eligible candidates, who are given hiring priority. According to Bashir (1977, p. 69), decisions about candidate selection are driven by sectarianism and the extent to which decision makers have discretion over the selection process. Consequently, even if a position is to be filled on the basis of merit, "the appointment will be made on the basis of ranking priority and within the sectarian frame of reference" (Bashir, 1977, p. 69). Once hired, public servants appointed in Grades III through V are given probationary status for a period of one year. If higher authorities do not take removal actions, these public servants become permanent employees at the end of their probationary period.

Individuals enter the civil service at the bottom rank of their appointed grade. According to Bashir (1977, p. 59), "after every two years of service, eligible civil servants are given an automatic pay raise [and] an advancement to the next rank [within their grade]." Civil servants become eligible for promotion as they reach the top of their grade. If promoted, a civil servant will be given additional responsibilities and may qualify for a salary adjustment. Promotion, however, is not guaranteed (Bashir, 1977, p. 59). OMSAR (2011) has reported that complications in the recruitment and promotion processes have caused shortages in the number of public servants throughout Lebanon's civil service ranks. In 2010, for example, 22,029 full-time civil service positions existed within the national bureaucracy; of these, only 6,685 or 30 percent were filled. When these data are broken down by grade, they suggest that the national bureaucracy suffers from a severe deficit of human capacity.

Remuneration

The Lebanese government does not publish public-sector remuneration data. However, insights into remuneration can be gleaned from United Nations reports, which state that Lebanon's public sector is not attractive to potential employees. Rather, individuals seek employment in the private sector because businesses offer higher levels of compensation (UNDESA, 2004b). Consequently, Lebanon's bureaucracy has a deficit in human capacity, especially in the areas of engineering, science, and information technology (UNDESA, 2004b).

Training

The Civil Service Board is responsible for maintaining and improving the capacity of public servants, which it does through the National School of Administration, known officially as the *École Nationale d'Administration* (ENA). The training activities undertaken by ENA are supported by a variety of international and domestic actors, including the European Union, the World Bank, and the United Nations Development Program. Such support is also provided to the OMSAR, whose mission includes the training of civil servants.

Gender and diversity

Lebanon's civil service regulations state that both men and women are guaranteed the right to work and the right to equal compensation (Legislative Decree No. 112 of 1959). While the government does not compile statistics on the demographic characteristics of public-sector employees, the number of men employed in the civil service probably exceeds those of women. This conclusion is supported by a United Nations International Children's Emergency Fund (2011) report that suggested that the participation rate for women in the Lebanese labor work force is only 22 percent, compared to the global rate of 53 percent.

Significant civil service reforms and developments

OMSAR (2011) reported that Lebanon's civil service suffers from several problems: an outdated employee grade and salary system; job descriptions and classifications that do not match position responsibilities; poor training and capacity-building opportunities; the lack of integration, evaluation, and performance management practices; and an absence of policies that specify employee rights and duties. Despite the persistence of these problems, the Lebanese government has not undertaken significant steps toward reforming the civil service over the last decade. Consequently, Lebanon's civil service continues to lack the human resource capacities needed to develop and support public-sector activities.

Public budgeting

Lebanon's public budgeting processes are rooted in Articles 83–87 of the constitution (Republic of Lebanon, 1926) and the Law on Public Accounting (Law 14969 of 1963). Under normal conditions, these processes would generate a well-formulated public budget. In times of governmental dysfunctionality and political uncertainty, however, these processes can break down. When such failures occur, Lebanon's public finance activities and budgetary reform processes suffer.

Budgeting praxis

Lebanon operates an incremental line-item public budgeting system. The budget process is initiated by the Ministry of Finance upon its receipt of procurement estimates generated by government ministries (Ministry of Finance, 2014a). These requests are aggregated to form the basis of the proposed budget. The proposed budget is submitted to the Council of Ministers by September 1 of every year, before the budget year begins. The Council then has two weeks to review and submit the proposed budget to the Chamber of Deputies. The Chamber reviews and votes on each article contained in the proposed budget during the general legislative session, which occurs between October 15 and December 31 (Ministry of Finance, 2014a, p. 62). If the budget is approved, the Ministry of Finance becomes responsible for its execution (Ministry of Finance, 2014a). If it is not approved, then the president works with the prime minister to convene a special session of the Chamber of Deputies, which must be held no later than January 31 of the proposed budget year, to consider the revised proposed budget. If this special session does not approve the revised proposed budget, then the president, with the approval of the Council of Ministers, can adopt the revised proposed budget (Ministry of Finance, 2014a, p. 62).

Between 2005 and 2016, political tensions prevented the Chamber of Deputies from adopting a public budget (Barrington, 2016). This did not mean that the central government was left without funds. According to the Ministry of Finance (2014a, p. 63), "in the absence of approved budgets ... government expenditures have been incurred and are currently incurred on the basis of the 'one-twelfth rule', pursuant to which the Government is authorized to spend monthly one twelfth of the last approved budget (i.e., the 2005 Budget) and other enabling legislation." In 2012, the parliament authorized the government to increase its legal spending beyond the limit established by the 2005 annual budget (Ministry of Finance, 2014a, p. 63). Political tensions eased slightly in 2016, thereby enabling the Chamber of Deputies to adopt budgets for 2017 and 2018.

Public finance

Lebanon's public finances are driven by economic factors that impact government revenues. Lebanon's economy averaged a 9.4 percent annual growth in GDP from 2007 to 2010 (World Bank, 2018). Between 2011 and 2017, Lebanon averaged a lower economic growth rate of 1.9 percent (World Bank, 2018). Several factors explain this reduced rate of economic growth, such as domestic political tensions, regional conflict, stagnation in the tourism sector, and a weakened global economy (Bank Audi, 2015). These factors seemed to have come to a head in 2015, one of Lebanon's worst years of economic performance over the past decade (Bank Audi, 2015).

The Ministry of Finance indicated that Lebanon's budget and treasury receipts have increased over recent years. For example, public receipts totaled LL 8,749 billion in 2007 (Ministry of Finance, 2009). By 2011, public revenues had surged to LL 14,070 billion, which totaled 23.5 percent of the GDP (Ministry of Finance, 2011). According to the Ministry of Finance (2011, p. 4, 6), this increase was driven by the receipt of arrears from the Ministry of Telecommunication and an increase in other non-tax revenues. After a period of stagnation, continued payments received from the Ministry of Telecommunication and increased administrative efforts to collect income tax arrears pushed public receipts to LL 16.4 billion in 2014 (Ministry of Finance, 2014b, p. 4, 6).

By 2016, the last year on which data are available, public revenues decreased to LL 13.989 billion. According to the Ministry of Finance (2016, p. 1), this decrease was caused by regional instabilities, which impacted economic growth and revenue collection.

Lebanon's annual public expenditures have also increased. For example, between 2008 and 2009, public expenditures rose from LL 14.96 billion to LL 17.17 billion, an increase of 14.77 percent. This growth was attributed to increases in personnel costs, interest payments, transfers to the National Social Security Fund, and treasury expenditures directed to the High Relief Committee, which is the Lebanese agency that provides aid to displaced Syrians (Ministry of Finance, 2009).

Another substantial increase in public expenditures occurred in 2012, when public expenditures totaled LL 20.08 billion. During this year, the government paid higher personnel costs and made additional financial transfers to *Electricite du Liban*, the state-owned electric utility company (Ministry of Finance, 2011, p. 4). By December 2016, the last month for which data are available, Lebanon's annual public expenditures totaled LL 22.4 billion or 29.4 percent of the GDP (Ministry of Finance, 2016). To fund these increases in public expenditures, the Lebanese government's fiscal policy has relied upon the accumulation of public debt, which totaled LL 119.90 billion by the end of 2017 (Ministry of Finance, 2017).

Significant budgetary reforms and developments

Lebanon faces several public budgeting challenges. These challenges include inefficient budgetary processes and procedures, capacity constraints that inhibit reform, and weak financial information management systems (World Bank, 2014, p. 15). These challenges continue to exist, even though public finance reform has been on the government's agenda for more than a decade. In 2005, for example, the government committed to a two-year program of public finance reforms, which were disrupted by the 2006 Lebanon War (Jauode & Morachiello, 2010, p. 42). Further attempts were made to advance public finance reform in 2011. These reforms were backed by the World Bank, the UNDP, and the International Monetary Fund (World Bank, 2014, p. 10). With their support, the Ministry of Finance advanced several budget reform recommendations in 2012: to create a unit for macro-fiscal analysis; to simplify the Public Accounting Law of 1963; to improve the budgeting processes; and to strengthen administrative capacity through training and international collaboration (Ministry of Finance, 2011, pp. 7–10; World Bank, 2014, p. 10). Like previous attempts, the success of these recommended reforms will depend on political support, administrative capacity, interdepartmental communication, and the efficient use of resources (World Bank, 2014, pp. 49–54).

E-government

OMSAR (2002) released the first e-government strategy for Lebanon in 2002. This document committed the government to the adoption of information and communication technology (ICT) strategies that would strengthen the government's capacity to disseminate public-sector information. The government also committed itself to use ICT to provide public services, to unify data collection and storage processes, and to improve procurement activities (OMSAR, 2002, p. 4). The OMSAR acknowledged, however, that the success of this strategy depended on political stability, effective resource mobilization, prompt enactment of the necessary legal and regulatory frameworks, sufficient ICT infrastructure, and the acceptance of the e-government by both civil servants and the general public (OMSAR, 2002, p. 15).

E-government readiness

The UNDESA defines e-government as "the use of ICT and its application by the government for the provision of information and public services to the people" (UNDESA, 2004a, p. 15). UNDESA's 2014 E-Government Development Index, which measures the willingness and ability of government to use e-government to deliver public services, ranked Lebanon the 89th out of 193 countries in "E-Government Readiness." These survey results suggest that Lebanon needs to strengthen its telecommunication infrastructure and the scope and quality of the online public services it offers. There are several reasons why Lebanon has struggled to increase its e-government readiness. Although most government agencies now have websites that provide the public with basic information, many of the government's ICT reforms have not yet been finalized (Choueiri et al., 2013). Indeed, Lebanon's ICT infrastructure has been constrained by the government's monopoly over the telecommunications sector until 2007, when the government decided to privatize the sector. Until the privatization process is completed, bandwidth limitations and the costs of internet access will inhibit the public's ability to take advantage of online services.

E-participation

E-participation is defined as the "process of engaging citizens through ICTs in policy and decision-making in order to make public administration participatory, inclusive, collaborative and deliberative for intrinsic and instrumental ends" (UNDESA, 2014a, p. 61). E-governance involves the government's use of online services to facilitate e-information sharing, e-consultation, and e-decision-making. According to the UNDESA's 2014 E-Government Survey, Lebanon ranked 110th globally in e-participation. While the survey revealed that Lebanon's public bodies were involved in e-information sharing, there was little or no government involvement in e-consultation and e-decision-making activities. These results further confirm that Lebanon needs to improve its online services, its telecommunication infrastructure, and its ability to use ICT to inform and engage with its citizens.

Significant e-government reforms and developments

Several of Lebanon's public agencies have sought to improve their e-government capacities (Choueiri et al., 2013). For instance, the National Archives and OMSAR have taken steps to digitize government documents. OMSAR has also worked with the Directorate General of General Security to create online information portals, to standardize the forms used to initiate online transactions, and to increase the public's ability to access client-oriented internet services. Additionally, the Ministry of Water and Energy is developing information systems that can be used to collect and distribute weather forecasting information. Finally, the Ministry of Finance has used the internet to provide e-taxation information and services to the public.

More broadly, the Lebanese government last updated its e-government strategy in 2008 (OMSAR, 2008). This update stressed that Lebanon had obtained several of its e-government goals and had developed a sizable pool of ICT expertise (OMSAR 2008, p. 12). Moving forward, OMSAR has committed itself to overcoming resistance to e-governance reform and pursuing ICT reforms that will change how the Lebanese government operates (OMSAR, 2008, p. 2). Despite the clarity and importance of these goals, Lebanese citizens remain hesitant to embrace e-government services (Fakhoury & Aubert, 2015; Harfouche & Robbin, 2012). In response, the government needs to take further advantage of ICT benefits, while at the same time, demonstrate that the information collected by, and transmitted through, its e-governance systems will remain confidential and secure.

Ethics in public administration

Lebanon's Public Sector Staff Regulations (Decree Law 112 of 1959, as amended) specify the boundaries of acceptable civil servant conduct. Accordingly, civil servants are expected to pursue the public's interest through the proper implementation of the laws, by being personally accountable for following lawful instructions and by completing their work effectively (Article 14). Civil servants must also act in accordance with Lebanon's constitution and the country's laws and regulations (Article 15). To this end, civil servants are also prohibited from joining political parties, undertaking employment not sanctioned by law, accepting positions and responsibilities that constitute a conflict of interest, divulging private information, and accepting bribes and gifts. Despite the specificity of these regulations and legal responsibilities, Lebanon's bureaucratic system has substantial problems with public officials who engage in activities that constitute ethical violations.

Ethics

Seeking to modernize Lebanon's Public Sector Staff Regulations, OMSAR developed a Code of Conduct for Public Servants that was approved by the Council of Ministers in 2002. Although not legally binding, the code informs public officials about their civic responsibilities and legal obligations. It is organized into multiple sections (OMSAR, 2001), which specify public employees' (1) general obligations to the state; (2) public service obligations; (3) responsibilities toward citizens; (4) responsibilities toward superiors, colleagues, and subordinates; (5) responsibilities toward conflicts of interests and outside activities; and (6) general rights in relation to the public bureaucracy. To facilitate adherence to these principles, all of Lebanon's public employees must formally declare their commitment to the code.

Corruption

Transparency International (2017) reported that Lebanon is perceived to have a high level of corruption, with the country ranked 143 out of 180 counties on Transparency International's Corruption Perceptions Index. The factors that influence this perception include a distrust of public institutions, the lack of awareness about the causes and consequences of corruption, domestic and regional instability, and the lack of anti-corruption mechanisms (Lebanese Transparency Association, 2009). Stated differently, Bou Jaoude and Morachiella (2012) argue that the Lebanese do not trust or have confidence in their civil service because public officials often act in pursuit of their sectarian or own interests, rather than in the public interest. Indeed, as Kisirwani (1997, p. 7) observed, "[h]ardly any public official in Lebanon is unaware of his rights, duties, obligations and the limitations imposed, yet employees' indulgence in offences and violations is phenomenal." Despite the impact that corruption has on Lebanese public institutions and society, corrupt and unethical behaviors remain public-sector problems.

Significant ethics reforms and developments

Lebanon's government has undertaken initiatives to eliminate corruption and unethical behavior within the public bureaucracy. These initiatives have included the adoption of reforms that have strengthened budgetary processes, the approval of legislation to create an Office of the Ombudsman, and the adoption of ICT practices that would improve the delivery of public services. The government has also established a ministerial committee to combat corruption, which was supported by the Minister of State for Administrative Reform. Finally, the government has ratified the United Nations Convention Against Corruption in 2008 and OMSAR joined the Arab Anti-Corruption and Integrity Network in 2012. To date, however, these anti-corruption initiatives have largely failed because they were pursued without political will or inter-agency support.

According to Antoun (2008), for an anti-corruption reform initiative to succeed in Lebanon, it must address five interrelated issues. First, the political system must be reformed to promote accountability and the rule of law. Second, administrative processes and procedures must become increasingly transparent and responsive to the needs of the public. Third, private sector organizations must adopt codes of conduct, track problems, and promote whistle blowing. Fourth, the media must be given access to public-sector information and the latitude to investigate allegations of corruption. Finally, the public must be made aware of the consequences of corruption, and, more importantly, become informed that their civic rights include "the delivery of public services … political freedom, representation, and participation" (Antoun, 2008, p. 29).

Conclusion

Not only has Lebanon's public bureaucracy survived 15 years of Civil War, it has continued to function during extended periods of political paralysis. This reality can be viewed from two different perspectives. One perspective is that Lebanon's bureaucratic deficiencies are a serious cause for concern, especially considering that the government does not always serve the public interest (AbouAssi et al., 2013; Hasbani, 2011; Youngblood Coleman, 2015). This concern is perhaps best exemplified by the detonation of more than 3,000 tons of ammonium nitrate at the Port of Beirut on August 4, 2020, which caused 200 deaths, thousands of injuries, and several billions of dollars of physical damage (Sherlock, 2020). Although "authorities from Lebanon's customs, military, security agencies and judiciary raised the alarm that a massive stockpile of potentially dangerous chemicals was being kept with almost no safeguard at the port in the heart of Beirut" multiple times (Karam, 2020), successive Lebanese governments failed to take action to eliminate the risk.

The other perspective is that the public bureaucracy has played an important role in the preservation and development of the Lebanese state, and has shown a willingness to, or has taken steps to, strengthen public institutions. This was strongly expressed after the Civil War, when the Lebanese government worked with international agencies to reform the Ministry of Finance and create

OMSAR, which was given a mandate to strengthen the capacity of Lebanon's ministries, public agencies, and municipalities. Over the last 25 years, OMSAR has supported the improvement of transparency and accountability, the adoption of information technology, and the use of managerialist processes and practices throughout the Lebanese bureaucracy.

While OMSAR may endeavor to strengthen Lebanon's bureaucratic capacities over the long term, there are a variety of threats that can undermine the success of its reform efforts. Historically, the most substantial of these threats has been domestic political tensions, which are encouraged by regional conflicts between Saudi Arabia and Iran. These domestic political tensions work to reinforce many of the bureaucratic deficiencies that OMSAR has sought to overcome, and if left unchecked, could undermine all the progress that OMSAR has made in recent years. To this point, Lebanon has experienced a series of political and economic crises since 2019, which have caused multiple governments to collapse, undermined the value of the Lebanese currency, depleted foreign currency reserves, and caused the country to default on a portion of its national debt. Additionally, pressures continue to be placed upon Lebanon by the Syrian Civil War, which some have suggested will bring about "the steady unraveling of the Lebanese state" (Trofimov, 2016).

Notwithstanding the significance of these threats, it is likely too premature to make predictions about the demise of the Lebanese state. Assuming that the current threats to the Lebanese state are overcome, there are opportunities to build upon OMSAR's bureaucratic accomplishments of the last 25 years. First, there are a growing number of universities in Lebanon that offer undergraduate and graduate degrees in public administration (Haase et al., 2018). As students graduate from these programs, Lebanon may see an increase in the number of individuals who possess the knowledge needed to design and implement bureaucratic reforms. Indeed, these individuals will be well-positioned to become Lebanon's next generation of public servants, provided that their recruitment is driven by merit and occurs within a stable political environment.

Second, Lebanon provides excellent opportunities for comparative public administrative research. The systematic investigation of Lebanon's public sector can help practitioners understand the constraints and opportunities that exist within the Lebanese bureaucracy. Such research may provide insight into how OMSAR might adapt its administrative practices and structures to fit Lebanon's local and regional contexts (Jreisat, 2005). Finally, and perhaps most importantly, the Lebanese are becoming increasingly frustrated by the limitations of their political and bureaucratic institutions. As these frustrations increase, the general public, domestic NGOs, and international actors have intensified their calls for politico-administrative reform in Lebanon. These pressures may encourage the Lebanese government to improve accountability and undertake the reforms needed to facilitate the development of public policies that align with the public's interest.

Acknowledgments

The author thanks Ashish Khemka for his efforts collecting the material used to complete this chapter. He also wishes to thank Samir Hankir and Melissa Ajamain for reading and commenting on earlier versions of this chapter.

Funding

This project was supported by the Department of Political Science and the College of Humanities and Social Sciences at Sam Houston State University.

Note

1 Substantially revised and updated from Haase, T. W. (2018). A challenging state of affairs: Public Administration in the Republic of Lebanon. *International Journal of Public Administration*, 41(10), 792–806. Reprinted by permission of the publisher Taylor & Francis Ltd., http://www.tandfonline.com

References

Abdel Samad, Z. (2007). Civil society in the Arab region: Its necessary role and the obstacles to fulfillment. *International Journal of Not-for-Profit Law*, 9(2), 3–24.

AbouAssi, K., Nabatchi, T., & Antoun, R. (2013). Citizen participation in public administration: Views from Lebanon. *International Journal of Public Administration*, 36(14), 1029–1043. https://doi.org/10.1080/01900692.2013.809585

AbuKhalil, A. (1989). Government and politics. In T. Collelo (Ed.), *Lebanon: A country study* (pp. 137–178). Library of Congress.

Adjamian, M., & Haase, T. W. (2018). Constraints to Lebanese nongovernmental organizations: A survey of the literature. In E. El Hindy & T. Haddad (Ed.), *Religion and civil society in the Arab world: In the vortex of globalization and tradition*. Routledge.

Adwan, C. D. (2004). *Corruption in reconstruction: The cost of national consensus in post-war Lebanon*. Center for International Private Enterprise.

Agence France-Presse. (2018, July). Lebanon questions activists over social media posts. *The DailyMail.com*. http://www.dailymail.co.uk/wires/afp/article-5990043/Lebanon-questions-activists-social-media-posts.html

Altan-Olcay, O., & Icduygu, A. (2012). Mapping civil society in the Middle East: The cases of Egypt, Lebanon and Turkey. *British Journal of Middle Eastern Studies*, 39(2), 157–179. https://doi.org/10.1080/13530194.2012.709699

Antoun, R. (1995). Municipalities in Lebanon: Past and present. *The Lebanon Report*, 4, 31–38.

Antoun, R. (2007). Innovating the organizational structure of the Ministry of Finance in Lebanon. In *Innovations in governance in the Middle East, North Africa, and Western Balkans: Making governments work better in the Mediterranean Region* (pp. 117–140). United Nations Department of Economic and Social Affairs. https://digitallibrary.un.org/record/607778

Antoun, R. (2008). *Towards a national anti-corruption strategy*. The Lebanese Transparency Association and United Nations Development Program. http://www.undp.org.lb/communication/publications/downloads/Final_book_en.pdf

Atzili, B. (2010). State weakness and 'vacuum of power' in Lebanon. *Studies in Conflict & Terrorism, 33*(8), 757–782. https://doi.org/10.1080/1057610X.2010.494172

Bank Audi. (2015). *Lebanon Economic Report: 4th quarter*. Author.

Barrington, L. (2016, March 25). World Bank warns Lebanon of dangers of political paralysis. Reuters. http://www.reuters.com/article/us-mideast-crisis-lebanonworldbank-idUSKCN0WR1FY

Bashir, I. E. (1977). *Civil service reforms in Lebanon: An evaluation of the Lebanese civil service system with special emphasis on the role of the Civil Service Board*. The American University of Beirut.

Bennet, J. (1995). Lebanon: The Lebanese NGO forum and the reconstruction of civil society, 1989–93. In Jon Bennett (Ed.), *Meeting needs: NGO coordination in practice*. Earthscan Publications.

Blominvest Bank. (2015, January). *The Lebanon Brief* (Vol. 903, pp. 1–18). Economic Research Department, Beirut.

Bou Jaoude, R., & Morachiella, E. (2012). Lebanon. In R. P. Beschel Jr. & M. Ahern (Eds.), *Public financial management reform in the Middle East and North Africa: An overview of regional experience* (pp. 126–134). The World Bank.

Central Intelligence Agency. (2015). *World fact book*. Central Intelligence Agency. https://www.cia.gov/library/publications/the-world-factbook/geos/print/country/countrypdf_le.pdf; Archived at Wayback Machine (citing a capture dated March 9, 2015), Retrieved March 5, 2023, form https://webarchive.org

Chaaban, J. (2013). *Public sector wages must be adjusted to save the middle class* (featured analysis). Lebanese Center for Policy Studies. http://lcps-lebanon.org/featuredArticle.php?id=17

Chaaban, J., & Seyfert, K. (2012). *Faith-based NGOs in a multi-confessional society: Evidence from Lebanon*. Arab Center for Research and Policy Studies. http://english.dohainstitute.org/file/get/6d3efaaf-fdd3-4c73-ac42-7fa220502abb.pdf

Choueiri, E., Chouieri, G., & Chouieri, B. (2013). An overview of e-government strategy in Lebanon. *International Arab Journal of E-Technology, 3*(1), 50–57.

D'Aspremont, G. (2011, December 23). *The development of civil society in Lebanon from the Ottoman Empire to the XXIst century: A driver of political changes?* European Institute for Research on Mediterranean and Euro-Arab Cooperation. http://www.medea.be/2011/12/the-development-of-the-civil-society-in-lebanon-from-the-ottoman-empire-to-the-xxist-century-a-driver-of-political-changes/

Elbayar, K. (2005). NGO laws in selected Arab States. *International Journal of Not-for-Profit Law, 7*(4), 3–27.

El-Husseini, H., Salamon, L. M., & Toepler, S. (2004). Lebanon. In L. M. Salamon & W. Sokolowski (Eds.), *Global civil society: Dimensions of the nonprofit sector* (2nd ed., pp. 227–232). Kumarian Press.

El-Saad, F. (2001). *Strategy for the reform and development of public administration in Lebanon*. Office of the Minister of State for Administrative Reform. http://www.omsar.gov.lb/SiteCollectionDocuments/www.omsar.gov.lb/PDF%20Files/ICT%20Strategies%20and%20Master%20Plans/Strategy_Reform_and_Development_English.pdf

El-Zein, F., & Holly Sims, H. (2004). Reforming war's administrative rubble in Lebanon. *Public Administration and Development*, *24*(4), 279–288. https://doi.org/10.1002/(ISSN)1099-162X

Fakhoury, R., & Aubert, B. (2015). Citizenship, trust, and behavioral intentions to use public e-services: The case of Lebanon. *International Journal of Information Management*, *35*(3), 346–351. https://doi.org/10.1016/j.ijinfomgt.2015.02.002

Gavin, J. (2012). Partnerships to replace privatization. *Economic Digest*, *56*(22), 34–35.

Gebara, K. (2007). *Reconstruction survey: The political economy of corruption in post-war Lebanon*. Lebanese Transparency Association.

Ghosn, F., & Khoury, A. (2011). Lebanon after the civil war: Peace or the illusion of peace? *The Middle East Journal*, *65*(3), 381–397.

Haase, T. W., & Antoun, R. (2015). Decentralization in Lebanon. In A. R. Dawoody (Ed.), *Public administration and policy in the Middle East* (pp. 189–213). Springer. https://doi.org/10.1007/978-1-4939-1553-8_11

Haase, T. W., Haddad, T., & El-Badri, N. (2018). Public administration higher education in Lebanon: An investigation into the substance of advertised courses. *Journal of Public Affairs Education*, *24*(1), 43–65. https://doi.org/10.1080/15236803.2018.1429820

Haase, T. W., Harb, M., & Atallah, S. (2016). Decentralization in Lebanon. In A. Farazmand (Ed.), *Global encyclopedia of public administration, public policy, and governance* (pp. 1–8). Springer. https://doi.org/10.1007/978-3-319-31816-5_2423-1

Habib, O. (2005, October 3). World Bank urges Lebanon to reduce size of public sector. *The Daily Star*. http://www.dailystar.com.lb/Business/Lebanon/2005/Oct-03/6392-world-bank-urges-lebanon-to-reduce-size-ofpublic-sector.ashx

Haddad, T., Haase, T. W., & Adjamian, M. (2018). Religion, relief and reform: The history of civil society in Lebanon. In E. El Hindy & T. Haddad (Eds.), *Religion and civil society in the Arab world: In the vortex of globalization and tradition*. Routledge.

Harb, M., & Atallah, S. (2015). Lebanon: A fragmented and incomplete decentralization. In M. Harb & S. Atallah (Eds.), *Local governments and public goods: Assessing decentralization in the Arab world* (pp. 189–225). Lebanese Center for Policy Studies.

Harfouche, A., & Robbin, A. (2012). Inhibitors and enablers of public e-services in Lebanon. *Journal of Organizational and End User Computing*, *24*(3), 45–68. https://doi.org/10.4018/joeuc.2012070103

Hasbani, K. (2011). *Electricity sector reform in Lebanon: Political consensus in waiting* (Report No. 124). University of Stanford, Center on Democracy, Development, and the Rule of Law. http://iis-db.stanford.edu/pubs/23465/No._124_Electricity_Sector_Reform.pdf

Human Rights Watch. (2018). *"Our homes are not for strangers": Mass evictions of Syrian refugees by Lebanese municipalities*. https://www.hrw.org/sites/default/files/report_pdf/lebanon0418_web.pdf

Jauode, R., & Morachiello, E. (2010). *Public financial management reform in the Middle East and North Africa: An overview of regional experience*. The World Bank. http://siteresources.worldbank.org/INTMENA/Resources/MENARegionalPFMOverviewPartIFinal.pdf

Joseph, C. (2010). The state of freedom of association in Lebanon: What prospects for the future? *Global Social Policy*, *2*(3), 319–342.

Jreisat, J. E. (2002). *Comparative public administration and policy*. Westview.

Jreisat, J. E. (2005). Comparative public administration is back in, prudently. *Public Administration Review*, 65(2), 231–242. https://doi.org/10.1111/puar.2005.65.issue-2

Karam, K. (2008, September). The downward path of the civil project for electoral reform: A critique of the cooperation between civil society, public authorities and international organization (in Arabic). *Al-Akhbar* [Daily Arabic Newspaper]. Akhbar Beirut.

Karam, Z. (2020, December 10). Lebanese judge charges caretaker PM in August port Explosion. *NPR News, Beirut*. https://apnews.com/article/middle-east-beirut-lebanon-explosions-28ab23c7ba7e3f9ac7c9cbcf86dfb3cd

Karam, K., & Catusse, M. (2009). Reforms at a standstill for the Ta'if government of Lebanon (Arab Reform Initiative Country Report, tr. William Peterson). Lebanese Center for Policy Studies. http://www.arab-reform.net/reforms-standstill-taef-government-lebanon

Kingston, P. W. T. (2013). *Reproducing sectarianism: Advocacy networks and the politics of civil society in postwar Lebanon*. State University of New York Press.

Kisirwani, M. (1997). Accountability of Lebanese civil servants: An overview of disciplinary mechanisms. In A. Amin Saikal & G. Jukes (Eds.), *Lebanon beyond 2000 (CMECAS monograph)*. Centre of Middle Eastern and Central Asian Studies, The Australian National University. http://almashriq.hiof.no/ddc/projects/pspa/lb2000.html#back-notes-42

Kisirwani, M., & Parle, W. M. (1987). Assessing the impact of the post-civil war period on the Lebanese bureaucracy: A view from inside. *Journal of Asian and African Studies*, 22(1–2), 17–32. https://doi.org/10.1177/002190968702200102

Lebanese Transparency Association. (2009). *National integrity system study 2009*. Lebanese Transparency Association. https://issuu.com/transparencyinternational/docs/2009_lebanon_nis_en?e=2496456/3673819

Leenders, R. (2012). *Spoils of truce: Corruption and state building in postwar Lebanon*. Cornell University Press.

Makary, M. (2007). Notification or registration? Guarantees of freedom of association in non-democratic environments: Case studies of Lebanon and Jordan. *The International Journal of Not-for-Profit Law*, 10(1), 77–108.

Makdisi, S., Kiwan, F., & Marktanner, M. (2011). Lebanon: The constrained democracy and its national impact. In I. Elbadawi & S. Makdisi (Eds.), *Democracy in the Arab World: Explaining the deficit* (pp. 115–141). Routledge.

Maktabi, R. (1999). The Lebanese census of 1932 revisited. Who are the Lebanese? *British Journal of Middle Eastern Studies*, 26(2), 219–241. https://doi.org/10.1080/13530199908705684.

Mansour, M. W., & Daoud, C. Y. (2010). *Lebanon: The independence and impartiality of the judiciary*. Euro-Mediterranean Human Rights Network.

Mehanna, K. (1993). *The role of civil society associations in disaster management: Experiences from the war*. Ministry of Health and Ministry of Social Affairs.

Ministry of Finance. (2009). *Public finance review 2009: Ministry of Finance Yearly Report*. Beirut, Republic of Lebanon. http://www.finance.gov.lb/en-us/Finance/Rep-Pub/DRI-MOF/Public%20Finance%20Reports/YR_2009.pdf

Ministry of Finance. (2011). *Public finance annual review 2011*. Ministry of Finance, Republic of Lebanon. http://www.finance.gov.lb/en-US/finance/ReportsPublications/DocumentsAndReportsIssuedByMOF/Documents/Public%20Finance%20Reports/Annual/YR_2011.pdf

Ministry of Finance. (2014a). *Lebanon Country Profile. Ministry of Finance, Republic of Lebanon.* http://www.finance.gov.lb/en-US/finance/ReportsPublications/DocumentsAndReportsIssuedByMOF/Documents/Sovereign%20and%20Invensment%20Reports/Country%20Profile/Lebanon%20Country%20Profile%202014.pdf.

Ministry of Finance. (2014b). *Public finance annual review 2014. Ministry of Finance, Republic of Lebanon.* http://www.finance.gov.lb/en-us/Finance/Rep-Pub/DRI-MOF/PFR/Public%20Finance%20Monitor/YR%202014.pdf

Ministry of Finance. (2016). Public finance monitor: December 2016. *Ministry of Finance, Republic of Lebanon.* http://www.finance.gov.lb/en-us/Finance/Rep-Pub/DRI-MOF/PFR/Public%20Finance%20Monitor/Monthly%20PFM%20-%20December%202016%20-%20Final%20Version.pdf

Ministry of Finance. (2017). Debt and debt markets: A quarterly bulleting of the Ministry of Finance. *Ministry of Finance, Republic of Lebanon.* http://www.finance.gov.lb/en-us/Finance/PublicDebt/DebtReports/Documents/Debt%20and%20Debt%20Markets%20QIV%202017.pdf

Ministry of Social Affairs. (2009). *The state of civil society organizations in Lebanon: Analytical report on the national survey results civil society organizations in Lebanon in 2005.* United Nations Development Programme.

Office of the Minister of State for Administrative Reform (OMSAR). (2001). *A code of conduct for public servants.* OMSAR http://www.omsar.gov.lb/SiteCollectionDocuFOMSARments/www.omsar.gov.lb/PDF%20Files/Miscellaneous%20Publications/Employee%20Behavior%20Guide%20-%20A%20Code%20of%20Conduct%20-%20English.pdf

Office of the Minister of State for Administrative Reform (OMSAR). (2002). *E-government strategy for Lebanon.* OMSAR http://www.omsar.gov.lb/Cultures/en-US/Publications/Strategies/Documents/0c1a2448c3f2450a94ccc000ed7234d2eGov_Strategy_Executive_Summary_En.pdf

Office of the Minister of State for Administrative Reform (OMSAR). (2008). *E-government strategy for Lebanon.* OMSAR http://www.e-gov.gov.lb/Cultures/en-us/Publications/UNPAN/Documents/fd3901b4c2244d87b32861a8dd0513c4eGovernmentStrategyforLebanonAM14Jan08withminister.pdf

Office of the Minister of State for Administrative Reform (OMSAR). (2011). *Strategy for the reform and development of public administration in Lebanon.* OMSAR http://www.omsar.gov.lb/SiteCollectionDocuments/www.omsar.gov.lb/PDF%20Files/ICT%20Strategies%20and%20Master%20Plans/strategy%20in_english.pdf

Organization for Economic Cooperation and Development (OECD). (2010). *Progress in public management in the Middle East and North Africa: Case studies on policy reform.* OECD. https://www.oecd.org/mena/governance/48634338.pdf

PresidentoftheRepublicofLebanon.(2016).*Secretariat–GeneralDivision.*http://80.83.20.5/English/PresidentoftheRepublic/PresidencyDirectorateGeneral/Pages/SecretariatBranch.aspx

Rached, C. A. (2008). *The "Paris III Conference" and the reform agenda. Social Watch. Montevideo, Uruguay.* http://www.socialwatch.org/node/11084

Republic of Lebanon. (1926). *Constitution of the Republic of Lebanon.* http://www.presidency.gov.lb/English/LebaneseSystem/Documents/Lebanese%20Constitution.pdf

Safa, O. (2010). Lebanon. In J. Dizzard, C. Walker, & S. Cook (Eds.), *Countries at the crossroads: An analysis of democratic governance* (pp. 341–360). Freedom House.

Salamey, I. (2014). *The government and politics of Lebanon*. Routledge.
Sherlock, R. (2020, December 25). In Lebanon, judge suspends inquiry into Beirut Port explosion. *NPR News, Beirut*. https://www.npr.org/2020/12/25/950314947/in-lebanon-judge-suspends-inquiry-into-beirut-port-explosion
Traboulsi, O. (2000). Mapping and review of Lebanese NGOs. In World Bank and Middle East and North Africa Human Development Group (Eds.), *Republic of Lebanon poverty review*. The World Bank. http://www.charbelnahas.org/textes/Economie_et_politiques_economiques/WB_CRI_Lebanon_Poverty_Review-Main_%20Report.pdf
Transparency International. (2017). *Corruptions perceptions index 2017*. Transparency International. https://www.transparency.org/news/feature/corruption_perceptions_index_2017#table
Trofimov, Y. (2016, May 5). Political deadlock leaves Lebanon to unravel. *Wall Street Journal*. http://www.wsj.com/articles/political-deadlock-leaves-lebanon-tounravel-1462440603
United Nations Department of Economics and Social Affairs (UNDESA). (2004a). *Global e-government readiness report 2004: Toward access for opportunity*. UNDESA. https://publicadministration.un.org/egovkb/portals/egovkb/Documents/un/2004-Survey/Complete-Survey.pdf
United Nations Department of Economics and Social Affairs (UNDESA). (2004b). *Republic of Lebanon: Public administration country profile*. UNDESA. Retrieved from http://unpan1.un.org/intradoc/groups/public/documents/un/unpan023179.pdf
United Nations Department of Economics and Social Affairs (UNDESA). (2014). *United Nations e-government survey: e-government for the future we want*. UNDESA. https://publicadministration.un.org/egovkb/portals/egovkb/documents/un/2014-survey/e-gov_complete_survey-2014.pdf
United Nations Economic and Social Commission for West Asia (UNESCWA). (2010). *Comparative analysis of civil society participation in public policy formulation in selected Arab countries*. UNESCWA. http://www.escwa.un.org/information/pubaction.asp?PubID=966
United Nations, High Commission for Refugees. (2016, April–June). *UNHCR Lebanon operational update: Syria refugee response*. UNHCR. http://data.unhcr.org/syrianrefugees/country.php?id=122
United Nations, International Children's Emergency Fund (UNICEF). (2011). *Lebanon: MENA gender equality profile*. UNICEF. http://www.unicef.org/gender/files/Lebanon-Gender-Eqaulity-Profile-2011.pdf
Wickberg, S. (2015). *Overview of corruption and anticorruption in Lebanon*. Transparency International. http://www.u4.no/publications/overview-of-corruption-and-anti-corruption-inlebanon
Wilson, W. (1887). The study of administration. *Political Science Quarterly, 2*(2), 197–222. https://doi.org/10.2307/2139277.
World Bank. (2005a). *Lebanon quarterly update*. The World Bank. http://siteresources.worldbank.org/INTLEBANON/News%20and%20Events/20666801/Q2-2005.pdf
World Bank. (2005b). *Lebanon: Public expenditure reform priorities for fiscal adjustment, growth, and poverty alleviation* (Report No. 32857-LB). The World Bank. http://www-wds.worldbank.org/external/default/WDSContentServer/WDSP/IB/2015/08/31/090224b0828b34b1/1_0/Rendered/PDF/Lebanon000Publ00poverty0alleviation.pdf

World Bank. (2014). *International bank for reconstruction and development project appraisal document* (PAD549). The World Bank.

World Bank. (2016). *The World Bank in Lebanon: Overview.* The World Bank, Lebanon Office. http://www.worldbank.org/en/country/lebanon/overview

World Bank. (2018). *Lebanon: Data.* The World Bank. https://data.worldbank.org/country/lebanon

Youngblood, C. D. (2015). *2015 Country watch: Lebanon.* CountryWatch. http://www.sciencedirect.com/science/article/pii/0969212693900159

4
PUBLIC ADMINISTRATION AND DEVELOPMENT IN JORDAN[1]

Jamil E. Jreisat[2]

Introduction

Historical and contextual analyses are important for understanding current challenges and evaluating reform strategies. Societies inherit laws, political relationships, management systems, and cultural norms (Pollitt, 2008, p. 2). Such traditional and contextual influences often shape public administration perspectives and applications. Certainly, "public administration does not operate in a vacuum but is deeply intertwined with the critical dilemmas confronting an entire society" (Stillman, 2008, p. 1). Autocratic rule often induces basic managerial attributes and practices that are incompatible with democratic values or the preferences of citizens. In many Arab states, autocratic governance and ineffective and corrupt public management provoked popular riots, protests, and finally public revolutions in 2010–2011, referred to as the "Arab Spring," which began in Tunisia and spread to other Arab countries. Economic growth in most Arab countries has not served well the cause of equity and social justice. An incredible waste of resources, mismanagement, and destructive military conflicts deprived the developmental policies of Arab countries of necessary human and financial resources.

With the end of the Ottoman Empire, the Arab region was divided into spheres of influence for the victorious Western colonial countries, mainly Britain and France. The secret Sykes-Picot Agreement, concluded at the end of WWI, between Sir Mark Sykes of Britain and Francois Georges-Picot of France, divided and kept most of the Arab world under British and French imperial control (Lenczowski, 1962). The British sought to extend their domination in several parts of the Arab world through treaties and connections with

DOI: 10.4324/9781003389941-5

loyal rulers even after the demise of the Western colonial order in the post-WWII era.

A hundred years later, the consequences of the Sykes-Picot Agreement continue to afflict the Arab world. It is baffling to explain "the burdensome, humiliating fact that the Arab region is the only part of the world where foreign armies today still regularly invade, occupy, and try to remake societies" (Khouri, 2005, op-ed). The constantly widening gap of perception between Arab people and the West is largely rooted in real experiences with Western domination that has revived Arab collective consciousness today. The invasion of Iraq in 2003 illustrates how the problems of the Arab region often seem to become much more complex and bear broader significance. Instead of making progress toward finding solutions for immediate problems, external and internal influences appear to derail the Arab world into a debilitating state of insecurity, institutional incapacity, and incessant foreign interference and/or occupation.

Jordan emerged in the 1920s as the *Emirate of Transjordan* and was under direct British hegemony until 1946, when the country became nominally independent and later was officially designated as the *Hashemite Kingdom* of Jordan. The political system in Jordan today is a constitutional monarchy with a parliament (Council of Deputies) elected through universal suffrage. A second chamber of the parliament is appointed by the king from senior public officials. Laws are approved by both chambers. Separation of powers among the three branches of government is fairly defined in the constitution. Municipal councils and mayors are directly elected by citizens with a minimum number of seats reserved for women. The prime minister is appointed by the king and confirmed by the parliament. Since the establishment of the state in 1921 as Transjordan, the country relied on vital external financial support (British, American, Arab, and European) to be able to maintain and manage its institutions and its economy. The need for foreign aid increased with the recent influx of refugees from Iraq, Syria, and Palestine, who presently constitute over 35 percent of the total population.

Despite poor natural resources and the constant need for external financial aid, Jordan has been able to make considerable advancements in national development. In contrast to the tumultuous politics of its neighboring countries, Jordan employed its strategic location, educated public, and stable governance to achieve a measure of domestic development and international recognition. As a member of the League of Arab States, Jordan shares with the Arab world similarities in language, culture, history, religion, and national aspirations as well as in various political and administrative aspects. Still, Jordan carries its own context, which shapes many current societal attributes and governance processes.

Public administration in Jordan includes many public organizations responsible for serving various aspects of public life. They are involved in developing the economy as well as ensuring safety, public health, education, transportation, quality of water, and other public services. Thus, seeking reform and improvement of performance are constant endeavors. In recent years, public bureaucracy in Jordan lost some grounds of authority and responsibility. Privatization limited certain traditional powers of the public bureaucracy, particularly in the economy. Political interference reduced discretion of public bureaucracy in personnel recruitment and in prioritizing public spending, even when public administration remains formally responsible for results. The frequent political meddling (by members of the cabinet and the parliament) in organizational management practices limits the professional discretion of public management.

The changing context of governance

At the initial phase, in 1921, the British colonial order set up a traditional system of governance in Jordan, providing financial subsidies, administrative know-how, and political support (Carroll, 2003; Cole, 2014). Independence from British rule instigated public demand for improvements in governance. Competence of public bureaucracy in law and order proved inadequate in delivering essential public services or leading developmental initiatives. Over time, public administration gained greater attention, increasingly becoming the main instrument for responding to public needs and demands, including in economic development and job-creation. While reform has been a common cry in Jordan, it has not been easy to break out of traditional political and administrative patterns that guide actions and influence public policymaking. The following contextual challenges have intensified incongruities between existing and needed processes of governance:

Demographic change

According to UNDP estimates, the population of the Arab countries by the end of 2015 was 395 million people, compared to 150 million in 1980. Rapid population growth has also changed the age distribution; about 60 percent of the population is under 25 years, making Arab societies among the most youthful in the world (AHDR, 2009, p. 2). Similarly, the last national census conducted in Jordan (end of 2015) showed that Jordan had 9.5 million residents, nearly 2.9 million of whom were non-Jordanians. The population within the capital, Amman, has more than doubled between 2004 and 2015 as it went up from 1.9 million to over 4 million, constituting around 42 percent of the country's inhabitants.[3] As a result, pressures on the capacity of the state to provide adequate resources for managing growing demands for public services are relentless (more below on citizen protests in 2018).

Socio-economic development

Jordan and most Arab states have been facing difficult challenges such as low economic growth, demographic pressure, expanded poverty, and increasing inequality of income. The broader experiences of developing countries indicate that development strategies did not often lead to the realization of development objectives. At one time, economists promoted the idea of economic growth as a linear process; all a country needs is to discover the proper mix of savings and investment to enable it to reach the "take-off" phase (Pye, 1962). The futility of the "linear" approach became apparent in the 1970s; it gave way to other competing perspectives (Sayigh, 1991).

The more recent and influential perspective, emerging from the United States, was presented by a neo-conservative movement and emphasized a free market approach, which relies on privatization and the dismantling of public ownership, public planning, and government regulation of economic activities (Todaro, 1989, p. 82). Reacting to the Third World debt crisis of the early 1980s, the International Monetary Fund (IMF) and the World Bank pronounced radical free market reforms via "structural adjustment programs"—a package of economic policies that included deregulation, privatization, cuts in government spending, and an emphasis on exports. These policies failed in many places and stimulated more corruption and more concentration of wealth. International Law expert Richard Falk summed up the situation and referred to this economic prescription as "predator" economics (Falk, 1999). During this period, Jordan privatized major public enterprises in phosphate mining, communications, cement manufacturing, and others.

The Human Development Index (HDI) of the United Nations Development Program (UNDP) is a composite index measuring average achievement in three basic indicators: per capita income, education, and health. In 2015, Jordan ranked 80 among 177 countries on the HDI. Two persistent economic problems face Jordan. The first is chronic budget deficit necessitating reliance on borrowing and foreign financial assistance. The budget deficit is about 7 percent of annual public expenditures without foreign assistance and borrowing. The second is unemployment that seems to have grown rather than subsided over the past few years. Recent data from the Central Bank of Jordan on unemployment reveal a far worse condition than is publicly known. The Central Bank reported that unemployment in the first quarter of 2016, among youth of 20–24 years of age, is at 33 percent. This high percentage seems to persist, and even increase to 37 percent, through 2018.

During the past many years, a significant source of economic sustenance for Jordan, in addition to foreign financial aid, has been the transfers and remittances from abroad. Remittances from about 350,000 doctors, engineers, teachers, and construction workers in the Gulf states exceed one billion dollars annually (AL-Oudat

& Khlaifat, 2011). Still, Jordanian economic prosperity remains precarious and the country is struggling to improve economic growth while problems of high unemployment and chronic budget deficits persist. The business sector in Jordan has not been a major contributing factor to the country's economic development. According to Katherine Carroll (2003, p. 6), the business community in Jordan "has been parasitic, relying on the state for protection, subsidies, and contracts."

Corruption and civic culture

Unethical conduct by public officials has been attributed to different factors. Low wages of public employees and poor transparency seem to induce unethical conduct of embezzlement, fraud, bribery, and similar irregularities (Rohr, 2000). Corruption in Jordan has endured due to additional cultural norms (Jreisat, 1997). Traditional tribal customs expect people in authority to support and do favors for their relatives, friends, and clan members, including providing employment in government. In addition, the education system in Jordan, particularly at the university level, does not infuse graduates—future public employees—with values of ethical behavior, serving common interests, compliance with the law, and other essential norms of democratic governance. The public education's deficiency in developing civic culture, a sense of commitment to ethical conduct, and an obligation to serving the common interests mirror the negative social conditions of a society with too many parochial, religious, regional, tribal, and gender divisions. At the same time, rather few bridges are introduced to cultivate cooperation, advance commitments to higher values, and encourage collective behavior for serving common objectives.

In concept and in practice, civic culture is shaped and promoted by various influences. What makes a culture consistent and supportive of democratic values, participatory governance, free association, and ethical behavior in public service is not instituted. Ethical standards and administrative reform are not foundational matters in education, tradition, religious beliefs, and political tradition. Generalizations repeated by average citizens when the subject of corruption in government is mentioned include: "everyone is corrupt." A survey by the Strategic Studies Center of the University of Jordan indicates that 61 percent of citizens believe that there is corruption in government.[4] The Corruption Perceptions Index of Transparency International ranked Jordan in 2021 as 58 among 180 countries and territories.

Globalization

Globalization conveys linkages and interdependence among economies, peoples, cultures, and countries. The widening and deepening global integration reinforced mutual relationships among countries to unprecedented levels of worldwide interconnectedness in all aspects of contemporary life. Market-driven economic transformation has been a potent force in extending and deepening global relationships. However, Arab states have not overcome crucial barriers to development within their own societies or altered persistent economic fragmentation among Arab countries. Arab markets remain underutilized and political feuds among leaders have been a major obstacle to trade and economic diversification. Political regimes have not been successful in negotiating and reaching agreements in economics, finance, environment, defense, and health.

Globalism also underscored a multitude of threats to human development in the Arab region and in Jordan. Issues of advancing development, security, good governance, and human rights are today seen under a different light. Human development is concerned with expanding the individual's capabilities and opportunities, while human security is centered on enabling people to contain or avert threats to their lives, work, and human dignity. Contextual changes created difficulties for public administration reforms in Jordan and demanded from public managers' knowledge and leadership skills that they were not prepared for. Moreover, recent developments in the region imperiled the human security of the country as never before. The political turmoil in surrounding states raised new risks for Jordan. The resulting refugee problems from these neighboring countries strained administrative capacities in rendering essential services and exhausted scarce resources.

Transition to effective democratic governance requires the development of indispensable managerial capacities. According to Farazmand (2009, p. 1016), "Nothing gets done without administrative capacity." Comparative public administration literature provides insights on practices that worked or did not work in implementing reform strategies in various countries (Pollitt and Bouckaert, 2011). Beyond the structural and behavioral attributes that shape capacity and professionalism in public management, success requires a rational legal and constitutional architecture that refines the processes and institutes an overall framework for governing. Formalistically, Jordan has a fairly developed constitutional foundation, even if vague on issues of distribution of powers, accountability, and protection of democratic values of freedom and equity.

Professionalizing public management also requires capacity rooted in knowledge, authenticity of values, a building of culture, and an essential "administrative space" to apply expertise and ethics (Argyriades, 2013). The development of administrative capacity, and steering it to serve the objectives of governance, has been a constant challenge. Management capacity is viewed as "the ability of governments to fulfil the responsibilities of democratic governance" (Ingraham, 2007, p. 3). Earlier public administration reform schemes in Jordan were primarily used to adjust the pay of certain groups of civil servants as well as elect and appoint political groups with a tangential focus on improving performance and eliminating corruption. Recently, in addition to ethical reform initiatives, various measures were adopted to introduce fundamental changes such as increasing the number of women employed in government and improving public services in general. It is too early to systematically evaluate results of many of these proposed changes, which were finalized only in 2015.

Enforcement of administrative change in Jordan faces many obstacles, particularly from traditional forces that have resisted checks and balances in the system and have continued to protect patronage practices. In the absence of an effective legislative branch to provide political and moral legitimacy to reform policies, resistance to change became formidable. In addition, for public administration reforms to succeed, appropriate conditions must prevail. Such conditions include a clear definition of the administrative problem with proposed solutions, a legitimate and transparent process that considers all possible options for the suggested changes, and a continuous monitoring and measuring of progress during the implementation process.

Public administration is inherently a dynamic field that routinely searches for improved performance. Yet, past experiences in reform implementation have been "so often disappointing," as Aberbach and Christensen (2014, p. 3) report. Public administration literature in Jordan that highlights reform and essential changes and modifications in governing lacks a clear understanding of the problems and how to solve them, given the country's traditional administrative practices. A reform strategy that is realistic and attainable requires the sound conceptualization of the problem in order to direct the development of effective solutions. A problem may be analyzed in different ways and may have different possible solutions. Leaders and managers of proposed solutions in Jordan usually come up short on explanations and analyses offered publicly about lack of reform progress.

Administrative solutions are not like spare parts of machines to be ordered and installed according to a manual. The design of an effective solution to an administrative problem should consider numerous contextual factors, including characteristics of the political and administrative systems. Depending on the type and magnitude of the problem, the process often encounters disagreements to be resolved through negotiations and an evaluation of facts and evidence. No single framework is sufficient for dealing with administrative reform in Jordan. In the past, most perspectives employed were grounded in foreign experiences, and possibly suggested by foreign consultants. Other major features of reform processes are a reliance on hierarchical orders more than discussions and negotiations among those involved in implementation of the intended change and the lack of skilled professional managerial and political leadership committed to reaching reform objectives.

Administrative reform failure: Two cases

The following two cases are illustrative of problems encountered when trying to implement administrative reform in Jordan. One lies in the ubiquitous area of the budgeting process; the other is a manifestation of the gravity of patronage and reliance on nepotism (*wasta*) in recruitment of public servants:

First case: Reforming public budgeting

Over the past two decades, many countries, developed and developing, have changed evaluation criteria in budgetary decisions and allocations from input-driven to output/outcome-driven measurements. Accordingly, the government of Jordan decided, in 1999, to change its budget system from the traditional input-oriented, line-item format, to a performance-based budget system. Jordan's Ministry of Finance, and the Department of Budgeting within it, requested help from the German Technical Cooperation (GTZ) in making this change. The reasoning stated by the Jordanian officials for seeking to change their budget system included what they perceived as expected benefits from this reform; adoption of performance budgeting would give them better information on results, improve accountability, and allow greater control over cost. The response of the GTZ program was to invite an "international team of experts" to develop a plan for introducing performance budgeting to Jordan. This author was invited to chair the team and to draft the final report.[5] After several meetings and interviews in Amman, a detailed report was submitted on the design and implementation of the proposed change.

Among the many points stressed in the report is that performance budgeting should provide better information about the effectiveness and efficiency of government services. It would allow public managers to view their operations methodically to identify problems and to deal with them promptly. Policymakers (the prime minister, cabinet, and parliament) would be able to improve the quality of strategic and operational decisions. The report stressed the following fundamental elements of the proposed reform:

- Central strategic policy direction at the initial phase of the annual budget process is essential for indicating national policies and priorities that need to be reflected in budget allocations. Primarily, this is the responsibility of the political leadership: the prime minister, the cabinet, the parliament, and senior public managers.
- Operational guidelines are crucial for instructing the central budget office (the Budget Department) on how to introduce the proposed changes and ensure compliance with relevant laws and regulations.

- Setting operational goals for determining outputs and outcomes and measuring them begins with identifying primary objectives of each public organization, particularly those specified in the enabling law. Operational goals are derived from a legitimate public policy; they must be manageable, measurable, and represent consensus.
- Performance indicators must be developed to facilitate data-gathering to gauge progress in reaching organizational goals. Work indicators are instrumental to measuring results and providing information on effectiveness, efficiency, quantity, and quality of services.
- Investing in an appropriate electronic management information system that provides for collection, recording, storing, classifying, summarizing, and retrieval of data about the indicators is essential.
- The legitimacy and sustainability of a shift from a line-item to a performance budget format would be far more authentic and reliable when the planned change is grounded in a legislative mandate that institutes the new framework.
- The designated body responsible for leading the implementation process of budget reform is the Budget Department, which operates as a semi-autonomous unit within the Ministry of Finance. The Budget Department plays a central role in the design of budget procedures that determine the form, the calendar, and the guidelines for the submission of estimates by line agencies. Its role, also, involves setting procedures and regulations, coordinating requests for funds, and evaluating and approving these requests.

The Minister of Finance has an influential position in the cabinet and among line agencies, not unlike the Chancellor of the Exchequer in the British system. The minister's special status in the cabinet is also enhanced by his responsibility to coordinate with the prime minister about setting limits and arbitrating disputes over funding among agencies, or between agencies and the Budget Department. The institutional framework for financial management in Jordan is set by the Ministry of Finance, which has major responsibilities regarding overall economic and financial policies, and oversees several other functions ranging from forecasting revenue to administering public debt and cash management. Line agencies are the main source of cost estimates for government operations. Although a high ratio of these costs is fixed as salaries, the rest of their expenditures are not based on real data or reliable measurements. Generally, the top leadership of each line agency determines how much money to ask for. Budget officers in each administrative unit may participate in the calculations of estimates but their role is usually limited to monitoring compliance and developing financial reports.

A permanent finance committee in the parliament reviews the budget request before sending it with recommendations for a vote by all members.

Typically, the conclusions of these debates do not result in increasing spending and rarely affect, meaningfully, the outcome. The vote usually is on the total budget bill. The cabinet on its own, if convinced during the debate in the parliament, may promise to increase or decrease spending decisions in the future according to appropriate procedures. As expected, exhortations from the parliament's podium, criticisms, questions, and requests for reduction or for additional funds are voiced. The government usually acknowledges "respectfully" the opinions expressed by the legislators and promises to take these views into serious consideration. The formalistic ritual is ill-defined and poorly understood by most members of the parliament. They have neither been effective in utilizing the power of appropriation nor educated in monitoring government within set rules (Jreisat, 2011b).

After executive and legislative approval, line agencies start the execution phase following elaborate procedures for payments, monitored from within each unit and from without by the Budget Department and the Bureau of Accounting and Audit. The bureau provides a basic layer of control on spending by monitoring compliance and by verifying conformance to the technical spending rules throughout the executive branch. The bureau submits its annual audit report to the parliament, the prime minister, and Minister of Finance simultaneously. In cooperation with the Budget Department and the Ministry of Finance, the bureau takes the lead in standardizing and enforcing generally accepted accounting principles (GAAP) in line agencies.

Several years after the submission of the Master Plan for Performance Budgeting in Jordan in 1999, a "follow-up" consultant's report concluded: "The current format of the Budget law does not support a result-oriented debate." Subsequent visits in 2008 and 2009 by this author also found out that "very little has been done" toward the operational implementation of a performance budgeting process in Jordan. The most compelling question, then, is why?

The answer is not simple or based on a single reason. Many mutually influencing factors create such a deadlock. The uncertainty caused by chronic structural deficits and the subsequent reliance on foreign sources to shore up these deficits have effectively prevented shifting the emphasis back to micro-budget negotiations. The political leadership has been using "lack of revenue" as a financial shield to deny or postpone urgent and popular requests for funding, regardless of output and outcome of the results. Other obstacles to implementation include lack of technical and managerial competence required for managing performance budgeting at the senior level of political and administrative leadership. Clearly, building a professional managerial competence in the leadership is difficult when the system of recruitment to senior positions is not merit-based. In addition, weak institutional capacities prevent deploying a sufficient level of resources to effectively guide the reform process. Subsequent behavior suggests that the political leadership never intends to loosen its grip on decision making, particularly where money is involved. At the end, few individuals in the executive branch of government ultimately determine the main allocations among public functions. Only recently, the financial system began to practice a modest measure of transparency. Line agencies prepare the estimates and execute the budget law but within careful administrative discretion. Jordan's public agencies and departments, including key institutions as the Budget Department and Bureau of Accounting and Audit, operate with narrow perceptions of their duties because of inadequate organizational capabilities and uncertain political support.

Second case: Nepotism: Impairing professionalism of civil service

An exchange on June 2016 between two top political leaders in Jordan illustrates, amazingly, a more serious problem than is publicly acknowledged. For a few days, the local press in Jordan allocated front page space to unpleasant the political and administrative issues of governance, namely, how persons in high public positions seem to ignore the rules of the competitive merit-based appointments to government jobs. One headline in *The Jordan Times* on April 12, 2016 was indicative of how deep the nepotism malady ran. It read: "Hundreds of MPs' relatives appointed as administrators at Chamber" (Obeidat & Omari, 2016). A document listing 109 people appointed to work at the parliament showed that 15 of them were sons of members of the parliament, while most others were relatives of lawmakers, adding to already "bloated" administrative staff in the legislative branch. The list was approved by the prime minister and his cabinet, but the approval was described in a letter by the prime minister to the speaker of the parliament as "made reluctantly." The latter word generated serious, protracted bickering between the prime minister and the speaker.

This case is illustrative of why administrative reforms in Jordan are much talked about, but things remain mainly the same. As reported, the large number of administrators in the parliament has been growing over the past six years due to a series of appointment cycles endorsed by speakers to "appease" fellow lawmakers, especially at time of imminent speakership elections. Nearly 800 persons have been hired by the House over the past years (Obeidat & Omari, 2016). One incongruity is that Jordan's budget continues to endure serious deficit and relies heavily on foreign aid. To secure future votes, members of the parliament generally do not reject requests from people in their constituencies for special favors, particularly jobs in government. Appointments, which mainly consist of relatives of lawmakers in the parliament, are not excluded from review by the Civil Service Bureau. Review, however, does not always mean approval and compliance with merit-based qualifications. Letters between the prime minister and the speaker, leaked to the press, show that both men are at odds. The prime minister wrote to the speaker saying: "For your information, the Cabinet, in a session on March 23, decided, reluctantly, to create jobs for the 109 persons..." The speaker conveyed his objection in using the word "reluctantly." In his letter, the prime minister added: "The Cabinet also decided to disregard all similar requests in the future because they deprive job seekers who have applied to the Civil Service Bureau from their rights" (Obeidat & Omari, 2016). The saga of the list of appointments brought to the surface tensions between leaders of the executive and legislative branches and underlined the shallow confidence of citizens in the integrity of the decisions made by their political leaders.

Analysis of public administration reform in Jordan indicates that the growth of public spending did not often translate into improved administrative performance. Central command and control models of governance reinforced corruption and bolstered many negative administrative attributes. Comparative analysis reveals that these ailments of public management in Jordan are widely prevalent throughout Arab systems of governance, hindering professional public administration performance (Hertog, 2010; Jabbra & Jreisat, 2009; Jreisat, 1997, 2006, 2009, 2011a; UNDP, 2006).

Obstacles to reform

The above two cases, (a) an attempt to implement budget reform, and (b) the debacle between the prime minister and the speaker of the parliament over patronage and nepotism in recruitment for public positions, illustrate some deep-rooted obstacles to public management reform. Public administration in Jordan remains captive to many traditional factors standing in the way of important management changes. The following summarizes the most relevant of such hurdles:

1   Excessive centralization of public management maintains central control over funds and fosters other problems such as micro-managing programs and circumventing accountability and transparency. Centralization provides public managers with justifications for inaction or poor decision making. Claims of compliance with orders of the central authority rather than achieving results and applying professional skills are routine explanations given for bad performance. Excessive centralization causes vague public policies and creates unnecessary ambiguities and bottlenecks that prevent the taking of initiatives and cause fear of risk-taking by public managers. A new law was passed by 2017 to decentralize and activate local authorities. Local councils, despite the decentralization efforts, remain without substantive powers and are often in conflict with central authorities who have the laws on their sides. Local councils lack an understanding of their functions, have limited staff support, and some do not even have headquarters to meet.

2   Weak institutional development is another major consequence of autocratic public decision-making processes. The style of decision making is individualistic rather than institutional. Softness of structures and diffuseness of functions below the dominating top leaders prevents the emergence of viable institutions that can exercise discretion, perform checks and balances, and represent diverse views. The personal squabbling between the prime minister and the speaker over appointments illustrates the concentration of power at the top and the absence of institutional input.

Traditional politicians, preoccupied with accumulating of personal wealth and gaining influence and power over appointments to government positions, have been basic impediments to the development of Jordan into a modern democratic state. In 2018, their influence has been challenged forcefully by the people of Jordan. The public demanded to see a transformation of the political and administrative governance system from one based on personal, tribal, regional, and religious politics to a collective of organization and management that puts higher emphasis on governing with integrity, transparency, equity, and justice for all citizens. No doubt, such successful transformation is not easy, but it is a start that does not seem reversible.

3   Professional appraisal of performance is a must. Improvement of administrative performance necessitates greater reliance on appraisal of results, inspections, independent performance audit, and performance measurement. Public managers must be committed to the values of improving performance by setting goals and regularly collecting data to gauge progress. In the centralized governance system of Jordan, what needs to be done, by whom, and at what cost are, often, not clear or defined. Within a context of deficient transparency, a lack of competent investigative mass media, and inaccessibility of real performance data, accountability tends to fade away.

4   Fighting corruption and ensuring ethics in public service is pertinent to a functioning system. Widely spread images of public officials portray public officials in a negative light. They are seen as enriching themselves rather than serving public interests. Stories of illegitimate acts of fraud, bribery, and influence peddling are often heard in social gatherings and in small group discussions. In 2011, demands for an investigation into corruption linked to decisions on privatization of major government companies at largely below market prices resulted in huge financial benefits to influential individuals. The companies were in communication, cement, potassium, and phosphate mining. Charges, voiced widely in society, simply accused previous governments of selling off public enterprises at low prices under clouds of suspicion. Consequently, in 2011, the government of Jordan drafted an anti-corruption law and submitted it to the parliament for approval, which passed

it expeditiously. Over the past few years, fighting corruption in Jordan has become one of the most supported public policies.

A new law was inaugurated earlier in 2016, replacing a previous statute on ethics and establishing what is named the Authority on Integrity and Combating Corruption, which is managed by a board and a president appointed by the prime minister for four years. The board and the president are entrusted with protecting integrity, fighting corruption, and achieving compliance with ethics and standards of professional public management. Maintaining ethical performance in governance is regarded as essential to serving the public with justice and equity. The law invites the public to submit information and to testify on corruption cases. It also provides for measures against what is called "assassination of character," a potentially intimidating provision aiming to protect those in power from false claims. This adds to public skepticism and doubt over the seriousness of enforcing this law.

5 Dependence on foreign financial aid and weak fiscal discipline are two other major hurdles. Diluting fiscal discipline is when autonomous components such as the military expenditures, security forces, intelligence operations, the judiciary, the Royal Court, and pension benefits are legally and/or politically assured of their fiscal status (non-discretionary). These expenditures are subjected only to the minimal scrutiny and evaluation by the central budget office. Their budgets are consistently determined at the top political level and consume over one-third of total public spending. Retirement expenditures, civil and military, make up over 21 percent of total operating budget. After adding debt service and other restricted expenditures, non-developmental budget allocations exceed 80 percent of total public spending. Thus, only a small part of the budget could be targeted for economic growth and job-creation.

In the long run, the consequences are gloomy without some radical reforms. Such reforms must achieve more efficient and effective delivery of public services, a reconsideration of the retirement system, and an enhancing of economic growth. The chronic dependence on foreign aid and loans is restrictive and creates formidable uncertainties. The financial condition of the government in Jordan undermines the independence of public decision making and discourages serious strategic planning. Moreover, Jordan's economy is burdened by the heavy weight of public debt, which reached almost 95 percent of GDP by the end of 2018.

Conclusions and synthesis

Public administration in Jordan remains short on strategic capacity to plan and implement public policies equitably and effectively. While public administration reform initiatives and claims are continuous in Jordan, only modest progress has been achieved. Operational, non-developmental public expenditures are largely fixed and difficult to change. They are mainly salaries, interest on public debt, retirement, military, security, and other fixed costs. In addition, Jordan is burdened by the responsibility of hosting large numbers of refugees from surrounding countries in political turmoil. Other administrative confines include lack of accurate information, weak transparency of public decision making, operational inefficiency, and absence of citizen-focused initiatives. Accountability of results, performance measurement, performance-based incentives, and employing cost-benefit analysis in making allocative decisions are rarely applied or practiced. Policies to control aggregate spending, improve efficiency, and initiate strategic prioritization have not been seriously employed. But, in many countries, information technology has already changed old habits of decision making and improved management capacity by expanding the knowledge base. Increasing reliance on data in policy making and assessing performance is becoming an almost universal management process employed to improve efficiency and effectiveness. Performance-based public management allocates responsibility and accountability for results (Bouckaert & Halligan, 2008, p. 2).

The Civil Service Bureau of Jordan plays a central role in building the administrative capacity of the government. The current CS Bureau began functioning in 1955. It is entrusted with applying laws and rules pertaining to civil service selection and staffing public jobs, developing processes, and building data base for human resources management. Government is the largest employer in Jordan. Interviews with senior officials of the Civil Service Bureau by this author (in Amman, June 13, 2016) revealed the following information: the 104 public organizations in existence employ 220,000 public employees, half of them in education. Public employees constitute 39 to 42 percent of total employment in the society. During 2016, the Civil Service Bureau had 320,000 applications on file for public jobs. The staff of the bureau had no convincing response when faced with the many exceptions made to merit-based appointment decisions.

The two cases presented above illustrate, from different angles, that administrative reforms in Jordan face difficulties at the political and administrative levels of governance. A major reason for poor implementation is inadequate knowledge and low skills within a culture of favoritism and cronyism in appointments. The civil service system remains without the essential elements of a professional management. The merit system remains unsteady, and standards of individual and organizational performance are not properly defined or reliably measured. Moreover, employing a systematic comparative analysis for discovery and application of best practices is rare. Relevant local knowledge and information are necessary for reducing reliance on generic prescriptions by foreign consultants that domestic traditionalists find easy to resist and not to enforce. The information and communication technology opened new channels for exchange of information on a variety of policy concerns. The liberating effect of the internet empowered organization management through immediate access to information and to citizens. The Jordanian bureaucracy has not increased its knowledge through use of technological tools and lacks proper training and development in the field electronic communication. It is also confronting the negative consequences of a fast-growing and generally unregulated social media spreading false rumors and distortive information.

The economic condition of Jordan remains a major challenge because of its increasing reliance on external aid and borrowing to fund the public budget. A chronic budget deficit often results in low capital investment in job-creation. Bureaucracy in Jordan does not seem to offer any credible analysis or successful solutions to alleviate the financial stress. Data, facts, and knowledge generated through research, bridging conflicting opinions and reaching a consensus over best policy options, are not taken seriously by the administrative system of the country. In Jordan, as in the rest of the Arab world, many assessments have concluded that a condition of poor knowledge and information "deficit" prevails (UNDP, 2006). Factual and data-driven public decisions are most effective methods for restoring citizens' satisfaction and trust and for professionalizing public management (Klingner, 2009).

Moreover, improving performance of public management in Jordan requires effective political and administrative leaders, willing and able to be responsible for the adoption and implementation of reform duties. Political and administrative leaders are responsible for sustaining and integrating the actions and outcomes of a functioning system. They inspire strategic initiatives and change, build the trust of subordinates and followers, demonstrate credibility, and transform a system to a better condition.

The main obstacles that obstruct the development of such a leadership in Jordan include (a) embedded patronage in recruitment, particularly in high positions; (b) deficiency of appropriate education and professional training and development; (c) traditional autocratic style of management that is hierarchical, personal, and non-institutional; and (d) fragile formal accountability processes inadequate to ensure commitments to common objectives and to serve citizens equitably. Consequently, development of competent and ethical leadership is possible only by limiting patronage and enforcing a firm merit system in recruitment as a precondition for ensuring ethics and compliance with the rule of law. Certainly, implementation of reform projects in Jordan requires organizational leaders, trained in professional modern management, not limited to traditional hierarchical command and control tools. The current "privileged circles" of influential persons in central authority resist change if viewed to limit their privileges. In the absence of organized massive political parties, many political leaders are supported by groups acting as lobbyists or special interest groups. They represent powerful relatives and associations of family and tribes seeking to perpetuate or enhance their special advantages far more than supporting values of equity and merit.

During 2017, the IMF forwarded to the government of Jordan a set of recommendations to be observed if it is to continue borrowing from IMF. The essence of these guidelines was to enhance domestic participation in the cost of governing and to reduce budget deficit and borrowing. The guidelines have been blamed for increasing prices in the marketplace and exacerbating negative economic conditions, particularly unemployment. Increasing domestic financial responsibilities under existing economic conditions has proven to be far more difficult than expected. Thus, when the government of Jordan submitted in May 2018 a new tax law to the parliament that was considered punitive to middle- and low-income people, citizens responded intensely. There were massive street demonstrations in most cities, demanding a change of policy and improvement of government. Labor unions, professional associations, students, and a variety of groups of citizens joined the protests. The people protested responsibly, without violence, resisting unpopular policies regarded unfavorable to the poor and unemployed.

Accordingly, the King of Jordan, in accordance with constitutional provisions, asked for the resignation of the prime minister and the cabinet and designated a new prime minister to form a new cabinet. After few days of consultation, the new government came into office by the middle of June 2018. The message from the king and the first pronouncement of the new prime minister emphasized certain principles and values of governing. They included improving the economy, taking into account all-relevant opinions and respecting citizens' views and demands, implementing transparency of government decisions, and the withdrawing the proposed tax law as submitted by the former prime minister to the legislature. The economic policies of the deposed prime minister and his cabinet instigated broad and deep public resentment, resulting in rising prices and a proposal for an unpopular new tax law. The change of political leaders in response to public demands was an effective response, attracting positive opinions across wide segments of the society. In addition, financial aid promised by the Arab states of Kuwait, Saudi Arabia, and the United Arab Emirates provided needed relief to the Jordanian budget and economy.

Finally, public administration in Jordan is facing complex challenges in implementing public policies of the country. The new prime minister gained considerable public confidence based on promises and public declarations he made. In a recent public opinion survey (*Alrai,* July 4, 2018, p. 1), the new prime minister was favored by 81 percent of those surveyed over the former one for doing a better job. The survey covered 1,524 men and women over 18 years old.[6] Clearly, administrative reforms in Jordan are a high priority for the government, but implementation remains in the formative phase. Political parties lack reliable ideological commitments, adding to the difficulty of predicting and evaluating expected future reform programs. Reducing the chronic budget deficit and curtailing public debt remain compelling objectives. The values emphasized by the new prime minister and his cabinet and the priorities for reforms, according to above-mentioned citizens survey (*Altai*, 2018), are as follows: (1) fighting financial and administrative corruption, (2) creating job opportunities, and (3) reducing inflationary prices of market products. Defined objectives are not, however, the same as defined policies and programs to achieve them. Overcoming old attitudes and oversimplified assumptions is a long-range strategy involving a constant search for appropriate policies and actions. A clear reform strategy includes programs of action with time, cost, and measurable expected results. Such actions are not presented yet, and only future analysis can assess and measure the end results of such reform ideas.

Notes

1 Revised from Jreisat, J. E. (2018). Public administration reform in Jordan: Concepts and practices. *International Journal of Public Administration*, 41(10), 781–791. Reprinted by permission of the publisher Taylor & Francis Ltd., http://www.tandfonline.com
2 Deceased.
3 Official census statistics as reported in *Jordan Times*, English daily newspaper, January 12, 2016, reported under the title "Non-Jordanians constitute third of population." http://www.jordantimes.com/#sthash.yfnEWtvr.dpuf
4 *Al-Arab El-Yaum*, daily newspaper in Jordan, May 8, 2015. A survey by the Center for Strategic Studies, at the University of Jordan in 2014, reported that "61% of Jordanians believe there is corruption in government institutions, and 87% regard the economic conditions (inflation, unemployment, poverty) as the greatest challenge facing the country."
5 The international team has membership of representatives from the UNDP, the World Bank, and experts from Germany, France, and New Zealand.
6 *Alrai*, Arabic daily newspaper. July 4, 2018, p. 1. *alrai.com/article/10442683*

References

Aberbach, J. D., & Christensen, T. (2014). Why reforms so often disappoint. *The American Review of Public Administration*, 44(1), 3–16.
AHDR. (2009). Arab Human Development Report. United Nations Development Program (UNDP), Regional Bureau for Arab States (RBAS), New York.
AL-Oudat, A., & Khlaifat, R. (2011). Jordan and Gulf crisis. *British Journal of Arts and Social Sciences*, 3(2), 165–179. http://www.bjournal.co.uk/BJASS.aspx
Argyriades, D. (2013). Pulling the threads together: An exit from the crisis restoring public trust with public service professionalism. In D. Argyriades, & G. Timsit (Eds.), *Moving beyond the crisis: Reclaiming and reaffirming our common administrative space* (pp. 327–374). Bruylant.
Bouckaert, G., & Halligan, J. (2008). *Managing performance: International comparisons*. Routledge.
Carroll, K. B. (2003). *Business as usual: Economic reform in Jordan*. Lexington Books.
Cole, J. (2014). *The new Arabs*. Simon & Schuster.
Farazmand, A. (2009). Building administrative capacity for the age of rapid globalization. *Public Administration Review*, 69(6), 1007–1020.

Falk, R. (1999). *Predator globalization: A critique.* Blackwell Publishers.
Hertog, S. (2010). *Princes, brokers, and bureaucrats.* Cornell University Press.
Ingraham, P. W. (2007). Studying state and local government management systems. In P. W. Ingraham (Ed.), *In pursuit of management systems in state and local government* (pp. 1–14). Johns Hopkins University Press.
Jabbra, J., & Jreisat, J. E. (2009). Administration of the Arab state: Synthesizing diverse traditions. In I. P. Pagaza & D. Argyriades (Eds.), *Winning the needed change: Saving our planet earth* (pp. 112–126). IOS Press.
Jreisat, J. E. (1997). *Politics without process: Administering development in the Arab world.* Lynne Reinner.
Jreisat, J. E. (2011a). Commentary—Comparative public administration: A global perspective. *Public Administration Review, 71*(6), 834–838.
Jreisat, J. E. (2011b). Budget discipline and undisciplined politics: The case of Jordan. In C. E. Menifield (Ed.), *Comparative budgeting* (pp. 221–236). Jones and Bartlett.
Jreisat, J. E. (2009). Administration, globalization, and the Arab states. *Public Organization Review, 9*(1), 37–50.
Jreisat, J. E. (2006). The Arab world: Reform or stalemate. *Journal of Asian and African Studies, 41*(5, 6), 411–438.
Khouri, R. G. (2005, August 23). When Arab democrats are denied democracy. *Jordan Times.*
Klingner, D. E. (2009). Using US public administration to support global development. *Journal of Regional Development Studies and Development, 18*(2), 1–30.
Lenczowski, G. (1962). *The Middle East in world affairs.* Cornell University Press.
Obeidat, O., & Omari, R. (2016, April 12). Hundreds of MPs' relatives appointed as administrators at Chamber. *Jordan Times.*
Pollitt, C., & Bouckaert, G. (2011). *Public management reform: A comparative analysis* (3rd ed.). Oxford University Press.
Pollitt, C. (2008). *Time, policy, management.* Oxford University Press.
Pye, L. W. (1962). *Politics, personality, and nation building: Burma's search for identity.* Yale University.
Rohr, J. A. (2000). Ethics, governance, and constitutions. In R. A. Chapman (Ed.), *Ethics in public service for the new millennium.* Ashgate Publishing.
Sayigh, Y. A. (1991). *Elusive development: From dependence to self-reliance in the Arab region.* Routledge.
Stillman, R. J. (2008). *Public administration: Concepts and cases* (9th ed.). Houghton Mifflin.
Todaro, M. P. (1989). *Economic development in the Third World* (4th ed.). Longman.
UNDP. (2006). *Capacity development: Lessons of experience and guiding principles.* Retrieved May 10, 2010, from http://mirror.undp.org/magnet/cdrb/CDPRIN1.htm

PART II
Public Administration in North African Countries

5
GOVERNANCE AND PUBLIC ADMINISTRATION REFORM IN MOROCCO

A "Glocal" Perspective

Rabia Naguib

Introduction

In light of waves of globalization, policies at national levels are highly influenced by actors at international levels, and the apprehension of the concept and praxis of governance and public administration must be put into consideration by both global and local factors. With the intensification of interdependence worldwide, national governments are voluntarily or coercively engaged in a complex system of "global governance," which implies "governing without sovereign authority" (Finkelstein, 1995, p. 369). Rosenau (2002) refers to a "bifurcated system" as the way governance is pursued in a new global order, where a multi-centric system interacts closely with the state-centric system. This model suggests the interference of global actors and supranational institutions in local governance with a "disaggregation of authority destined to weaken sates" (Rosenau, 2005, p. 79). Undeniably, Arab countries are subject to mainstream "global governance." They are caught between local demands from their citizens and global pressures from supranational institutions. Public administration in such contexts is affected by national and international actors and is subordinated to intrinsic and extrinsic factors. In fact, the Arab uprisings consisted of local demands made by citizens for better living standards through job creation and putting an end to corruption and unequal treatment by national administrations.

Meanwhile, external pressures were exercised by global forces and international donors imposing their own conditionalities and "encouraging their client states to reconfigure public institutions and build rule-bound systems that are responsive and accountable to citizens" (Brinkerhoff & Goldsmith,

2005, p. 200). The proposed models and approaches to public administration reforms and good governance are largely grounded in Organization for Economic Co-operation and Development (OECD) and US experiences and may have limited applicability in developing country contexts, requiring a "hybrid" approach to enforce adaptive responses to complexity (Robinson, 2015). As pointed by Jreisat (2018, p. 784), "the design of an effective solution to an administrative problem should consider numerous contextual factors, including characteristics of the political and administrative system." Administrative reforms are to a large extent dependent on politics that determine the policy priorities of a country and the level of support for their implementation (The Commonwealth, 2016). In fact, "political regimes crucially influence the system of governance," since the rules and principles that lay the foundation for good governance (for example, transparency, accountability, and participation) are "framed by the nature and interrelations of the political institutions, and the extent to which the regime respects these principles in its public decisions" (Benhlal, 2014, p. 3). Therefore, politics, policy, and administration are interdependent, and so, the exploration of governance and public administration reform should be sensitive to the local context while considering the influence of international actors.

Morocco offers a striking example of the importance of taking into consideration the local context with its peculiarities. It illustrates the concept of duality in governance and public administration, having to continuously juggle tradition and modernity in a longstanding monarchical regime. This unique case necessitates the adoption of a hybrid approach and eloquently reflects and translates what Pal (2019, p. 77) refers to as "an amalgam of effects and legacies, a complex DNA sequencing of local conventions and practices, Islamic principles, and Western influences." Therefore, a glocal perspective will be adopted in this paper to understand governance and public administration through reforms undertaken in the Moroccan context. The concept of governance and its application will be explored first, before delving into the salient aspects of public administration reform in the Kingdom of Morocco, notably through the over-sought organizational, managerial, digital, and ethical transformations, translating into the respective strategies of decentralization, rationalization, digitalization, and moralization of the public sector. This will be followed by a retrospective and a general conclusion.

Governance: Between global design and local reality

The concept of governance has been widely disseminated, since the 1990s, by Western development agencies such as the World Bank and the OECD, through governance reform seeking "the promotion of universal values such as freedom and democracy in the political realm, and effectiveness and responsiveness in the administrative realm" (Pal, 2019, p. 47). Western-led governance reform projects in the world and in Arab countries resulted in a regime of global governance with distinct Western accents. Global governance is defined as "formal institutions and regimes empowered to enforce compliance, as well as informal arrangements that people and institutions either have agreed to or perceive to be in their interest" (Commission on Global Governance, 1995, p. 4). Governance has become a new orthodoxy replacing the neo-classical "get prices right" approach to "get institutions right first," which perceived better-run public institutions as the most important instruments for fostering national development (Brinkerhoff & Goldsmith, 2005).

Therefore, "good governance" has become an instrument of public affairs and an indicator of political development as well as a mechanism to enhance the legitimacy of the public sphere. It moved to the forefront of public policy debates as international donors encouraged their client states to reconfigure public institutions and build systems that are responsive and accountable to citizens. The emphasis was put on the improvement of public services through adequate systems of public administration such as budgeting, human resource (HR) management, decentralization, service delivery, IT, and financial management. Good governance seems to have been commonly accepted as a critical element in driving the modernization and reform of public administration. Meanwhile, it has become obvious that "good governance" incontestably implies a "Euro-American monopoly" (De Jong, 2013, p. 99). Therefore, its implementation requires degrees of modification depending on cultural and institutional differences.

Governance in context

As pointed by Joffe (1988, p. 201), "in the context of North Africa and the Middle East, modern Morocco is, in many respects, a unique state." Morocco is one of the oldest monarchies in the world with a political tradition dating back to the origins of the modern Moroccan state in the ninth-century Idrisid dynasty. The current Alaouite dynasty has been ruling since the seventeenth century. It draws on the power of religious and symbolic legitimacy with proclaimed lineage from the Prophet Mohamed. The nature of the constitutional monarchy in Morocco differs from that of the European monarchies (e.g., Britain and Spain) since the king holds real rather than symbolic powers (Benhlal, 2014). Hence, in the Sharifian kingdom, the monarchy is a ruling institution where the monarch constitutionally combines political/secular power and religious authority. Brinkerhoff and Goldsmith (2005, p. 200) use the term "institutional dualism" to refer to the "tension between intended new performance-enhancing institutions and unwanted old and deeply embedded practices." The Moroccan political system provides a good illustration of such institutional dualism and complexity where change and status quo coexist within institutions (Naguib, 2020).

Morocco is defined by its constitution as both a "modern democratic state" and an "Islamic sovereign state." This identity translates into an institutional dualism, combining modern and imported institutions, such as parliament, with deeply rooted institutions such as the *Makhzen*. The latter is an institution developed throughout the history of Morocco and is "deeply rooted in Islam and informed by political practices" (Daadaoui, 2011, p. 42). It evolved into a powerful informal system and political and administrative structure involving submission, rituals, and the paying of tribute (Maghraoui, 2012). Noteworthy, Morocco also has a dual legal system drawing on the French code and the Islamic law codified in the *Mudawana* (the family code that deals with issues such as marriage, divorce, child custody, and inheritance).

Since independence in 1956, Morocco had to manage the challenging and complex cohabitation of two contrasting systems of power, one infused and diffused by the French colonization (1912–1956) and another inherited from a deeper unbroken political tradition. According to Daadaoui (2011, p. 41), the first "corresponds to modern state function of bureaucratic and administrative governance," while the latter, referring to the concept of *Makhzen*, represents "an ancient mode of government being traditional in nature and contributing to reinforce patrimonial practices and symbolic political power in Morocco." This reality illustrates what Riggs (1964) refers to as "prismatic society"—where a synthesis of ostensibly incongruent institutions can exist. In such a context, a hybrid approach is essential and a glocal perspective has not been encountered to understand the adopted governance mode and administration system. The Moroccan system is highly affected by a deeply rooted and persistent interplay between global trends and local reality, and between modern and traditional institutions. Despite many initiatives promoting institutional reforms and good governance in Morocco, the regime remains caught between the driving forces of modern and democratic changes and the pervasive power of traditional and authoritarian rules (Naguib, 2017).

Following this perspective, public service performance represents a key variable in the good governance equation. Therefore, like many counterparts in the region, the Moroccan government has been strongly encouraged by aid donors to undertake necessary reforms of the public administration sector to modernize and strengthen its capacities and capabilities notably through the decentralization of its services, the rationalization of its resources, the digitalization of its processes, and the empowerment of women.

Public administration reforms: An insidious path to modernization

The core objective of public administration consists primarily of efficiently delivering basic services to the public. Concretely, this is far from the case in most Arab countries and in Morocco in particular. Given the direct effect of access to basic public services on the living conditions of citizens and on their social and economic well-being, deficiencies in their provision contribute to sustaining poverty (UN, 2000). Brixi et al. (2015, p. 15) underline "a relation between state's performance and citizens' trust and engagement at the national and local levels affecting in turn institutional development and performance." They consequently refer to a cycle of poor performance in the Middle East and North Africa (MENA) region perpetuating a culture of privilege and cronyism that needs to be broken by improving the quality of public services and accountability in order to retain citizens' trust. Therefore, in partnership with European donors and supranational institutions, a series of public sector reforms were initiated in most developing countries as an "integral part of governments' efforts to modernize the public sector, making it more citizen-centric and responsive" (The Commonwealth, 2016, p. 5).

However, as underlined by Bilbao (2019), the assumption by Western donors and foreign experts that a pre-formed set of administrative reform processes will solve the particular problems of any specific government is not realistic. Successful public sector reforms should take into account the economic, social, cultural, constitutional, and political contexts of the state in which they are implemented. Hence, analysis of the current situation of public administration in Morocco requires an understanding of its genesis and legacy. Its structure and organization date back to the colonization era with the creation in 1913 of the first body responsible for state personnel under the General Secretariat of the Protectorate. Since then, it has fallen under an independent ministerial department. Following independence in 1956, a Minister of State for the Public Service was appointed, before a Minister of Public Service and Administrative Reform was nominated in 1960. Hence, the need for reflecting on administrative reforms has started since the sixties with the construction of a modern state faced with a dual heritage (*makhzenian* and protectoral).

In the seventies, reforms evolved around decentralization, while public service remained highly centralized. In the eighties, as structural adjustment programs were imposed, the focus came on macro-economic and budgetary aspects of the reform following a neoliberal logic. In the nineties, an Economic and Social Reform Program (ESRP) backed by the World Bank was adopted, and a Strategic Committee of the administrative reform was created under the supervision of the prime minister. With a political transition from King Hassan II to Mohamed VI taking place in 1999, administrative reforms focused on the modernization of public services. In 2002, a ministry responsible for the Modernization of the Public Sectors was appointed, and in 2013, a Minister Delegate to the Head of Government responsible for the Public service and the Modernization of the Administration was nominated. The Ministry for the Modernization of the Public Sector (MMPS) is a key actor in public administration reform. Its mission is to develop and ensure the implementation of a government policy on civil service and public sector modernization, with a view to strengthen good governance and lay the foundations for a modern, effective, transparent, and competent administration.[1]

In addition to the national government, international organizations and foreign partners (i.e., the World Bank, IMF, UNDP, OECD, the European Union, the African Development Bank, UNESCO, and UN Women) are involved in public administration reforms in Morocco. The country participated in many programs and initiatives seeking the improvement of public services. However, due to a lack of follow-up, most of the programs did not achieve the expected results. Since 2002, the Moroccan government has embarked on a comprehensive Public Administration Reform Program (PARP) with assistance from the World Bank, which incorporated governance-related conditions within its development loans policy, requiring governments receiving loans to demonstrate effective performance and pursue deep reforms. At the heart of this program was the modernization of the human resources management system, particularly using tools to assess skills and performance. Through this program, Morocco's administrative tradition aspired to move from strict and rigid legal compliance to a search for better performance and more effective public service (World Bank, 2010). Once again, the reforms failed to achieve their objectives. Given the critical socio-economic conjuncture, the Moroccan government initiated in collaboration with the World Bank Country Partnership Framework (CPF) covering the fiscal years 2019–2024. The goal of this program is to improve social cohesion by addressing inequalities and promoting economic growth and job creation. It aims to achieve this by focusing on improving education and healthcare outcomes, establishing innovative social protection programs, and promoting good governance and citizen engagement, which are essential foundations for implementing the CPF (World Bank, 2019).

The dysfunctions attributed to the Moroccan public administration have amply been diagnosed and solutions have been proposed without much positive impact on the ground (Ben Osmane, 2004). The undertaken administrative reforms did not translate into concrete changes and improvement of the public sector. This sector has been the subject of harsh criticism by different actors at various levels. In a letter addressed to the participants of the National Forum of the High Public Function in 2018, the king stated that "the imperative of efficient resource management and the necessary satisfaction of global development pose the fundamental question of the efficiency of public administration." He also asserted that "the reformation of public administration is acutely essential as a sine qua non condition for the outcome of public policies aimed at improving the living conditions of citizens in accordance with the constitution."[2] The minister of the MMPS also admitted the "illness" of the administration, which suffers from a heavy bureaucratic apparatus with a high level of authoritarianism and centralization of decision-making and a lack of meritocracy. He also highlighted the need for a paradigm shift and a new public service and administrative model.[3] This model is reflected in the National Plan for the Reform of the Administration (2018–2021), which targets four structural transformations covering the organizational, managerial, digital, and ethical dimensions. The first one is related to decentralization and deconcentration, the second to rationalization and HR management, the third to digitalization and e-government, and the fourth to moralization by fighting corruption and inequalities.

Decentralization and advanced regionalization: Organizational "transformation"

Following the Arab uprisings, Morocco initiated a decentralization reform effort aimed at responding to protesters' demands requesting more participative governance and efficient and accountable public services, as well as the modernization of the administrative and political system. The new constitution laid the foundation for advanced regionalization and decentralization as key to administrative reform and as a tool for a democratic system of governance. In addition to their domestic imperatives, decentralization reforms were also demanded by external donors as preconditions for the granting of funds (Houdret & Harnisch, 2017).

In their Country Partnership Strategy for Morocco, the World Bank (2013) emphasized decentralization reforms in order to promote a neoliberal approach that would improve private-sector-led competitiveness and global integration. Meanwhile, the focus is on improving governance and strengthening the accountability and capacity of institutions that manage public resources and deliver basic services, particularly at the local level. Hence, there are intrinsic and extrinsic factors pushing for administrative reforms through decentralization. The former emphasized the conditions of a substantive democracy, while the latter advanced conditionalities for an advanced economic liberalization and procedural democracy.

The first article in the 2011 constitution describes Morocco's territorial organization as "decentralized, based on an advanced regionalization." The constitution introduced seven new articles dealing with state efforts to foster local citizenship and human development across the country's regions, and assuring an "equitable allocation of resources, in order to reduce disparities between regions."[4] The new constitution also introduced the principle of "advanced regionalization" intended to provide more administrative self-determination at the local and regional levels and enable citizens to participate in political decision-making processes.

Morocco championed decentralization in the MENA region as it had previous experience with it in 2004. However, the practical implementation of this key component of public administration reform has been delayed several times and remains the function of a set of laws yet to be written (Silverstein, 2011). In 2015, new laws for decentralization reform were issued to specify and operationalize the constitution at the municipal, regional, and prefectural levels. Still, regional inequalities and grievances persist, and the uprisings in the Rif region in 2016 are symptomatic of related dissatisfaction. The protest movements advocate for local and regional development, highlighting the persistence of issues related to decentralization, participation, and public service provision.

In an examination of the recent reforms pertaining to decentralization in Morocco, Zaki (2019) states that legal changes remain largely theoretical and very limited in practice. The new constitution placed transparency and citizen as key principles of good governance. It replaced the concept of "tutelle," under the administrative authorities of the Ministry of Interior, with the principle of "administrative freedom" of local governments. However, municipalities lack the financial and technical means to implement their mandates and remain subject to the strong control of central and deconcentrated authorities (Zaki, 2019). While municipalities endorse increased legal responsibilities, the control of the central government and its representatives persists on the ground. This reality is informed and shaped by historical legacies of a monarchical centralized power and a colonial heritage engendering the concept of institutional dualism and a "double-headed administrative system."

As mentioned earlier, the administrative and political system in Morocco is embedded in a historical context. It dates from the colonial period when French rulers adopted a strategy seeking to preserve their interests by notably dividing Morocco into two parts (i.e., useful and useless), strengthening local regional authorities, and weakening national resistance movements (Bouabid & Iraki, 2015). This strategy was further adopted by King Hassan II and consolidated the alliance between the monarchy and rural elites to dilute the influence of urban and partisan elites and counter any potential opposition. It produced parallel institutions and structures at all levels of the state apparatus under the highly centralized control of the king via the Ministry of Interior (Houdret & Harnisch, 2019). Through different mechanisms operating regionally, the *Makhzen* has been able to control local elites by appointing local governors and supporting rural notables, thus allowing this institution to dominate elected bodies and informal decision-making (García & Suárez Collado, 2015). Houdret and Harnisch (2017,

p. 17) depict the double political administrative structure in Morocco by writing that "the elected representatives have counterparts at all levels in the form of representatives of the *Makhzen*, appointed by the King." Thus, there is on the one side the elected institutions (i.e., regional, provincial, prefectural, and municipal councils/parliaments) and on the parallel side, the representatives nominated by the palace (i.e., regional Walis, provincial governors, municipal Caids/Pachas, and Sheikhs/Moqadems at the district level).

This structure illustrates the dualism and double-headed administrative system where modern constitutional institutions coexist with traditional and ancient ones. It also highlights the tension between control and authority and a paradoxical logic reinforcing the center as the "unique driving force behind the reform of regional administration" (García & Suárez Collado, 2015, p. 46). In order to assess public administration reform in Morocco, understanding this system and the relationship between these institutions is fundamental for structural change and not just a procedural one. As highlighted by Houdret and Harnisch (2017, p. 18), "the limitation of the autonomy and scope of action of the elected institutions has not been addressed in the various decentralization reforms initiated since the 1970s." Therefore, Morocco's decentralization program has not experienced a devolution of power, resulting in expensive double structures (BTI, 2020). These structures were effectively revealed to be very costly and their inefficiency has been translated in the need to modernize and streamline public administration through a rationalization policy seeking a "managerial transformation" in line with the national plan that seeks to reform the administration.

Rationalization of public administration: Managerial "transformation"

Given the important role the public sector plays in the development process, the improvement of its managerial capabilities and resources represents a national priority for many countries. As highlighted by Robinson (2015), in developing countries with bloated and inefficient bureaucracies, some measures of downsizing and efficiency reforms will continue to remain a priority to bring spending on public administration within manageable fiscal limits. Such reforms are driven by a shifting logic from an old public administration to a "new public management" (NPM). This paradigm shift has been promoted and diffused by Western donors and lenders and is infused with a performance culture, market logic, and a "results-oriented" approach. It is based on an economic rationality which seeks to reduce budget deficits and fiscal imbalances in order to serve customers through decentralized public organizations; it is also based on the efficient use of resources, and a government playing a "steering" role and serving as a catalyst to unleash market forces.

From this perspective, the United Nations system offers to support the public administration of interested member states in becoming "sound, efficient and well equipped with the appropriate capacities and capabilities through capacity-building, access and utilization of technology, providing an enabling environment for private sector activities, involvement of women, and the promotion of opportunities for all to participate in all spheres of the public sector" (UN, 2000, p. 58). Therefore, a greater emphasis on results and better value for money, with a larger delegation of authority and flexibility, and the introduction of competition and market rules became part of the "new public management" reforms and a condition imposed by International Financial Institutions in their loan policy to beneficiary governments (Lahjouji, 2019).

Hence, with the technical assistance and financial loans of three donors, notably the World Bank, the European Union, and the African Development Bank, the Moroccan government devised a PARP based on a matrix of measures, seeking to fulfill four objectives related to the improvement of the budget, HR management, the control of wage bill, and the simplification of administrative formalities and procedures (African Development Bank, 2006). The program started in 2003 with pilot ministries on the basis of "voluntary" adherence before applying the reforms to all ministries in 2008. The budget reforms aim was meant to make policies more open through decentralization, to increase accountability for results, and to improve ministries performance through internal audit and evaluation. For that, a system of "contractualization" of budget allocations was introduced progressively, through which performance measures were attached to budgets. The objectives of HR reform were to create a better match between job requirements and the skills of the workforce, to improve and create greater transparency in promotion, appraisal, and pay, and to build a coherent and continuous training policy (Hennebert, 2008).

Compared to other MENA countries, Morocco's public sector wage bill represents a large portion of its GDP, exerting financial pressures on the government's budget. The public sector played an important role in reducing unemployment among graduates until the mid-1980s, resulting in a considerable increase in the number of civil servants. Moreover, to tackle this structural constraint, initiatives to contain the cost of civil service through the rationalization and downsizing of the workforce were undertaken. Prior initiatives led by the government, notably in 1998, failed to bring any real change as they faced opposition from interest groups and resistance from the trade unions. As an alternative, a Voluntary Retirement Program (VRP) was designed to implement administrative reform within the framework of the PARP. According to El Massnaoui and Biygautane (2011, p. 23), "the VRP resulted in significant financial and economic gains to the Moroccan economy, through savings in the government's wage bill, as well as through the retirees' investments in the private sector and the creation of new SMEs."⁵

However, the results were mixed as the VRP did not improve the geographic distribution of the workforce, contributing to localized overstaffing and generating chronic redundancies and underemployment. In fact, while the program was an opportunity to restructure employment policies within the public sector and to recruit younger civil servants, it created a big gap in organizations where the most skilled senior employees retired and the remaining ones needed substantive training sessions to strengthen their skills. The program helped shed light on the broader structural challenges facing public administration reform such as "poorly targeted recruitment, overstaffing, competence deficiencies, unbalance geographic concentration, ineffective training, and subjective evaluation," and helped the government adopt reforms in "a number of important aspects of human resources management ranging from recruitment and training, to performance evaluation and monitoring, to redeployment" (El Massnaoui & Biygautane, 2011, p. 25). Such reforms require new legislations or an update of old ones, especially in the matter of the General Statute on the Civil Service dating from 1958. The statutory basis for HR management is clearly outdated and would not help in the modernization process of the public administration in Morocco.

On the Moroccan experience, Hennebert (2008) concludes that comprehensive reform requires government-wide support to have an impact, patience to design and enforce new laws, as well as strict regulation and a robust monitoring system. Moreover, for reforms to be effective, they require the internalization by public servants of technical knowledge related to the fields of budget management, public expenditure control, and HR management, and also a good grasp and use of information technology to provide better services to citizens.

Digitalization of public services: Digital transformation

Digital transformation is a key component of the modernization process and public administration reforms. It promotes the use of information and communication technology (ICT) and e-governance policies to improve the transparency and openness of governments in becoming "a platform" with a "user-driven" administration (OECD, 2018). Such a transition is not only about the digitization of paper-based service delivery processes. It requires organizational and managerial changes that are customer/citizen-centric involving broader cultural and mind-set shifts. Like incentives used to promote good performance in the public sector, the incentives for digitalization and e-government come from international institutions that support government agencies' use of information technologies for the provision of public service to citizens and encourage e-participation allowing citizens to get involved in the policy-making process.

In this logic, the World Bank (2019) asserts that "transitioning to digital platforms in government, finance and public services will help Morocco develop new drivers of growth by supporting e-transactions, and e-government." Therefore, Morocco has invested in ICT to support human development and public sector efficiency. The e-government program succeeded in the digitization of several public services through online portals. However, it faces many challenges related to the capacity and flexibility to change the workflow from an archaic manual service delivery to an automated one (Kettani et al., 2008). In fact, limited internet access and the high rate of illiteracy represent serious obstacles and challenges to the widespread use of ICTs. Therefore, "investing in human capital and financial resources is necessary to improve co-ordination and integration of ICTs initiatives across government" (OECD, 2015, p. 20).

However, while there is an official discourse and a moral engagement from the public authority to promote the use of IT in the public sector, there is little evidence to support the formal rhetoric. A field investigation exploring the perceptions and opinions of users of public services in Morocco shows that perceptions of public service users remain generally negative (CESE, 2013).

Since 1999, several strategies and plans related to digital reform have been designed. A new strategy called "Maroc Digital 2020" has been introduced in 2016 and has been criticized for presenting very general guidelines without a plan on how to support them. In 2017, the Digital Development Agency was created under the Ministry of Industry, Trade, Investment, and the Digital, with the general mission of implementing the state's digital development strategy and promoting digital tools to users. Although the legal framework of the agency has been finalized, it has not yet been fully operational (Sigma, 2019). According to the electronic government of the United Nations, Morocco made progress between 2010 and 2014, going up in rankings from 126 to 82, before falling back to 110 in 2018.[6]

The dematerialization of administrative procedures and digitalization of public services, if applied effectively, can be powerful levers in the fight against corruption, which is another pillar of public administration reform.

Moralization of the public administration: Ethical transformation

Pervasive corruption represents a systemic problem in most developing countries. Across the MENA region, Arab citizens perceive public institutions and governments officials as most corrupt (Abbott & Sapsford, 2016). Since the Arab uprisings, they have been protesting to "voice their anger at the corruption they see and experience in their daily lives: from the highest levels of government to accessing basic public services" (Global Corruption Barometer, 2019, p. 3). Systemic corruption has been identified as "a major impediment to sustainable development," and countries have to "prove themselves capable of containing the corruption that undermines public trust and confidence in the public institutions" (Denoeux, 2000, p. 156). Therefore, fighting corruption is widely considered a salient public policy issue.

In this vein, several initiatives have been undertaken in Morocco to strengthen the integrity of civil servants, promote ethical behavior within public institutions, and improve government-citizen relationship in order to address this problem. The 2011 constitution explicitly raised the issue by articulating principles of transparency and accountability (Article 15) and establishing public institutions in charge of fighting corruption. However, Despite its advisory role toward public, private, and nongovernmental actors in anti-corruption policies, Morocco's Central Instance for Corruption Prevention (CICP) is hindered by unclear regulations and lacks the necessary power and independence from the executive branch to effectively investigate and prosecute corruption charges (BTI, 2018). In June 2014, it was announced that the CICP will be replaced by the National Authority for Integrity and the Prevention and Fighting of Corruption. But its prerogatives have not been defined, and it is unlikely that this body will have a much greater impact.[7] Apparently, while progress has been made through the constitutional establishment of dedicated institutions to fight corruption, the drafting of relevant laws, and the formulation of national strategies, the moralization of the public sector is far from being internalized and adopted. Transparency International's Corruption Perceptions Index (2018) ranked Morocco the 80th out of 180 countries (score 41/100), highlighting a range of persistent institutional issues, notably the lack of transparency, lack of political will, low accountability, and a weak judicial system.

In an effort to fight corruption and promote transparency and integrity in public administration, bodies such as the Moroccan Court of Accounts (MCA) were established to ensure the principles of good governance. Noteworthy, the professional staff and magistrates of this supposedly independent entity are appointed by royal decree. The MCA publishes well-documented reports showing mismanagement and widespread misconducts involving corruption, bribery, nepotism, and patronage. However, following up remains largely at the discretion of the authorities and depends on political considerations. In fact, "the handling of corruption cases reveals a gap between leaders' promises and real actions" (GCB, 2019, p. 13). It highlights the importance of political will in fighting corruption. Based on the Global Corruption Barometer (2019), an overwhelming majority of surveyed Moroccan citizens (74 percent) think that the government is not doing enough to tackle corruption, and 53 percent think that corruption is increasing. Among MENA countries, Morocco has the second highest bribery rate (after Lebanon) which is revealing of the systemic and social nature of corruption and the abuse of power from civil servants. Citizens reported that they have to pay bribes and use their informal connections (*wasta*) to "access basic public services provided as a private favor" (GCB, 2019, p. 31).

Hence, the moralization of the public sector requires a fundamental change in the mind-sets of public officials (Robinson, 2015). Cognitive and normative changes are therefore necessary to any ethical transformation seeking to improve the country's governance. Moralization also requires necessary reform of the judicial system. Without efficient justice, there are significant risks of abusing power and not applying anti-corruption strategies, which can jeopardize the whole administrative reform (CESE, 2013). This situation can produce a vicious cycle, where corruption weakens public institutions, and, in turn, institutions are less able to control corruption (GCB, 2019). Therefore, like for the other dimensions of the undertaken administrative reform in Morocco, the process and outcomes are not clear, and the assessment of their impact reveals many contradictions as well as a widening gap between rhetoric and practice.

Retrospection: Between rhetoric and reality

The Moroccan government has undertaken many initiatives in partnership with international institutions to reform the public sector. Many dysfunctions have been identified by expert groups involving international bodies (i.e., the World Bank, UNDP, OECD, and the EU) and Moroccan entities (i.e., the Supreme Council of Accounts, the Economic, Social and Environmental Council, and local NGOs). Those consist of excessive centralization with heavy and retrograde bureaucracy hindering the quality of public services, lack of trust between public servants and citizens, lack of independence of the administrative domain from the political and economic spheres, and a lack of accountability and impunity, to name a few. Others include the predominance of the logic of power and patronage, an opaque and unequal remuneration system, an inoperative monitoring and evaluation system, a very slow legislative process, and a non-adapted judicial system.

The king, in a speech addressed to the members of the two houses of parliament, pointed to the "many shortcomings" of the public administration that relate to "the poor performance and quality of the services provided to citizens, the plethora of staff, the lack of competence and the lack of sense of responsibility among many public servants." He highlighted the "need to seriously consider the real questions and concerns of citizens, to stimulate the public service action of the administration and to improve the quality of its services." To do that, he asserted that "access to the public service must be based on competence, merit and equal opportunities."[8] Such ideas are in line with the principles of good governance and the "new public management" promoted by aid donors and Western-led organizations, and to which Morocco had to subscribe to address the local grievances of social movements and the global pressures of loan policies. Morocco relies on Development Policy Loans and external financing to support reforms. These reforms seek to foster a competitive private sector to improve the competitiveness and global integration of the kingdom, and to bolster an efficient public administration to provide better services at the local level through good governance and democratic participation. Therefore, liberalization and modernization are the targeted objectives of the reforms made in Morocco.

In this vein, the kingdom had to closely adhere to the neoliberal philosophy supported by the World Bank and the IMF through structural adjustment programs. According to Maghraoui (2002), Morocco signed a series of aid and loan conventions with the World Bank and the IMF to strengthen private entrepreneurship since the 1960s. These conventions focused on budgetary savings through higher taxes and cuts in social programs and subsidies. In the 1980s, under the supervision of the Bretton Wood institutions, the kingdom pursued structural adjustment programs involving privatization, the ending of subsidies, and a lowering of trade barriers. Such economic reforms came with conditions involving considerable social costs, political risks, and administrative changes. Hence, the country had to embark on reforms seeking the modernization of the public administration and a shift to the "new public management" system. The new reforms evolved around four axes: decentralization, rationalization, digitalization, and moralization of the public sector, requiring respective organizational, managerial, digital, and ethical changes.

However, despite several initiatives to modernize the administrative government apparatus, the old approach of public administration and the traditional administrative model persist in Morocco (Naguib, 2017). Given its history and legacy, the Moroccan political system permanently strikes a delicate balance between tradition and modernity, with Makhzenian practices and authoritarian values infiltrating the institutions of a modern constitutional system (OECD, 2015). Moreover, in the context of "transitional continuity" in which a process of change is displayed consistently over time (Naguib, 2020, p. 404), there is a need to question the degree of applicability of any effective transformation. According to the Bertelsmann Transformation Index (BTI), Morocco ranks 62 out of 120 countries in economic transformation, 104 in political transformation, and 88 in the Governance Index (BTI, 2020). Morocco is performing better in the economic indicators than in political participation and rule of law.[9] These results reveal the long-term impact of the reforms promoted by the Bretton Woods institutions that are based on a neoliberal and free market approach via structural adjustment programs focusing notably on deregulation, privatization, and the controlling of public expenditures.

While these reforms resulted in a decrease in the public sector, a reduction in social benefits, a rise in unemployment and falling middle-class incomes, they also contributed to a rise of crony capitalism, enabling the elite to capture the benefits of privatization and allowing the monarchy to retain a strong power base (Sapsford et al., 2016). Thus, as confessed by Western experts, "effects of structural adjustment programs have sometimes weakened the capacity of the public sector to perform its missions effectively" (UN, 2000, p. 61). Furthermore, as observed by Jreisat (2018, p. 783), these imposed policies "stimulated more corruption and concentration of power." In many cases, the strategy of economic liberalization proved to be ineffective in the social development of the country compared to its economic growth, which have to be in tune in order for Morocco to achieve sustainable development (Naguib & Smucker, 2010).

Hence, Morocco does not lack reform or development initiatives, but many strategic plans remain ambitious projects with lagging implementation and little follow-up. Many of the reforms undertaken also reveal an inner incoherence due to the contradicting logic between externally driven principles and the internally oriented reality. A marked example lies in the decentralization- and rationalization-promoting reforms. They assume the existence of transparent, technocratic, and relatively autonomous state institutions to implement them, but this is not the case in Morocco. Morocco's decentralization program has not experienced a devolution of power, resulting in expensive double structures where every representative institution, such as municipal councils, is monitored by the equivalent of a regime-appointed executive (BTI, 2020). In this context, decision-making power on significant political change does not lie in the hands of the elected. A separation of powers is not in place; the judiciary is not independent from the executive; and the latter is centralized in the palace, which has remained untouched (Kausch, 2008).

Therefore, the effective implementation of the outlined reforms remains strongly dependent on the political will of the king and a real political commitment to bring change, notably in the matter of decentralization through a concrete transformation of the power structures (Houdret & Harnisch, 2019). Indeed, as stated by Yom and Gausse (2012, p. 79), "the institutional capacity to reform does not always result in the will to reform." In the case of Morocco, the reforms are hampered not only by a lack of political will and resistance to change, but also by a weak institutional capacity and inefficient resources compensated by foreign development assistance contributing to the reinforcement of dualism and ambivalences. Teti et al. (2017) report, based on the survey on

Arab transformations and the specific question of "how democratic is your country?", that the highest levels of ambiguity with 62 percent of respondents considering the country to have hybrid values. This result is in line with the statement Maghraoui (2002, p. 25) made that "support for democratic principles [in Morocco] remains sparse and ambivalent." Also, as pointed by the OECD (2015, p. 26), "Morocco's inadequate governance structures and weak co-ordination mechanisms are hampering the achievement of tangible results." In this case, a mind-set change, solid leadership from the top, strong political support, realistic goals, and clear performance indicators are required to institutionalize and implement effective governance and public administration reforms.

Concluding comments: The way inward

The case of Morocco clearly illustrates how international development agencies and Bretton Woods institutions are concretely leading the good governance discourse worldwide, and how most reform programs are outsourced to foreign consultancy firms. It shows the global-local dichotomy and the strong imbrication of endogenous and external factors, as well as the interplay between national and international actors. Moreover, it highlights an externally driven and oriented development model that generates internal ambivalences and incoherent strategies and public policies. The Moroccan government has undertaken many initiatives, whether imposed or devised, in partnership with international institutions and aid donors to reform the public sector, in order to improve its governance. The reform they are seeking is the modernization of the Moroccan public administration through a multi-dimensional transformation in the organizational, managerial, digital, and ethical fields.

However, this reform is facing serious challenges consisting of the capacity to translate the pronounced principles and discourses into operational policies, functioning institutions, and measurable results. Robinson (2015) asserts that effective public administration reforms require reform-minded public officials committed to a very different vision of the public service that moves away from market-oriented "new public management" reforms. Following this perspective, the approach to public sector reform in developing countries should not be grounded in models that have evolved under the political and economic conditions of advanced industrialized countries. Hence, a more localized and contextualized approach should be globally adopted. Furthermore, from a historical perspective tracing good governance in the United States, Brinkerhoff and Goldsmith (2005, p. 220) show that the "supposedly modern institutions, evolved incrementally and during a long period, and that the outcomes of reform were mixed as good governance practices did not let bad governance to entirely disappear." Thus, a policy learning rather than a policy borrowing approach should be locally embraced.

Hence remains the puzzling question for Morocco, as for many Arab countries, about what is the right development model, where to begin changes, and how to "get to Denmark"? Or in other words, how to become a law-abiding, democratic, prosperous, and well-governed polity like Denmark, which has some of the world's lowest levels of political corruption? According to Fukuyama (2011, p. 449), "the story of the rise of Danish democracy is full of historical accidents and contingent circumstances that cannot be replicated elsewhere." The factors contributing to the distinctive development path of Denmark consist of a protestant/religious reformation, the encouragement of peasant literacy, and the adoption of enlightenment views by Danish monarchy. The influence of Martin Luther's ideology and the spread of the ideas of the French Revolution stimulated class-based demands for political participation on the part of the bourgeoisie and peasantry and were accepted by a series of Danish monarchs in the eighteenth and nineteenth centuries. In addition, schools were set up very early in every village so that by the eighteenth century, "the peasantry emerged as a relatively well-educated and increasingly well-organized social class," and "the literacy allowed peasants to improve their economic conditions, communicate among themselves and organize as political agents" (Fukuyama, 2011, p. 447). In sum, the birth of new ideas and education were critical to the Danish success story.

Therefore, an important lesson to draw from the Danish case is the salience of education and cognitive and normative factors that would pave the way to a sustainable development. In the case of Morocco, it is a sine qua non condition to any seriously envisaged reform, given the very high illiteracy rate and very low human development level (UNDP, 2019), which represent the most hindering and hampering factors to good governance and effective public administration. Without literacy and good education, no digitalization or moralization transformations of the Moroccan public sector can be possibly and reasonably achieved. Consequently, for changes to be effective and coherent, they should be internally driven and oriented. Furthermore, they should be based on home-grown policies rather than borrowed ones. As pointed by Jreisat (2017, p. 4), in the case of Jordan, "no single framework for implementing administrative reform can be relied upon as most perspectives employed were grounded in foreign experiences and possibly suggested by foreign consultants." This observation resonates as a reality across the Arab countries, unlike some countries which have opted for more adapted reforms. Buckley and Fitzgerald (2017, p. 22) pertinently note that "policies developed abroad are rarely likely to be adopted and enforced with the enthusiasm and rigor of those developed at home. This is a simple fact of human nature. We all do more willingly what we choose to do, rather than what we are told to do." Therefore, rather than being designed outwardly and imported locally or imposed by external and international pressures, administrative reforms and adequate governing modes should emerge from within and keep adapting to respond to the internal needs and demands of Moroccan people.

Notes

1. https://www.mmsp.gov.ma
2. https://www.mmsp.gov.ma
3. https://www.fnh.ma/article/economie/administration-publique-grand-corps-malade
4. https://www.bladi.net/IMG/pdf/Constitution-maroc-2011.pdf
5. https://atlasinfo.fr/Le-Maroc-s-offre-une-fonction-publique-qui-depasse-les-moyens-de-son-economie-Cour-des-comptes_a87399.html
6. https://publicadministration.un.org/Portals/1/Images/E-Government%20Survey%202018_FINAL%20for%20web.pdf
7. http://www.business-anti-corruption.com/country-profiles/morocco
8. http://www.maroc.ma/fr/discours-royaux/texte-integral-du-discours-prononce-par-sm-le-roi-louverture-de-la-1ere-session-de
9. https://www.bti-project.org/en/reports/country-report-MAR-2020.html

References

Abbott, P., & Sapsford, R. J. (2016). *The Arab Transformations Project. After the Arab uprisings: Political, social and economic attitudes in the MENA Region in 2014* [Arab Transformations Working paper 6]. University of Aberdeen.

African Development Bank. (2006, June). *Kingdom of Morocco: Public Administration reform support programme (PARAP I). Completion report.* Country Operations Department North, East and South Regions.

Ben Osmane, K. (2004). *Priority areas in reforming governance and public administration in Morocco.* http://unpan1.un.org/intradoc/groups/public/documents/un/unpan016523.pdf

Benhlal, M. (2014). *Governance in Morocco discourse, policies and reality.* Arab Reform Initiative. Policy Alternatives. https://www.researchgate.net/publication/271853293

Bilbao, J. R. (2019). *History and track records of decentralization reforms.* https://europa.eu/capacity4dev/public-pub.sector-reform-decentralisation/wiki/11-history-and-track-records-decentralisation-reforms

Bouabid, A., & Iraki, A. (2015). Maroc: Tensions centralisatrices. In M. Harb & S. Atallah (Eds.), *Local governments and public goods: Assessing decentralization in the Arab world* (pp. 47–90). The Lebanese Center for Policy Studies.

Brinkerhoff, D. W., & Goldsmith, A. A. (2005). Institutional dualism and international development: A revisionist interpretation of good governance. *Administration & Society, 37*(2), 199–224.

Brixi, H., Lust, E., & Woolcock, M. (2015). *Trust, voice, and incentives: Learning from local success stories in service delivery in the Middle East and North Africa.* International Bank for reconstruction and development. The World Bank.

BTI. (2018). *Morocco country report.* https://bit.ly/2PZ3oNM

BTI. (2020). *Morocco country report.* https://www.bti-project.org/en/reports/country-report-MAR-2020.html

Buckley, R. P., & Fitzgerald, S. M. (2017). An Assessment of Malaysia's Response to the IMF during the Asian Economic crisis [*Singapore Journal of Legal Studies*, 96]. University of New South Wales law Research Series (UNSWLRS) 41. Sydney, Australia.

Commission on Global Governance. (1995). *Our global neighbourhood: Report of the commission on global governance*. Oxford University Press.

Conseil économique, social et environnemental (CESE). (2013). *La Gouvernance des services publics*. http://www.ces.ma/Documents/PDF/Avis-AS13_2013-VF.pdf

Daadaoui, M. (2011). The Makhzen and state formation in Morocco. In M. Daadaoui (Ed.), *Moroccan monarchy and the reference Islamist challenge*. Palgrave Macmillan.

De Jong, M. (2013). China's art of institutional bricolage: Selectiveness and gradualism in the policy transfer style of a nation, *Policy and Society*, 32 (2), 89–101.

Denoeux, G. (2000). The politics of Morocco's "fighting against corruption". *Middle East Policy*, 7(2), 165–189.

El Massnaoui, K., & Biygautane, M. (2011). *Downsizing Morocco's public sector: Lessons from the voluntary retirement program. Case studies in governance and public management in the Middle East and North Africa*. Dubai School of Government. http://www.mbrsg.ae/getattachment/60db517c-ffd4-4053-9cf6-7fe6175b9cd1/Downsizing-Morocco%E2%80%99s-Public-Sector-Lessons-from-th.aspx

Finkelstein, S. L. (1995). What is global governance? *Global Governance*, 1(3), 367–372.

Fukuyama, F. (2011). *The origins of political order: From pre-human times to the French revolution*. Farrar, Straus and Giroux.

García, J. R., & Suárez Collado, A. (2015). The project of advanced regionalization in Morocco: Analysis of a Lampedusian reform. *British Journal of Middle Eastern Studies*, 42(1), 46–58.

Global Corruption Barometer (GCB) Middle East & North Africa. (2019). Citizens' views and experiences of corruption. *Transparency International*. https://images.transparencycdn.org/images/2019_GCB_MENA_Report_EN.pdf

Hennebert, P. (2008). *Partage d'expérience sur la gestion du programme d'appui à la Réforme de l'Administration publique au Maroc*. https://europa.eu/capacity4dev/article/public-administration-reform-morocco

Houdret, A., & Harnisch, A. (2017). Decentralisation in Morocco: The current reform and its possible contribution to political liberalization, Discussion paper, 11/2017. German Development Institute.

Houdret, A., & Harnisch, A. (2019). Decentralization in Morocco: A solution to the Arab spring? *The Journal of North African Studies*, 24(6), 935–960.

Joffe, G. (1988). Morocco: Monarchy, legitimacy and succession. *Third World Quarterly*, 10(1), 201–228.

Jreisat, J. E. (2018). Public administration in Jordan: Concepts and practices. International Journal of Public Administration , 41(10), 781–791. https://doi.org/10.1080/01900692.2017.1387991

Kausch, K. (2008). *Morocco: Negotiating change with the Makhzen*. Project on Freedom of Association in the Middle East and North Africa [Working Paper 54]. FRIDE.

Kettani, D., Moulin, B., Gurstein, M., & El Mahdi, A. (2008). E-government and local good governance: A pilot project in Fez, Morocco. *The Electronic Journal on Information Systems in Developing Countries*, 35(1), 1–18.

Lahjouji, K. (2019). Reflection on the new public management, case of Morocco. *Journal of Business and Management*, 21(6), 16–22.

Maghraoui, A. (2012). The perverse effect of good governance: Lessons from Morocco. *Middle East Policy, 19*(2), 49–65.

Maghraoui, A. M. (2002). Democratization in the Arab world? Depoliticization in Morocco. *Journal of Democracy, 13*(4), 24–32.

Naguib, R. (2017). Public administration in Morocco. In A. Farazmand (Ed.), *Global encyclopedia of public administration, public policy, and governance* (pp. 1–6). Springer.

Naguib, R. (2020). Legitimacy and "transitional continuity" in a monarchical regime: Case of Morocco. *International Journal of Public Administration, 43*(5), 404–424.

Naguib, R., & Smucker, J. (2010). When economic growth rhymes with social development: Malaysia experience. *Journal of Business Ethics, 89*(2), 99–113.

OECD. (2015). *Open government in Morocco, OECD public governance reviews.* OECD Publishing. https://read.oecd-ilibrary.org/governance/open-government-in-morocco_9789264226685-en#page48

OECD. (2018). *Digital government review of Morocco: Laying the foundations for the digital transformation of the public sector in Morocco.* OECD Digital Government Studies, OECD.

Pal, L. A. (2019). Reforming governance in Muslim-majority states: Promoting values or protecting stability? In L. A. Pal & M. E. Tok (Eds.), *Global governance and Muslim organizations* (pp. 45–82). Palgrave McMillan.

Riggs, F. W. (1964). *Administration in developing countries: The theory of prismatic society.* Houghton Mifflin Company.

Robinson, M. (2015). *From old public administration to the new public service: Implications for public sector reform in developing countries.* UNDP Global Center for Public Service Excellence.

Rosenau, J. (2005). Illusions of power and empire. *History and Theory, 44*(4), 73–87.

Rosenau, J. N. (2002). Governance in a new global order. In D. Held & A. McGrew (Eds.), *Governing globalization: Power, authority and global governance* (pp. 70–86). Polity.

Sapsford, R., Abbott, P., Teti, A., Lomazzi, V., Luguzan, C., Sarnelli, V., Xypolia, I., & Vincent, K. (2016). *The Arab transitions report on political, economic and social attitudes, 2014: Morocco.* University of Aberdeen.

Sigma. (2019). *Principes d'administration publique- Prestation de services administratifs: Maroc, Initiative conjointe de l'OCDE et l'UE.* p. 59. https://www.mmsp.gov.ma/uploads/documents/RevuePrestationServicesAdministratifs26Juin2019.pdf

Silverstein, P. (2011). *Weighing Morocco's new constitution. Middle East research and information project.* http://www.merip.org/mero/mero070511

Teti, A., Maggiolini, P., Talbot, V., & Abbot, P. (2017). *MENA populations' perceptions of key challenges, international context, and role of the European Union* [Arab Transformations Working paper 9]. University of Aberdeen.

The Commonwealth. (2016). *Key principles of public sector reform: Case studies and frameworks.* Commonwealth Secretariat. http://bibliotheque.pssfp.net/livres/KEY_PRINCIPLES_OF_PUBLIC_SECTOR_REFORMS.pdf

Transparency International. (2018). *Morocco—Corruption Perceptions Index.* https://www.transparency.org/country/MAR

UNDP. (2019). *Inequalities in human development in the 21st century.* Briefing note for countries on the 2019 Human Development report/Morocco. hdr.undp.org

United Nations (UN). (2000). *Professionalism and ethics in the public service: Issues and practices in selected regions.* United Nations, Department of Economics and Social Affairs, Division of Public Economics and Public Administration. ST/ESA/PAD/SER.E/5.

World Bank (2010). *Morocco – Public Administration Reform IV*. https://projects.worldbank.org/en/projects-operations/project-detail/P112612

World Bank (2013). *Morocco: Country Partnership Strategy 2014–2017*. https://www.worldbank.org/en/news/feature/2013/09/13/morocco-consultations-country-partnership-strategy-2014-2017

World Bank. (2019). *The World Bank in Morocco*. https://www.worldbank.org/en/country/morocco/overview

Yom, S. L., & Gausse, F. G. (2012). Resilient royals: How Arab monarchies hang on. *Journal of Democracy*, *23*(4), 74–88.

Zaki, L. (2019). *Decentralization in Morocco: Promising legal reforms with uncertain impact*. Arab Reform Initiative. AAA Bawader.

6
INSTITUTIONAL AND ECONOMIC REFORMS CHALLENGES DURING A DEMOCRATIC TRANSITION

A Case Study from Tunisia

Nizar Jouini and Taoufik Rajhi

Introduction

In most democratic transition countries, governments face many political and economic pressures with contradictory objectives during an unstable cycle of public management. In Tunisia, given the political and economic shocks it has faced, the government is engaged in restructuring the economy through pro-cyclical macroeconomic policies. At the same time, it has to respond to high demands from marginalized groups and resolve socio-distributional problems, the main reason behind the outbreak of the revolution. Hence, a package of reforms has to be put in place in order to maintain the sustainability of the fiscal space, which is highly needed to respond and redress all economic deficiencies that have been accumulating. In this regard, the development of public policies and major reforms is a challenge in itself, which must be stood up and promoted by adopting consensual mechanisms rather than a direct implementation approach based on the state authority and the enforcement of its powers.

The transition, with few successes, combines the institutional dimension as a key foundation of democratic transition, along with the economic dimension as a prerequisite for the sustainability of any democratic system. Although the process of consensus on economic and social choices is slow, it undoubtedly has the advantage to overcome difficulties, thanks to the coordination between the most important stakeholders. The formulation of reforms in this context is not straightforward but is rather based on engineering and deep analysis methods taken from rational and applied modern economic approaches as well as best-practice comparative experiences. It takes into account the reality of the Tunisian economy, its potential, its specific challenges, and the economic stakes of the different partners.

Between 2015 and 2019, the Tunisian government conducted 53 reform projects under six different reform pillars, namely capacity-building and the establishment of constitutional bodies, economic and institutional reforms, finance and banking reforms, public finance reforms, social reforms, and cross-cutting reforms. A significant number, 43, of the projects have been legalized by the parliament, while their progress was significantly affected by institutional and political factors (Figure 6.1).

Furthermore, the capacity to accelerate reforms requires a good understanding of the steps and dynamics of a reform project from its inception till its implementation. We will present in this paper a case study of the reform system adopted by the Tunisian government as well as the processes implemented for its evaluation and follow-up, as designed by the last two elected governments with the help of the IMF program. We limit the scope of this analysis to major reforms, or those which have had a structural and sustained impact on the major economic sectors; which have helped achieve the main objectives of the transition phase; and which were subject to laws voting and legalization under the parliament. To build an efficient reform agenda, the Tunisian government has developed a process of national evaluation and follow-up with the participation of different stakeholders from the legislative and the executive, and civil society. Given the new political context and unsuccessful legislative depolarization, a consensual reform strategy is needed to enhance the efficiency of political institutions and government leadership in order to improve the coordination, sequencing, and follow-up of the reform cycle to effectively support the national evaluation system.

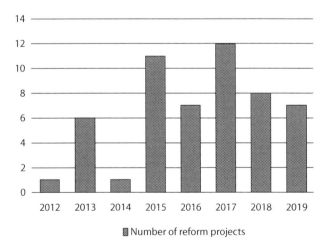

FIGURE 6.1 Number of Yearly Legalized Reforms within the Parliament

Source: The authors

Political and economic context

Since 2011, political support needed to endorse reforms represented a significant barrier to legalizing most of the bills in the parliament. The October 2014 marked the beginning of a consensus process aimed at overcoming a serious deterioration in political life; disagreement between political rivalries could have possibly led to a civil war and resulted in an agonistic debate and a conflict of objectives (Murray & Stigant, 2017). The consensus also aimed to attenuate waves of demonstration hitting the whole country, which had strong economic and social demands.

The overweighed political discussion taking place throughout the transition period has affected the economic public debate and did not help build the momentum needed to prioritize economic reforms. The transition period has marked a drop in growth performance as a result of political, institutional, and social shocks, which led to an increase in fiscal spending and the deterioration of public financial balances. The fiscal deficit averaged 5 percent of the GDP over the past years, and external debt has increased from 57 percentage points of GDP to 85.5 percent of GDP between 2013 and 2019 (IMF article IV, 2020). The growing financial dependence on external funds reflects a situation where public and private consumption absorbed almost 89 percent of the wealth created. This led to a weakening of the gross national saving capacity to fill the investment gap, steadied at 10 percent of GDP in 2017 compared to 24 percent of GDP in Morocco for the same period (World Development Indictors, 2017). Obviously, this unsustainable economic path requires a strategy to rethink the public spending structure more efficiently and to expand substantially production in the strategic sectors with high value added.

Public spending is mainly driven by the high salary bill, the state-owned enterprises (SOEs) deficit, and social security imbalances. The wage bill increased dramatically after the revolution having absorbed 15 percent of the GDP in 2017 (IMF country report, 2017). The average salary in the public sector is almost double that of the private sector. Besides that, SOEs are identified as a significant barrier to the compensation of public financial balances as government subsidies increased by 144 percent (5.3 percent of GDP) in 2017. This affected national debt sustainability as SOE loans, guaranteed by the government, made up 12 percent of GDP, and the cumulative amount of external loans transferred to SOEs comprised $126 million in 2016. Further, the social security system is underfunded and the deficit, including stock of arrears and cash needs, accounts for more than 5 percent of the GDP. A consolidation of financial needs is required as the situation is likely to worsen in the years ahead; the growing life expectancy and weak cash flow of many SOEs may affect contributions to social security funds (IMF country report, 2017).

The compensation of the public deficit accumulated after 2011 increased the country's dependence on external funds and the use of unconventional tools for resource mobilization. As a result, Tunisia has consumed most of the allowed quotas allocated by international financial institutions (IFIs) and the possibility of obtaining loans with the reasonable cost is now more limited than ever. Apart from that, the deterioration of the country's ratings by international rating agencies has limited the possibility of fund-raising in international markets without hindering debt sustainability. This debt crisis was behind a political movement speaking up against any increase of external debt at the expense of future generations, which makes it difficult for the government to close the yearly budget gap.

Clearly, economic prosperity in Tunisia can only be attained through economic reforms and political stability. The implementation of prerequisites needed for productivity such as governance, infrastructure, global value chains, and others can structurally transform the economy. In this regard, economic reforms seem to be a complicated mission but a key step to overcoming the rough transition in Tunisia.

Literature review

There is an ongoing debate among economists around the best strategy to conduct reform in terms of macroeconomic stabilization policies (see Sturzenegger & Tommasi, 1998, p. 3); reform speed (Åslund et al., 1996; Murrell, 1993; Roland, 1994, 1994a); the sequence and the timing of reforms (Alesina et al., 2006, for an empirical literature review; Gray & Hendley, 1997; Kolodko, 1999; Murrell, 1996; Poznanski, 1996; Sachs, 1993; Sachs & Pistor, 1997); and political power conflicts (Acemoglu, 2003).

For the purpose of this chapter, we focus on economic reform approaches, highlighting governance and institutional challenges. Specifically, the political economy approach is the most adapted to the context of building a political consensus during a reform transitional period like in Tunisia. This methodology stands out for its flexibility and positive approach compared to the first best normative approach emanating from economic modeling and technical frameworks. According to this framework, reform success depends on the ability of stakeholders to engage and support the reform path by highlighting the most feasible solutions rather than the first best solutions (Fritz et al., 2017). Several contributions have highlighted the necessity to consider political economy factors and engage with insights from the political economy research field in particular during structural changes such as fragile and conflict situations, revolutions, or even political developments (Acemoglu & Robinson, 2012; Rodrik, 1995).

According to the literature, two important variables should be considered when analyzing the political economy of reform by new democratic governments. The first is whether the economy will be hit or not by the economic crisis, since when that happens, governments would lose the support of groups sympathetic to the previous authoritarian regime on the one hand and meet high pressing demands from revolutionary groups on the other. The second variable is related to the polarization and fragmentation of political parties, which increases political disputes and encourages executives to bypass legislative institutions (Haggard & Kaufman, 2018).

The World Development Report (2017) highlighted the importance of the distribution of power in the policy arena and how it affects policy reform and changes. The higher inclusion of actors who have a high level of legitimacy and cooperation increases participation (contestability) and gives actors more incentive to comply with agreements. However, conflict of interests between organized socio-political groups explains why some groups reject reforms and benefit from the status quo (Khemani, 2017). Reforms are likely to occur when the cost of political bargaining between elite rival groups and delaying reforms exceeds the cost of implementing reforms specifically during an economic crisis or when a government acquires sufficient political strength to overcome the opposition (Alesina et al., 2006), or even when the elite accept to renounce some benefits in exchange for more public goods (Lizzeri & Persico, 2004; North et al., 2007). Conversely, when the elite reject changes and refuse any reduction of their benefits, a revolution is likely to be the only way for them to renounce their bargaining power and to agree to a redistribution of power (Acemoglu & Robinson, 2000).

New public management reform literature has contributed to this debate by arguing that reforms have been successfully implemented in majoritarian democracies than in consensus democracies. However, little attention is paid in the literature to the role of policy entrepreneurs and political leaders in reform implementation (Christensen & Lægreid, 2001). This area of the literature shows that, compared to majoritarian institutions, consensus institutions are more likely to become a political asset in the hands of those who implement policy because the consensual management style that emerges from these institutions may produce successful reforms (Bovens et al., 2001; Nagel, 1998; Yesilkagit & De Vries, 2004).

Various empirical evidence have confirmed that a broad-coalition government and weak executives are negatively associated with reform progress (Alesina & Perotti, 1995a, 1995b; Grilli et al., 1991; Roubini & Sachs, 1989), while other further evidence has alternatively shown that a broader coalition positively correlates with progress reform (EBRD, 1999; Hellman, 1998). The reason behind this is that negative results happen when a broader coalition tends to paralyze policy-making because of "wars of attrition" (Alesina and Drazen, 1991), while positive results happen when there is value to consensus building created by broader coalitions and more closely checked executives.

The efficiency in implementing reforms depends primarily on the extent to which reforms were subject to consensus and institutional capacities were available to execute different programs. In fact, many obstacles were identified whether at the technical, institutional, or political levels which decelerated the reform process, from their design to their implementation, and negatively impacted the stabilization of the democratic transition as a whole. The following analyzes the obstacles and discusses reform problems and presents solutions to overcome them.

Inducing the reform project cycle

Before discussing reform implementation, it is important to understand the reform project cycle (Figure 6.2) itself in order to identify obstacles in each stage starting from reform design to its implementation. In Tunisia, the reforms cycle includes three phases: a ministerial phase involving government, a second legislative phase through the assembly, and a third phase when the proposal returns to the government again. Only a few of these reforms escape the second legislative phase and do not require to be enacted by law; instead, they are processed only through governmental decrees or application orders. An example is the reform of the "public transaction system." Given its importance, an evaluation was conducted in partnership with the World Bank and the African Development Bank according to the OCDE-DAC methodology

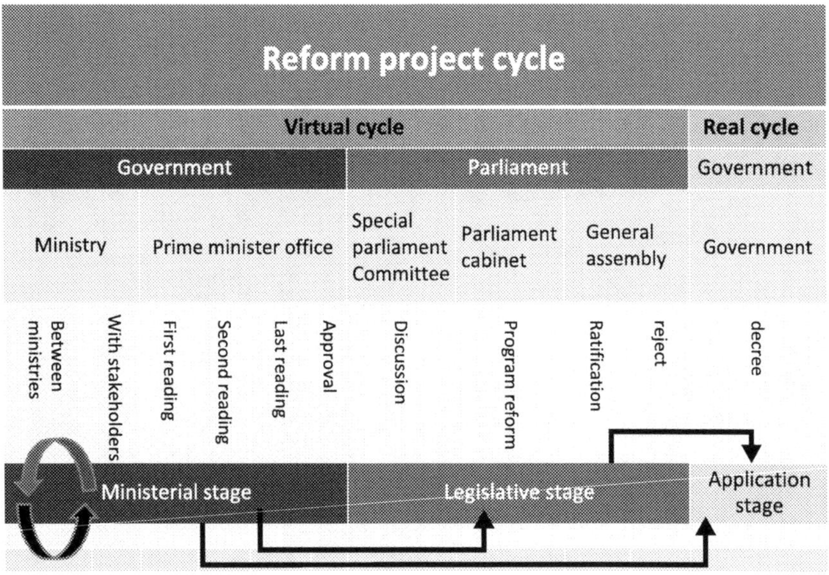

Reform project cycle

Virtual cycle						Real cycle
Government			Parliament			Government
Ministry	Prime minister office	Special parliament Committee	Parliament cabinet	General assembly		Government
Between ministries / With stakeholders / First reading / Second reading / Last reading / Approval		Discussion	Program reform	Ratification	reject	decree
Ministerial stage			Legislative stage			Application stage

FIGURE 6.2 Reform Project Cycle

Source: The authors

in 2012; then, a reform plan was launched in 2013 by a national committee following consultation with various actors from the field, including civil society. A year later, the application order to regulate the public transactions was issued in March 2014. More broadly, the different stages leading to the completion of the reform, including the existing barriers rooted in each phase, are summarized in Figure 6.2.

The first phase, defined as the ministerial phase, is when the reform project is launched, starting with a preliminary draft at the level of the supervising ministry and then submitted to the ministers' council for approval. The draft proposal is usually submitted first to a smaller Ministers' Council with limited number of ministers involved, then to the general minister's council. If approved, the draft is sent to the assembly for voting. In fact, the speed with which the project draft is ultimately approved is essentially related to its quality and the value of its contribution, but also to the extent to which social parties, political actors in the parliament, and officials are involved. However, projects that have not been well-prepared at the level of the supervising ministry are presented more than once to the Council of Ministers, which reflects negatively on the pace of the reform project's progress in its early stages.

The second phase starts with an examination of the reform project by a special committee at the level of the assembly. Similarly, at this stage, the quality of the reform project determines how quickly a plenary session is scheduled for ratification. Finally, the third phase starts when the adopted law returns to the government from the parliament and is issued an application order. Unless the reform passes through these three sessions, it remains a hypothetical reform and has no effect on the ground. It turns out that accelerating the reform decree means shortening the duration of the various stages, moving it quickly from a theoretical public policy formulation to its real execution. However, in practice, this process contains a number of obstacles at different levels, which include the following:

Weak technical capabilities of the ministry concerned

The lack of institutional capacity and technical capabilities to design an appropriate and comprehensive reform project is a significant barrier that slows down the first stage of a reform project. Design project weaknesses include unclear zones, cavities, and unanswered questions such as the impact on main stakeholders, underestimated financial implications, and the absence of cost-benefit analysis. In these cases, the draft will be presented several times to the Council of Ministers with all the correspondence and paperwork required and may result in a disagreement between the different ministries involved or the dissociation of other important actors. In this context, institutional capacity-building is one of the challenging conditions that needs to be developed during the transition. The following include factors affecting institutional capability components that are related to the state's abilities:

1   the size of the institution;
2   the quality of the institution;
3   the logistical capacities of the institution; and
4   the leadership in conducting the reform process.

Lack of consensus at the level of the assembly

The lack of political consensus could be the reason most of the cases are rejected by the committee in charge at the assembly, despite its validation by the government. This phase represents the most important step because any failure will lead the reform bill to undergo another round of ministerial council validation. To some extent, this reflects obstacles related to the lack of communication within the government, but more importantly, to the weak endorsement of the governmental coalition's deputies of the proposed reform. It turns out that communication and consultation with political partners are crucial to overcoming this roadblock in light of the consensus approach preferred in the management of the democratic transition in Tunisia.

The agenda inside the assembly does not fit with the government's agenda

During the transition period in Tunisia, political legislative agenda dominated the activity of the parliament, which made it difficult for the economic reform agenda to receive enough attention despite the urgency of economic challenges. Given political turbulences, the government failed to fit its economic program into the assembly's busy and dictated political agenda. It significantly affected the implementation of reforms that have been initiated since 2012. Meanwhile, some of these reforms are still pending on the council's agenda until today. The solution to this lack of coordination between the legislative and executive branches of the government was to translate the outcomes of the Carthage agreement[1] into a strategy that united executive and legislature branches of the coalition around a unique pragmatic and practical action plan.

Procedural challenge and delay of the executive orders issuance

In most of the cases, bills are often submitted to the assembly without application orders, before ministries get the approval of the legislative to start working on the application orders. This step is time-consuming and causes a delay in the execution of the reform, in particular when the reform requires a very high number of application orders. To ease this procedural difficulty, it is proposed that the draft preparation of application orders be initiated right away after the approval of the Council of Ministers, without waiting for the legislative ratification. Besides that, the number of accompanying application orders should be limited and the capacity of administrative legislation units within the ministries should be increased.

Governmental leadership in supporting reforms

The implementation of the reforms requires the government's mobilization to support the reform project and the participation of various actors, including political coalition actors. This requires, first, a strong political leadership and a good understanding of the reform objectives, second, a social dialogue discussion with different partners, and third, the development of an evaluation system and follow-up process to adjust any discrepancies that could emerge from implementing the reform.

First, with regard to governmental leadership, this requires a high level of coordination between the different ministries and the prime minister's office since reforms are most of the time unsynchronized (some reforms just being started and others have been initiated for years), and can overlapping and cover many sectors. In particular, coordination is highly required when the subject of reform focuses on social protection plans, including the reform of social security funds, resources mobilization to finance the economy, the reforms related to the budget and human resources, and the reform of the financial sector. For example, the advanced tax reform, which began with a discussion in 2008, has culminated in 2013 with a distinction made between governance issues on the one hand and structural economic reform on the other hand, and then adopted in 2015, after a marathon of coordination efforts between different ministries and relevant authorities.

Second, stimulating social dialogue through intensive consultations with relevant actors is important. The adoption of a step-by-step approach has the advantage of instilling trust between parties and helps incorporate amendments throughout the dialogue and reduce the uncertainty of risk emanating from the participatory process. The success of social dialogue requires the development of tools and processes of evaluation in order to convince different partners of the sustainability of the reforms. This cannot be done without supporting or creating permanent institutions responsible for designing and implementing evaluation methods, and sharing information related to reform sustainability.

Third, although the participatory approach and governmental leadership remain the real driving forces for the success of the reforms, it is expected that the government will be more exposed to criticism, reservations, and demands for compensation. Compensation appears to be necessary in reducing concerns and minimizing the immediate side effects of reform but should not affect the spirit and the nature of the reforms themselves. For this reason, the existence of a fiscal space increases the chances to adopt reforms by allocating compensation for the benefit of the losers following the adoption of the reforms.

Coordinating reforms

A large number of proposed reforms require consultation and coordination between the various stakeholders in the Tunisian economy, specifically among the prime minister's office, the different ministries, market stakeholders, social partners, and donors.

To a large extent, the follow-up unit for reforms created in the prime minister's office helps in developing comprehensive reform as well as in the follow-up processes. To have a successful reform mandate, it is recommended to develop a detailed outline—with measurable "key indicators" that can be assessed and reviewed with the advantage of facilitating reform prioritization. Besides that, it is essential to create a high task force committee to lead reforms and extend the mandate of the follow-up unit to cover coordination duties as a key step to speed up the reform process. Some reforms such as the financial sector reform require multi-sectoral coordination, given its strategic importance and the multiplicity of initiatives and actors involved. Sectors that should be prioritized for coordination include the most important sectors in terms of their size, their contribution to the state resources, and their effects on employment and job creation such as tourism and real estate. Others to be considered include strategic public companies active in the sector like the phosphate Gafsa company, the Tunisian Chemical company, and others.

Sequencing reform priorities

The implementation of the reforms raises questions related to the methodologies adopted to prioritize them, particularly their sequencing and evaluation. Whatever strategy the government adopts, it is important to regularly review the progress of reform implementation based on a clear framework and objective indicators. In this context, there are a number of questions that need to be answered such as what assessment methods should be developed and what indicators can be used to assess the effectiveness of reform governance (progress and improvement achieved, sources of disruption, etc.). Furthermore, what budget should be allocated for future periods and what kind of resources should be mobilized to finance the different steps whether at the internal or the external levels.

Sequencing priorities for reforms are essential for efficiency since the number of reforms are huge and varied, while resources are limited in the context of transition. Moreover, the intersection between reforms requires the ordering of steps in an integrated framework to avoid overlapping actions and a waste of resources needed for similar reforms. For example, redrafting the investment law requires prior reflection and an accompanying commitment to tax reform. Therefore, if reform of the investment law is a priority, then tax reform is also a priority, given the importance of financial incentives for investment. Moreover, reforms of an institutional, regulatory, and orderly nature remain a priority, given their nature. The role of institutions (and the regulatory environment) is fundamental to adopting, implementing, and translating sound policies into positive results on the ground. In the absence of such reforms, even sound policies do not have a shot in achieving the desired goals in the short-, medium-, or long-term perspectives.

Finally, the chronological sequencing of reforms is important; specifically, reforms should be prioritized according to the time schedule of their expected outcomes. Notably, in a context of transition where short-term impact is privileged over medium- and long-term impacts, it is important to consider the social cost-benefit dynamics of any reform project, including the capacity to achieve the reform objectives at the micro level as well as broader objectives at the macro level. Hence, the chronological consistency of the reforms and optimality of its sequencing are prerequisites to achieving reform credibility with high efficiency.

The example of social security reform

One example of fundamental reform priority in Tunisia turned to be the social security reform, given its impact on fiscal sustainability. The social fund arrears and cash needs accounted for more than 5 percent of the GDP in 2017. The quality of social fund equities has significantly deteriorated, especially the National Pension and Social Security Fund (Caisse Nationale de Retraite et de Prévoyance Sociale, CNRPS). At the beginning of 2018, this situation provided the government with a good reason to prioritize and discuss with all stakeholders the various components of the social security reform. The government consulted with its main partners, the workers union (UGTT) and the employers union (UTICA), to find adequate solutions by developing a review process under a comprehensive framework. The objective was to build a consensus around proposals and scenarios that ensure the balance of the pension system in the short, medium, and long terms, without breaking the terms of the social contract and while respecting equity matters within and between generations. The review committee also benefited from a series of meetings held by the Social Protection Subcommittee in 2016 and 2017, which studied possible options for pension reform and has concluded the following:

1. adopting an internal policy to regulate the work of the review committee;
2. agreeing on the diagnostics and documentation of the reasons behind the deterioration of the financial imbalances of public and private pensions funds;
3. studying and developing a number of scenarios and policy choices to reform the pension systems in the public and private sectors and assess their expected financial consequences;
4. agreeing to create a solidarity social contribution aiming to diversify the social security sources of funding;
5. agreeing to create a higher council of social protection funding;
6. working on the draft charter to reform public and private pension systems;
7. agreeing to develop a new law on public and private pension systems.

The national review and evaluation systems

The evaluation of public policies and their systematic review constitute the pillars of modern public affairs management and provide decision-makers with the effective tools to analyze the problems and formulate the most effective solutions. The new Tunisian constitution reinforced this principle through Chapter 15 (Tunisia Constitution, 2014), which states: "Public administration remains at the service of the citizen and the public interest, it regulates and operates by the principles of neutrality, equality, and continuity of the public facility, and under the rules of transparency, integrity, efficiency, and accountability."

The national review and evaluation system reinforces the evidence-based approach of public management affairs, strengthens accountability, oversight of public projects, and informs decision-makers on the efficiency of policies and resource allocation. It should be emphasized that there is no single definition of the peer-review-based evaluation system, but in general, it can be defined as "a systematic approach that goes beyond the simple sharing of information about performance ... to provide and build a solid argument (by presenting information and data) that is credible and useful (at the level of those who request the information) and determine the relevance and fulfillment of objectives, developmental efficiency, effectiveness, impact and sustainability of a policy or project" (Organization for Economic Cooperation and Development [OECD], 2009).[2]

The national evaluation system

According to DAC OECD evaluation criteria, evaluation is an assessment "to determine the relevance and fulfillment of objectives, developmental efficiency, effectiveness, impact and sustainability" of efforts supported by aid agencies (OECD, 1992, p. 132).[3]

Institutional and economic reforms challenges 117

In Tunisia, a high committee is in charge of the monitoring and evaluation of public policies. Attached to the Cabinet of the Prime Minister, it was created in August 2015 and has developed the following process (see Fig. 6.3):

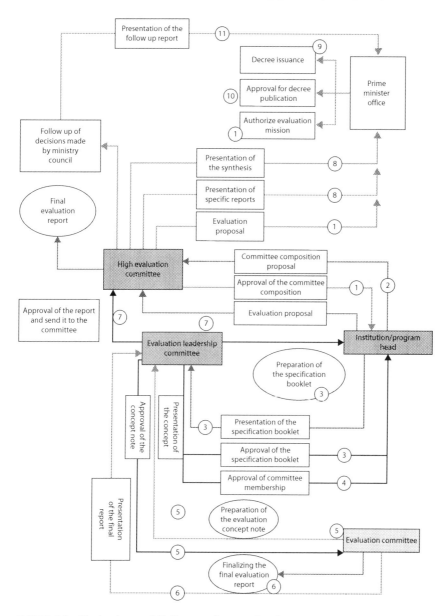

FIGURE 6.3 Evaluation and Follow-up System Graph

Source: The authors

The process is divided into two main phases:

The evaluation phase

This phase is coordinated between the high evaluation committee and the supervisory public entity in charge of the evaluation of the policy subject. The topic of the evaluation process is selected in coordination with the supervisory structure or as per the priorities of the government's agenda, while the task mission is issued by the prime minister. This phase is characterized by the adoption of a participatory approach through the creation of an intermediary-led committee, including various actors in the field and representatives of civil society to monitor the evaluation process. The role of the high evaluation committee is limited to accompanying the supervisory public entity in the evaluation process, from the drafting of terms of reference to the selection of experts. It ensures compliance with international standards and good governance as stipulated by the constitution. Apart from that, the commission monitors and ensures the upholding of the participatory approach and the publication of the evaluation report, including applicable recommendations. This monitoring process holds the objective of conducting sound policies by improving public projects' life cycles and facilitating the conceptualization of reforms based on scientific evidence and evaluation.

On October 20, 2017, the government issued permissions to the high committee to conduct its first mission on evaluating youth social inclusion policies. The evaluation process will result in formulating a national strategy along with an action plan to promote youth inclusion.

Follow-up of decisions emanating from the evaluation process

This phase is considered as the most effective step. It aims to enhance the effectiveness and the feasibility of the entire evaluation process. It also shows the extent to which evaluation is rather a process for making real change and adapting policies to overcome deficiencies and fit to reality on the ground, based on comparative experiences. It is a continuous and systematic process of collecting information made in accordance with a clear framework and well-defined indicators that provide the policy-maker with data on progress made, objectives achieved, and funds allocated.

In addition to collecting information at the macro level, the follow-up strategy also focuses on collecting information at the micro level through a well-developed e-information management system established since 1990. This system, called "INJAZ," is now expending to cover project monitoring and evaluation and helps in disaggregating macro policy at the macro level into programs and projects for each locality by incorporating the geographical information system (GIS).

In addition, a new public financial management by objective (performance-based budgeting) has been established by voting on a new law on February 13,

2019. This new law aims to include more public financial accountability and transparency and facilitate the follow-up of public financial management by moving toward a fully operation-based performance system of budgeting, improving multi-year budgeting, and streamlining public finance control at the local level.

The coordination process

Coordination is key to accelerating democratic transition and determining the pace of structural reforms. It consists of promoting communication between the different levels of decision-making at its normal vertical hierarchical path (vertically), along with horizontal integration of the different decision-making centers (horizontally) in order to achieve the same goals set by government agenda.

In addition to the old administrative mechanisms of coordination (cabinet of the prime minister, ministerial working sessions, etc.), a new mechanism has been created to help coordinate external financial development assistance to fund major reforms through international cooperation. This mechanism is considered a communication tool between the Tunisian state and international financial partners and provides a data dashboard that aims to facilitate the process of resource mobilization. Therefore, all these above-mentioned components constitute an integrated system aiming to improve government action at various levels, from the development of the strategy, its conceptualization, implementation, and follow-up up until the evaluation of policies, programs, and projects. Worth noting at this stage are the key steps used to facilitate the implementation of the follow-up and evaluation system:

Vision

The reform vision has been translated through an initiative launched by the prime minister in 2015 into a national follow-up and evaluation system. The objectives and expectations are well-defined under this initiative as well as the creation of a ministerial position in charge of reforms in 2017.

Diagnosing the system

In order to institutionalize the channels by which information is provided and used for decision-making in order to enhance the effectiveness of the information system in the long run, the last diagnostic process was conducted in 2016. It identified many deficiencies and a plan has been developed to strengthen the capabilities of multiple structures by training about 30 teams at the central and regional administrations levels. In addition, a National Capacity Development Program was developed and organized during the period from September 2016 to April 2017 to enhance public servants' capacities. Similarly, a training course in evaluation has been offered by INA Canada (National School of Public Administration in Canada) where ten judges from the Accounting Department, ten public controllers, and another ten employees from administrative structures were trained. Finally, many international forums have been organized to increase awareness about public policy evaluation.

Developing an action plan

Given the importance of building a reliable system that reflects Tunisian specificities, the authorities have adopted a participatory approach, using the input of different actors, including comparative experiences from countries in the region. The plan included the strengthening of the information system through a systematic and periodical review, the development of a policy against unsafe information use as well as the institutionalization of a permanent structure in charge of implementing the action plan. This plan was intended to be enforced within the framework of the 2016–2020 National Development Plan and in upcoming development plans.

Conclusion

Conducting reforms in a period of transition calls for an inevitable multidimensional approach in order to meet challenges and develop economic, political, and institutional immunity. This is important in a period characterized by uncertainty and conflicting objectives between different stakeholders. Building on the Tunisian "exceptional" political consensus as crowned by the "Carthage plan" and the Nobel Prize, the reform strategy followed the same path by opening a dialogue with different parties and reinforcing a transparent and participatory process. In particular, the following actions were key to building the reform strategy:

1 Building institutional capacities, including enhancing management system efficiency and sectoral deployment, in accordance with reform axes developed within the reform strategy.
2 Deepening the consensus among the different actors involved in the reform process with respect to the new constitution principles and based on a participatory approach, aimed to overcome fundamental political conflicts and to achieve democratic transition objectives.
3 Like experiences of other countries, the reforms process in Tunisia encountered heavy risks related to economic fragility and the difficulty of establishing coordination between all actors. Certainly, the importance of promoting transparency in the official discourse and introducing reforms to citizens gradually is fundamental, given that citizens have become more vigilant to public affairs participation and government activity monitoring.

Notes

1 For Tunisia, the political agreement in 2015 is formulated by the Carthage document and the government of national unity.
2 Evaluation policy and guidelines for evaluations (OECD, 2009).
3 OCDE (DAC).

References

Acemoglu, D. (2003). Why not a political Coase theorem? Social conflict, commitment, and politics. *Journal of Comparative Economics, 31*(4), 620–652.
Acemoglu, D., & Robinson, J. A. (2000). Democratization or repression? *European Economic Review, 44*(4–6), 683–693.
Acemoglu, D., & Robinson, J. A. (2012). *Why nations fail: The origins of power, prosperity, and poverty.* Crown Publishing.
Alesina, A., Ardagna, S., & Trebbi, F. (2006). Who adjusts and when? The political economy of reforms. *IMF Staff Papers, 53*(1), 1–29.
Alesina, A., & Drazen, A. (1991). Why are stabilizations delayed? *American Economic Review, 81*(11), 70–88.
Alesina, A., & Perotti, R. (1995a). Fiscal expansions and adjustments in OECD countries. *Economic Policy, 10*(21), 205–248.
Alesina, A., & Perotti, R. (1995b). The political economy of budget deficits. *IMF Staff Papers, 42*(1), 1–31.
Åslund, A., Boone, P., Johnson, S., Fischer, S., & Ickes, B. W. (1996). How to stabilize: Lessons from post-communist countries. *Brookings Papers on Economic Activity, 1/1996*, 217–313.
Bovens, M., 'T Hart, P., & Peters, B. G. (Eds.). (2001). *Success and failure in public governance: A comparative analysis.* Edward Elgar.
Christensen, T., & Lægreid, P. (2001). A transformative perspective on administrative reforms. In T. Christensen & P. Lægreid (Eds.), New public management: The transformation of ideas and practice (pp. 13–39). Ashgate.
EBRD (European Bank for Reconstruction and Development). (1999). *Transition report 1999: Ten years of transition.* EBRD.
Fritz, V., Verhoeven, M., & Avenia, A. (2017). *Political economy of public financial management reforms: Experiences and implications for dialogue and operational engagement.* The World Bank.
Gray, C., & Hendley, K. (1997). *The rule of law and economic reform in Russia.* Westview Press.
Grilli, V., Masciandaro, D., & Tabellini, G. (1991). Political and monetary institutions and public financial policies in the industrial countries. *Economic Policy, 6*(13), 341–392.
Haggard, S., & Kaufman, R. R. (2018). *The political economy of democratic transitions.* Princeton University Press.
Hellman, J. S. (1998). Winners take all: The politics of partial reform in post-communist transitions. *World Politics, 50*(2), 203–234.
Khemani, S. (2017). *Political economy of reform* [Policy Research Working Paper No. 8224]. The World Bank.
Kolodko, G. W. (1999). *Ten years of post-socialist transition: Lessons for policy reform.* The World Bank.

Lizzeri, A., & Persico, N. (2004). Why did the elites extend the suffrage? Democracy and the scope of government, with an application to Britain's "Age of Reform". *The Quarterly Journal of Economics*, *119*(2), 707–765.

López-Calva, L.-F. et al. (2017). World development report 2017: Governance and the law. *No. 112303*. The World Bank.

Murray, E., & Stigant, S. (Eds.). (2017). *National dialogues in peacebuilding and transitions: Creativity and adaptive thinking*. United States Institute of Peace.

Murrell, P. (1993). What is shock therapy? What did it do in Poland and Russia? *Post-Soviet Affairs*, *9*(2), 111–140.

Murrell, P. (1996). How far has the transition progressed? *Journal of Economic Perspectives*, *10*(2), 25–44.

Nagel, J. H. (1998). Social choice in a pluralitarian democracy: The politics of market liberalization in New Zealand. *British Journal of Political Science*, *28*(2), 223–267.

North, D. C., Wallis, J. J., Webb, S. B., & Weingast, B. R. (2007). *Limited access orders in the developing world: A new approach to the problems of development*. The World Bank.

Organization for Economic Cooperation and Development. (1992). Development assistance manual: DAC principles for effective aid. Organization for Economic.

Organization for Economic Cooperation and Development. (2009). Evaluation policy and guidelines for evaluations. *Bing*. Retrieved March 4, 2023, from https://www.bing.com/search?q=OECD+2009+evaluation+policy+and+guidelines+for+evaluations&cvid=a5497498e386455cb8a2ddef7a5d2845&aqs=edge..69i57j69i60j69i11004.422j0j1&pglt=41&FORM=ANNAB1&DAF0=1&PC=U531

Poznanski, K. Z. (1996). *Poland's protracted transition: Institutional change and economic growth, 1970–1994* (Vol. 98). Cambridge University Press.

Rodrik, D. (1995). The dynamics of political support for reform in economies in transition. *Journal of the Japanese and International Economies*, *9*(4), 403–425.

Roland, G. (1994). On the speed and sequencing of privatisation and restructuring. *The Economic Journal*, *104*(426), 1158–1168.

Roland, G. (1994a). The role of political constraints in transition strategies. *Economics of Transition*, *2*(1), 27–41.

Roubini, N., & Sachs, J. (1989). Political and democracies. *European Economic Review*, *33*(5), 903–933.

Sachs, I. (1993). *L'écodéveloppement, stratégies de transition vers le XXIème siècle*. Syros.

Sachs, J., & Pistor, K. (Eds.). (1997). *The rule of law and economic reform in Russia*. Routledge/Taylor and Francis.

Sturzenegger, F., & Tommasi, M. (1998). *The political economy of reform*. The MIT Press.

Tunisia Constitution. (2014). Retrieved March 4, 2023, from https://www.constituteproject.org/countries/Africa/Tunisia?lang=en

Yesilkagit, K., & De Vries, J. (2004). Reform styles of political and administrative elites in majoritarian and consensus democracies: Public management reforms in New Zealand and the Netherlands. *Public Administration*, *82*(4), 951–974.

7
THE EROSION OF PUBLIC ADMINISTRATION IN SUDAN

Ibrahim Elnur

Introduction

The period from 1989 to 2019 has been marked as a radical departure from all forms of past state interventions, including the Abboud (1958–1964) and Nimery (1996–1986) regimes as well as the short-lived second post-independence parliamentary system (1986–1989), in the operation of the statecraft by installing a "one-party" rule in Sudan. Since its independence in 1956, Sudan is largely managed/controlled by the military and civil elites, who are the core of the upper echelon of society. During both colonial and post-colonial periods and throughout different regimes, democratic and authoritarian alike, the country was essentially run by Northern Sudan's educated elites. After that, the model established by the Islamists closely resembled the Russian and Eastern European experiences where the state became a monopoly of the ruling party. The privatization of state functions mimicked this model, which depended on oligarchies and deepened graft and corruption. Consequently, the challenges of returning to old state management in Sudan present an enormous task, if at all feasible, without further power fragmentation, as in the case of Southern Sudan. While there are some commonalities between post-independence regimes, the 1989–2019 marked an alternative conceptual framework, not only in terms of state control of the economy but also in terms of emergence of a new ideologically led one-party system that controlled the whole economy and the state apparatus by its members and followers at all levels. Despite the post-Islamist efforts to eliminate state-led corruption, this chapter emphasizes that despite the rigorous steps taken by the transitional government to eliminate state-led corruption, the "deep state" seems to persist.

Some historical notes on the unmaking of Sudan

This section highlights on the processes that led to the unmaking of Sudan (Elnur, 2008). The focus is on two periods of active state intervention in the economy and society which radically transformed the processes of capital accumulation. This is not to deny that a certain continuity exists in the post-colonial policies of the Sudanese state from colonial times, notably in preserving the lopsided development model. But rather, it is to emphasize that the two authoritarian regimes of Nimeiri (1969–1985) and the National Islamic Front (NIF)-dominated regime (1989–2019) stand out distinctively because of their roles in crisis making. Both regimes, beyond the sheer relative time length (totaling 32 years, 1989–2019), brought about irreversible structural transformations that undermined the relatively "stable" and "manageable," albeit stagnant, post-colonial structures of capital accumulation and social reproduction. These structures exhibited predictable and manageable flows of population, relatively sustainable mechanisms of surplus extraction, and a great deal of stability in the efficiency of state capacity, despite regular civilian–military shifts in state control.

Hence, if the Nimeiry period of 1969–1985 was associated with crisis making, the Islamist-dominated regime of 1989–2019 triggered processes that brought the crisis to its ultimate demise. The main emphasis is on the role of the state and its relative autonomy because of its direct bearing on the central theme of this discussion. This chapter asserts that the accumulation crisis, which became apparent in the late 1970s, was fundamentally different from that of the early post-independence period of the 1960s, with respect to its breadth, severity, and the role of various actors in the process of capitalist accumulation (whether state, foreign, or indigenous).

A comprehensive review of the 1960s accumulation crisis is beyond the scope of this chapter; it is important, however, to point out that the accumulation crisis in agriculture and the early exhaustion of the "easy" phase of import substitution industrialization brought a contradictory dimension to the relationship between indigenous capital and foreign capital. On the one hand, foreign trade and finance, a domain of foreign capital, were obvious targets for indigenous capital control. On the other hand, because of its relative weakness, foreign capital was indispensable to the manufacturing sectors.

This contradictory relation explains, to a great extent, the hesitant policies of the post-colonial state in indigenizing finance and foreign trade activities. More importantly, it gives coherence and logic to post-1969 policy changes. The period from 1960 onward is especially different from the preceding post-independence years. It particularly is marked by the intensification of the political struggle over the future path of development in the country. Subsequently, a disjunction in the political and socio-economic spheres occurred, and external factors played a far more important role in the shaping of national policies and strategies. We may broadly divide the 1969–1983 period into three distinct phases as follows:

1 The 1969–1971 period
   This brief period stands out as a very distinct phase because a new coalition made up of social forces came to play a decisive role in the economy and society. The polarization and intensification of the struggle within the new coalition over the future path of development were very pronounced. In essence, this was a replication to a great extent of the Nasserite-model with almost identical build-up of state-repressive apparatus. This struggle came to a dramatic conclusion following the defeat of the July 1971 coup led by the left-wing (mostly members of the communist party) members of the Free Officers Organization, which had initiated the May 1969 coup d'état.
2 The 1972–1976 period
   The period after 1972 witnessed a sharp departure from the declared "socialist"-oriented policies of the preceding period. This was a period of transition. On the one hand, it coincided with the process of political hegemony initiated by the military–civilian bureaucratic bourgeoisie (basically the military but in alliance with the civilian elites), whose goals were to reorient the regime's policies toward the adoption of its new socio-economic program, the Interim Action Program, promulgated in 1972. On the other hand, this process, which essentially built a "conducive" atmosphere with politics involving denationalization and de-confiscation, suppression of trade unions, and the introduction of new investment acts, was in preparation for the next period, the "open-door policy."
3 The 1976–1983 period
   The post-1976 period was characterized by the large role played by foreign capital within the broader framework of a tripartite coalition. Foreign capital was by and large based on the Organization of the Petroleum Exporting Countries (OPEC) surplus based on economies which played a leading role as providers of aid and investment. In examining the Sudanese version of the Egyptian "infitah" policy, one must take into account the complex interaction of both internal and external forces which contributed to the policy in the first place: the impact of the 1973 oil price rise and the need for the recycling of OPEC surplus both regionally and internationally. Conceptual frameworks put forth at the time such as the "Afro-Arab Cooperation," "Pan-Islamic Solidarity," and "Pan-Arab Strategy" must also be considered since the latter is related directly related to the food strategy of major Arab oil exporters, in which Sudan figures as the most important partner in what was largely known as "The Breadbasket Strategy." From 1978, however, a new phase can be discerned within the open-door policy. The direct and

indirect reshaping of strategic policy was largely a result of pressures from multi-national donors and investors primarily through the IMF and the International Bank for Reconstruction and Development (IBRD).

This chapter addresses only briefly the period of 1983–1989 as a period of crisis management through its three political phases: the last year of Nimeiry's authoritarian regime, the transition to democracy of 1985–1986, and the third parliamentary democracy of 1986–1989. The shrinking state—exacerbated by declining extractable surplus, dwindling external support, and external pressures from IMF and other donors—merely pursued a survival strategy that neither halted the crisis nor dramatically reshaped it. Similarly, the post-2000 period witnessed a shift away from commodity production to more of a rentier economy. Extractivism became the dominant mode of economic activity, with oil production in South Sudan being carried alongside nationwide gold-mining operations. The latter functioned as a quasi-alternative for oil, albeit far less significant in terms of financial returns to the state. More recent updated work on the "Rentier State" is very useful in understanding its multiple forms and models of application (Yamada & Hertog, 2020).

The 2007 privatization program: Dismantling state control over the economy

State policies of privatizing the public sector started as early as 1989. This includes the "Law for the Release of State Control over the Public Sector" of 1990 followed by the "Law for the Privatization of the Public Sector" of 1992, and was finally concluded in October 1997 with the establishment of "The Technical Committee for the Release of Public Sector Entities" (TCRPSE). The 1997 TCRPSE document openly stated that:

> Based on most of the studies that took place, there was an agreement to sell public textile factories; Sudanese Marine Company; Sudan Airways and most of the banking system; and while Sudan Railways has maintained all productive units belonging to it should be sold or held in partnership with the private sector.

In 2007, the regime after it created dominant and leading strata of business community shifted to full integration in the global economy. In chapter one of the 1997 TCRPSE which presents the concept of privatization (pp. 13–18), the document concludes in no uncertain terms that all previous forms of state-led development were no longer valid and that full integration into the world economy was the only reasonable option.

Ironically, the first (1990–1996) and second waves (1997–2000) of denationalization were accompanied simultaneously by an undercurrent of clientelism and a thinly veiled transfer of ownership from the federal level to the state through what is known as the "al-Aylula" policies. Widely referred to as the period of "*Tamkeen*," these sub-sets of policies resulted in consolidation of economic power in the vein of the aforementioned Interim Action Program of 1972. At the same time, it eroded state control over vital functions within the Sudanese economy as the neoliberal policies of liberalization, concurrent with the development of the oil sectors, soon followed the second wave.

The first wave followed the announcement of Three-Year National Salvation Economic Program (NSEP) whereby the program called for fundamental reform of the parastatal sector through liquidation, privatization or turning public enterprises into joint ventures with domestic and private sector participation (Bechtold, 1990). After the evaluation of state-owned enterprises (SOEs), the implementing bodies responsible identified 88 enterprises as potential targets for privatization. However, only 64 enterprises were privatized between 1992 and 1997 (Elbeely, 2015).

Meanwhile, the government imposed rapid reform in the education and trade union sectors to weaken opposition groups and extend its reach to civil society. University spaces were purged of political influence, their curriculums "Arabized" and "Islamized." Similarly, trade unions were first abolished and then consolidated into a single entity, the Sudanese Workers' Trade Union Federation (Mann, 2014). These changes were a hallmark of the "Tamkeen" policies, which also involved a major reshuffling of all branches of government: "military, civil service, parastatal companies, universities and even some private businesses" (Mann, 2014). These concurrent trends of the decentralization and political consolidation produced serious tensions as the economic performance of the country's economic sectors continued to suffer. This was especially true, given the weakness of domestic capital and financial institutions in supporting policy implementation at a time when the country was under political and economic sanctions from both Western and Gulf states, as well as international financial institutions (Elbeely, 2015).

Compounding these tensions was the wide adoption of the "al-Aylula" formula in the privatization program. This formula, which involved transferring certain enterprises from the federal government to state entities and local charitable organizations, "accounted for 53.1% of the implemented privatization forms" of the first wave (Elbeely, 2015). At the same time, the rapid changes made in the education and civil service sectors to bring them closer to sites of patronage networks debilitated the private sector. On the one hand, "Tamkeen" accelerated the flight of skilled labor as qualified professionals were replaced with loyal supporters in universities and government institutions. On the other hand, "constant shuffling of civil servants had the effect of compressing the regime's time frame, encouraging short-term corruption over long-term vision" (Mann, 2014). Hence, the country's public institutions were being expanded at the same time as they were being degraded. These competing dynamics nurtured an environment that called for a shift toward further liberalization and, with the discovery of significant oil reserves in 2000, the development of the rentier state.

The neoliberal rentier economy

The second wave of denationalization was carried over a more fragmented and drawn-out period, though written into law mainly within the period of 1997–2000. However, given considerable challenges from further sanctions and weak economic performance, the remaining 24 enterprises identified in the first phase were not liquidated until the middle of the following decade. Among those were "large, complex units like Sudan Airways, Sudan Railways, and Public Corporation for Electricity," as well as some local banks, and textile and cement manufacturing operations (Elbeely, 2015).

In the meanwhile, the ruling Islamic party was reorienting itself toward partnerships with foreign investors, contributing further to the weakening of indigenous capital and state institutions. As oil discoveries were announced in October 2000, Islamist rule turned to reliance on foreign capital and even labor to accelerate resource extraction activities. As oil production started to flow, a pattern of "exogenous modernization" was pursued in order to sustain the unprecedented levels of oil revenue (Abbink, 2004). The government helped establish the Greater Nile Petroleum Operating Company (GNPOC), a consortium composed of four foreign producers: Chinese CNPC, Malaysian Petronas, Indian GNC, and Sudan's state company, Sudapet (Mann, 2014). Heavily reliant on foreign expertise, and even labor, this shift magnified the patronage potential of this economic model and is what contributed to its success.

During the same period, public expenditure increased dramatically as substantial funding was redirected to civil service employment, the transfer of federal funds to local governments, and increases in federal salaries in the security and defense sectors (World Bank, 2007). At the expense of a diverse economic base and a healthy gradual privatization process, the second wave of denationalization saw an already bloated bureaucracy continue to invest in economically non-productive public sectors. This ill-advised model is attributed to the weak regulatory frameworks under which privatization was implemented, absent of any legal or institutional reform, the purpose of which would be to safeguard accountability and transparency (Elbeely, 2015). Additionally, by disproportionately shifting the focus to strategic (i.e., lucrative) segments of the economy, through exogenous modernization, less involved ministries and local governments were excluded from the fiscal windfall. This resulted in a "shifting of responsibilities" onto local governance structures to provide public services, address employment gaps, or sustain some semblance of a social safety net (Mann, 2014). Beyond the scope of this chapter, it is easy to see how political instability and the secession of oil-rich South Sudan quickly threatened this fiscal bubble and led to further institutional collapse.

Toward plans to eliminate state-led corruption

Borrowing from similar debates on Russia, Sudan's post-colonial period and especially the Islamist phase of 1989–2019 can be understood within the framework of state-sanctioned corruption at best and a modern kleptocracy at worst. In fact, in comparison to the post-Soviet experience, I would argue that the Islamist case has been far more extreme. The extent of state-led corruption in Sudan was recently laid bare in the aftermath of Omar Al Bashir's removal from power in April 2019. In his study of the corruption, Elamin (2019) concluded by suggesting a "holistic strategy that includes legislative, educational, business, and economic dimensions to fight corruption."

Suffice to note that a Sudanese court found Al Bashir guilty of corruption and sentenced him to two years in jail. However, the 75-year-old dictator is spending his sentence in a social reform facility, since under Sudanese law, a septuagenarian cannot serve jail terms. After having ruled the country for three decades, Al Bashir was arrested in April 2019 on charges of corruption. Infamously, Al Bashir is also wanted by the International Criminal Court for alleged war crimes, genocide, and crimes against humanity in the Darfur region. Authorities seized from his residence more than $113 million dollars in cash, including $25 million dollars he received from Saudi Crown Prince Mohammed Bin Salman. He denied having used any of it for himself and claimed that it was intended for private donations to individuals and organizations. He further explained that he was to allocate these funds to the Military Hospital, the International University of Africa, the Islamic media channel. He allegedly gave some $5.4 million to the Rapid Support Forces (RSF)—the government-aligned militia (OCCRP, 2020).

Similarly, in February 2020, Sudan's transitional government formed the Empowerment (*Tamkeen*) Elimination, Anti-Corruption, and Funds Recovery Committee. *Tamkeen*, roughly translated as empowerment, was the name given to a similar set of policies undertaken by the National Congress Party in the early period of their rule (1998). The committee was charged by the attorney general with dismantling the system developed by Al Bashir and government cronies. It oversees investigations into crimes involving the use of public funds and corruption by the former president, members of his extended family, and other individuals affiliated with the old regime. Their findings provided a wealth of evidence on how the old post-colonial state apparatus was replaced by a tiny new elite military group that allied itself with the civilian one. Despite alleged denationalization and privatization of state institutions, the committee's reports confirm that the National Congress Party, headed by Al Bashir, continued in the vein of the Interim Action Program of 1972 which sought to consolidate power and control through the capture of critical organizations and various economic functions of the state.

The transitional government announced its plans to form state sub-committees under the larger *Tamkeen* committee at the federal state level to be chaired by the governor of each state. Between February and April 2020, these anti-graft sub-committees issued a great number of decisions to counter and eliminate economic corruption. Their announcements provide some insight, albeit incomplete and inexhaustive, as to the scope of state corruption during this period of Islamist rule. They also foreshadowed the oncoming challenges of dismantling the "deep state" left in the wake of 30 years of single-party rule in Sudan. These included[1]:

- The seizure of all assets of El Maaraj Peace and Development Organization (a state-led NGO) and assets of the El Nour Islamic Complex, including 28 plots of land in the Kafouri district in north Khartoum, and 12 vehicles. Ownership of said assets would be transferred to the Ministry of Finance.
- Issuance of directives to suspend all state propaganda owned and operated by members of the previous regime and their affiliates. Media suspensions included El Sudani and El Rai El Aam newspapers, as well as Ashorooq and Teiba TV satellite channels. Based on the committee's findings, these media institutions were the beneficiaries of suspicious sources of funding by the Islamist regime. Committee spokesperson, Salah Maana, pointed out that the committee decided to appoint a commissioner to manage media institutions and review their finances. He also explained that the committee would make sure that the rights of the employees are respected and that the salaries of employees in these institutions would be paid from the accounts of the media organizations where they work. "We have no quarrel with the employees. It is the entities we are after," he concluded. Additionally, the general manager of the popular Al Nil Al Azrag TV channel, Hasan Fadlelmawla, would be dismissed and replaced because of his deep ties to the previous regime.
- Confiscation of properties belonging to former president Al Bashir's brother-in-law, nieces, nephews, as well as a former defense minister and close ally of Al Bashir. The committee transferred ownership of a total of around 92,000 square meters to Sudan's Ministry of Finance. In a separate decision, the committee dissolved the boards of the Khartoum International Airport Company and the Sudan Airports Holding Company, in connection with allegations of corruption.
- The committee also instructed the removal of 51 employees from the Ministry of Finance, and another 51 employees from the Ministry of Youth and

Sports. The directors of the Land Authority, the Housing Unit, and the Urban Planning Department were also to be dismissed. Furthermore, the committee decided on the removal of the Secretary General of the National Student Trust Fund, as well as the Funds' deputy secretaries in all 18 federal states of the country.

- In addition, the registration and licenses of several organizations and companies were withdrawn. These include a number of private hospitals, including the Elban Jadeed Hospital of the Mamoun Hemeida University, set up by the former State Minister of Health, Mamoun Hemeida. The academic teaching hospital would also be confiscated.
- The funds and assets of the Aviation Club in Khartoum would be transferred to the Ministry of Finance and the Civil Aviation Authority. The registration of the Islamic Daawa Authority would be cancelled, and all its real estate assets are to be seized and handed over to the Ministry of Finance.
- The committee spokesperson also announced the dissolution of several public and private institutions set up by members of the former regime, such as the Industrial Oil Producers Authority, the El Gezira and El Managil Scheme Producers Association, the El Rahad Agricultural Producers Association, and the El Junaid Sugar Producers Authority. The board of directors of the El Souki Agricultural Company for Investment and Services and El Khayari for Agricultural Services Ltd. would also be dissolved, and the funds and assets of these companies confiscated.
- The amount of resources smuggled outside Sudan (bank deposits and real estate across the Middle East, Western Europe, and Asia) is not known. The estimate of those smuggled resources is very high. Sudan Anti-Corruption Committee has to date confiscated 390 properties—collectively 248,894 square meters in some of the most prestigious neighborhoods of Khartoum that were registered under the names of officials, families, and affiliates of the deposited Al Bashir regime (Ljubas, 2020).

The oncoming crisis of contemporary Sudan

Despite the rigorous steps taken by the transitional government to eliminate state-led corruption, the "deep state" seems to persist through its domination of the administrative structures of the state. This applies not only to administration but also to all forms of state apparatus, including military and armed organizations, whether formal or informal.

In addition, according to virtually every available social and economic indicator applied to Sudan, dramatic declines in both levels of economic activity and the standard of living have been recorded during Islamist rule from 1989 to 2019. Every key indicator has been affected, causing a crushed economy, negative growth rates, falling gross investment, deteriorating health and education services, to falling enrollment rates and dropped standards of living and growing poverty, with approximately 65 percent of the population living below poverty line (almost three times over the developing countries average and double that of Sub-Sahara Africa (SSA)) (Elnur, 1999). Moreover, civil war and ethnic conflicts in Sudan may have deprived the rural communities not only of a substantial part of their assets but of their physically able bodies. To date, past development efforts at both the domestic and international levels have failed to develop a set of policy alternatives capable of reversing the current process of decline and restating a process of economic growth and raising the standard of living.

In addition to these challenges, the current global crisis caused by COVID-19 and its oil price and supply shock components merit special attention. In a country where the export of labor is a major source of national income, remittances are sure to decline drastically as workers are laid off following a contraction in the industry. More concerningly, return migration from the oil-producing countries would constitute a major challenge to the local economy in terms of income, employment, and further economic displacement of youth. These questions await the yet unborn bureaucracy of a new post-Islamist Sudan. Decidedly, they are likely to pose serious challenges to the transformative phases of socio-economic and political state organs of both the transitional and post-transitional regimes.

In conclusion, a wide range of policies are needed to overcome the declining state capacity to control its state administrative capacity, particularly in terms of re-establishing state control over administrative entities still dominated by the old regime (of Al Bashir); ensuring a wide range of policies to overcome low economic growth challenges; developing viable financial and economic policies targeting the suppressed regions particularly in Western and Eastern Sudan; and the rehabilitation of the productive capacity of the economy.

Note

1 This was published in Arabic and in English by the official TV and public media.

References

Abbink, J. (2004). Violence and state (re)formation in the African context: Global and local aspects of crisis and change. In R. E. Westerfield (Ed.), *Current issues in globalization* (pp. 137–149). Nova Science.

Bechtold, P.K. (1990). More turbulence in Sudan: A new politics this time? Middle East Journal, 44(4), 579–595. https://www.jstor.org/stable/4328191

Elamin, N. (2019). A theoretical analysis of corruption in Sudan: Causes, diagnostics, consequences, and remedies. *African Journal of Political Science and International Relations*, 13(2), 4–16. https://doi.org/10.5897/AJPSIR2018.1134

Elbeely, K. H. (2015). Sudan privatization program: Putting the cart before the horse. *International Journal of Business and Social Research*, 5(2), 32–41.

Elnur, I. (1999). Alternative development policies for Sudan. *Review of African Political Economy*, 26(82), 508–512. Retrieved March 25, 2020, from http://www.jstor.org/stable/4006484

Elnur, I. (2008). *Contested Sudan: The political economy of war and reconstruction*. Routledge. https://doi.org/10.1604/9780415476454

Ljubas, Z. (2020, May 8). *Sudan's anti-graft body to seize property of the Bashir family*. Retrieved March 5, 2023, from https://www.occrp.org/en/daily/12304-sudan-s-anti-graft-body-to-seize-property-of-the-bashir-family

Mann, L. (2014). Wasta! The long-term implications of education expansion and economic liberalisation on politics in Sudan. *Review of African Political Economy*, 41(142), 561–578.

The Technical Committee for the Release of Public Sector Entities (TCRPS). (1997). An evaluation of the Sudanese privatization Experience. (In Arabic). The Ministry of Finance and Economic Planning, the Republic of Sudan.

World Bank. (2007). Sudan: Public expenditure review, synthesis report. *The World Bank*. https://openknowledge.worldbank.org/handle/10986/7672

Yamada, M., & Hertog, S. (2020). Introduction: Revisiting rentierism—With a short note by Giacomo Luciani. *British Journal of Middle Eastern Studies*, 47(1), 1–5. https://doi.org/10.1080/13530194.2020.1714267

Additional References

Anti-Corruption Committee dissolves boards of Central Bank of Sudan and 11 other banks [Radio broadcast]. (2020, February 9). Khartoum, Sudan: Radio Dabanga. https://www.dabangasudan.org

Economist: Plunging Sudanese Pound leading to economic collapse [Transcript, Radio broadcast]. (2020, February 25). Khartoum, Sudan: Radio Dabanga. https://www.dabangasudan.org

Sudan anti-graft authority seizes 390 plots of prime Khartoum real estate [Radio broadcast]. (2020, April 19). Khartoum, Sudan: Radio Dabanga. https://www.dabangasudan.org

Sudan dissolves central bank board, governor remains. (2020, February 20). Retrieved March 20, 2020, from https://www.reuters.com/article/us-sudan-economy-banks/sudan-dissolves-central-bank-board-governor-remains-idUSKBN2002NW

Sudan government seizes assets of Islamic movement leaders [Radio broadcast]. (2020, April 24). Khartoum, Sudan: Radio Dabanga. https://www.dabangasudan.org

Sudan's Anti-Corruption Committee suspends media outlets [Radio broadcast]. (2020, January 8). Khartoum, Sudan: Radio Dabanga. https://www.dabangasudan.org

8
LIBYA'S PUBLIC ADMINISTRATION
Burdens of the Past and Challenges of Transition[1]

Youssef Mohammad Sawani

Introduction

Public administration in Libya has undergone a number of changes that affected its structure, role, levels, and relationship with the populace (El-Fathal et al., 1977). These have been a reflection of changes in the political system, the deep-seated colonial tradition, the move from federalism to a unitary system during the monarchy (after independence in 1951), the Gaddafi rule (from 1969 until his fall in 2011), and an unstable transition thereafter. The shape, structure, and functions of public administration have been shaped by, and sometimes continue, the different, and at times similar, policies adopted by authorities during Libya's modern history. Despite variations in the different systems of public administration employed by the country, public finance and the role of central authorities in controlling public administration have remained almost intact. Moreover, changes in the political system notwithstanding, economic and social factors related to the rentier economy and to the tribal nature of the society have come to weight down more on public administration than the merits of any politico-administrative model. This would have hampered the success of any model that could have served the objectives of development.

The 1951–1969 monarchy maintained a simple administrative model, the ability of which to infiltrate the society was limited by shortages in both finance and human resources. During the Gaddafi era, public administration became more sophisticated and expanded to become the largest employer and item in the national budget (El-Fathaly et al., 1977; Metz, 1987). Muammar Gaddafi, as early as 1973, introduced a politico-administrative model that rested upon

DOI: 10.4324/9781003389941-10

decentralization. He claimed this to be a unique form of direct democracy, but it was, in fact, only a façade—a disguised mode of authoritarian rule.

During the uprisings against the Gaddafi regime in the 2011 and afterward, local non-state actors sprang up almost haphazardly adding to the already cumbersome situation. Self-appointed local councils, revolutionary bodies, councils of elders, and *Shura* councils, as well as armed militia prevailed, becoming the *de facto* regional and local governments of Libya and expanding at the expense of formal state organs. Tribes also regained some of their lost functions and became more resilient, adding more chaos to an increasingly ineffective, corrupt, and fragile system of public administration. The post-Gaddafi tumultuous phase made Libya an undeniably weak and fragmented state reflecting the increasing influence of both armed groups and the periphery. The country continues to suffer from devastating impacts of an ongoing conflict, which has paralyzed public administration by crippling its already-strained resources and capabilities of dispersing public services particularly at the provincial and local levels. The fact that Libya remains very much a country in a fragile transition emphasizes the need for state-building and a reinvigorated focus on human rights, reconciliation, and a new social contract.

This chapter attempts to provide a detailed analysis of public administration in Libya. It introduces the country's contemporary history of governance and public administration, starting with the Gaddafi era since Libya's public administration owes much of its characteristics to that period. It, then, provides a profile of the current situation and analyzes the components most relevant to governance and public administration in the post-Gaddafi transition. It ends with an analysis of challenges ahead and future prospects and offers some policy suggestions.

Development of public administration in Libya

Gaddafi era: The Jamahiriya unique governance system

Despite Gaddafi's claim of building a direct democracy, his era was strongly marked with pushing a system of centralization rationalized by a populist discourse. The Gaddafi regime embarked on a unique model of governance as early as 1973, but particularly after 1977, when the Jamahiriya system—literally, a state of the masses—was established. This system purported to abolish the traditional governmental structure and establish a bottom-up direct democracy with extensive devolution and de-concentration of power. A populist administration model had replaced the traditional public administration system (CAIMED, 1990). This unique system mocked popular administration and local governance in favor of clientelism and subordinate elites (El-Fathal et al., 1977; Obeidi, 2001). Though a formal, sophisticated public administration existed, it faced strong competition from powerful, informal, and personal power arrangements (Mattes, 2008).

Gaddafi realized during his regime's later years that politico-administrative reforms were badly needed. Regime legitimacy was eroding rapidly and there was a need to avoid further damaging international isolation. The reforms coincided with a global trend toward reducing the gap between state and society, a democratic third wave, and a movement toward decentralization. Reforms, however, were more a result of being a prerequisite for Libya's rehabilitation on the world stage and its rapprochement with the West, although they were well suited to serve the regime's own security and existence. In a 2013 report, the United Nations Economic and Social Commission for West Asia (UNESCWA) concluded, "for decision-makers in the Arab region, institutional restructuring by de-concentrating powers and resources was deemed beneficial for enhancing the state's infrastructural power ... [and] consolidating the state's legitimacy and authority" (UNESCWA, 2013, p. 6).

Although the ideological premises expressed in Gaddafi's *The Green Book* were arguably associated with ideals of democracy, justice, and egalitarianism, actual policies revealed a contradiction between ideology and lived experience, obliging Libyans to live in a peculiar confluence of three simultaneously overlapping systems (Sawani, 2012).The first was what may be termed an *ideological system* as outlined in the *The Green Book*, which focused on paths toward the realization of democracy, justice, equality, and an overall scheme of ethical and moral values that could be shared by humanity at large. This system was utilized as a justificatory mechanism and a basis for supporting the legitimacy of the regime as well as that of its leadership.

The second was the *formal system* that involved the "official" and "proforma" application of the mechanisms recommended by *The Green Book* in government. It took the form of political and administrative institutions, local government, and other units. Accordingly, after March 1977, when the *Jamahiriya* or the "state of the masses," as coined by Gaddafi, was announced, a host of official "institutions" came into existence. Theoretically, these institutions were created to put the *Jamahiriya* into practice, but in reality, these institutions and associations were dysfunctional and bereft of any real power. In other words, they camouflaged the reality that real power resided elsewhere.

The third system, however, was an *informal* arrangement of power and influence that Gaddafi was keen to set up at all levels of political, economic, social, and military life. Such informal arrangements brokered real authority and they reflected a pattern of carefully crafted political, military, tribal, and economic alliances that in terms of *realpolitik* created a hegemony over and above formal politics. Those dictated and controlled every major political action or policy. This third system appropriated the other two systems and employed them for various ends. It is in this context that it may be possible to understand the role of Gaddafi's family and the most prominent men of his al-Gadadafah tribe in addition to the role played by those who had become to be known as the "men of the tent" (Crisis Group, 2011). The latter term refers to the inner circle of the Gaddafi regime who were in constant consultation with him and who were involved in all matters of consequence. This inner circle was composed of those who typically, and quite literally, gathered in Gaddafi's tent, including his own family, his tribe's leaders, and some members of the defunct Revolutionary Command Council that had been organized in the aftermath of the September 1, 1969 coup that had brought him to power. Others, including some prominent and loyal individuals with personal ties to Gaddafi, heads of the security apparatus, prominent social or tribal leaders, and trusted members of the revolutionary committees, also joined this group (Shalgam, 2012).

The focus of public administration and its civil servants was to maintain whatever advantages that were made possible by the informal system that profited through rent-seeking and patronage. Public administration provided low-quality services for the population as a whole while simultaneously being employed for political purposes and operated for the consolidation/empowerment of allies or clients. However, the two parts of the dual system—the formal and informal—were mutually dependent. The formal system could not be executed without the intervention of the informal system to drive results. Conversely, the system as a whole—including the informal system—relied on the formal system for whatever legitimacy it enjoyed.

Local governance and the dynamics of authoritarianism

The *Jamahiriya* model maintained a decentralized structure that still relied on civil servants, and so, lost its independence when its administration became part of the national machinery of government. Heads of administrative units were no longer selected based on merit but on managed or controlled popular selection and political loyalty. The 1990s and early 2000s saw the introduction of formal decentralization. The number of ministries and central departments or authorities was reduced to a handful, while central providers were haphazardly distributed regionally. The real *raison d'être* was to absorb the shocks of the sanctions and international isolation, which caused wide popular dissent. Therefore, the country was divided into a number of provinces (*shabiyyat*). Public administration was under great pressure to adopt the new dynamics and to adapt to the whims of an autocrat whose imagination saw no limit.

The overall system was a sham—one that only obscured authoritarianism—and was destined to fail (Sawani, 2013). Consequently, public administration was rendered almost obsolete. The dual system of government with strong informal structures frequently overrode formal state structures in ways that made effective government unattainable. While the dual system consisted of a relatively weak, atomized, and disorganized formal system, the informal system was powerful and centralized. The formal system was characterized by poorly defined decision-making rights and an emphasis on deliberation and consensus building, which meant that all actions must be extensively debated at all levels before being agreed upon. The multiple and extensive level of debate rendered the system inefficient and opaque, with national decisions often appearing to reflect little of the decisions taken at lower levels (Halm, 2013). In most instances, the views of the civil servants and technocrats were either dismissed or totally ignored.

Structures of local government

The concept of popular administration and Jamahiriya governance was based on the gradual dissolution of the central organs of government and the consolidation of the local and regional organs. Gaddafi claimed that each governorate would become a self-managed mini state. At the local level, each unit had defined roles, functions, and responsibilities, which included the management of all services and the right to raise local revenues. Budget allocations were included in the national budget, limiting the local level's capacity to act. At the regional level, each *shabiyyat* acted as an independent legal personality and had its own budget approved by the national legislature, making up one single administrative unit with employment and budgetary functions (Sawani, 2012).

Each *shabiyyat* was considered a local decentralized government, one that resembled that at the national level. Each one had a legislative people's conference, and had administrative bodies and execution agencies to deal with all socioeconomic matters. These covered all aspects of policies other than foreign and defense policies, which were under the preview of the central government. However, such local governments were the epitome of corruption and the squandering of public resources, which only helped the Gaddafi regime maintain the power and legitimacy that comes with attaining the loyalty and allegiance of the people (Sawani, 2013).

Widespread corruption and the lack of accountability notwithstanding, such top-down decentralization built on ambitious ideological claims of grassroots, direct democracy proved to be nothing more than centralization par excellence. The regime was only able to distribute administrative functions and operations and spread them geographically. Therefore, the central authority expanded its reach and quiet extensively infiltrated society. Agents of the regime and members of the revolutionary committees at the governorate, municipal, and sub-municipal levels provided most of, if not all, the public services under central supervision and tightly controlled resources and public finances.

Real devolution was, thus, not realized, despite being advocated as a goal. An alarming degree of disparity existed among the different regions, especially in the fields of human resources and local revenue. The so-called development plans drawn up by provinces and submitted to the central government were nothing more than shopping lists where the objective was gaining access to more funding rather than capacity building and development. The informal system was more capable of efficient and decisive action. It intervened in governance in a manner that appeared both chaotic and illegitimate—chaotic because the informal system encompassed divided power and illegitimate because it contradicted the formal system's claim of direct democracy. Public administration was becoming less capable of implementing policies nationally, while at local levels it was not effective. Local governance bodies were not given the information they needed for effective policy-making and execution. People's conferences made requests (such as for a new school) with little sense of what these requests would cost or of what other resources (such as a hospitals) would have to be traded off in order to deliver on the request. The center, propped up by intervention from the informal sector, primarily managed citizens' needs. Local government was not able to make any operating decisions affecting citizens' lives (Sawani, 2013).

The consequence was a public administration unable to formulate or execute policy effectively. The concept of the common good lost its place and value, since the interaction between the formal and informal systems leads to a distributive form of politics focused on group or individual self-interest. Because the formal system of decision-making at the three-tier system of people's conferences merely aggregated local and regional decisions at the national level, there was no mechanism for identifying and deciding on the common good. The focus, too often, was on dividing the economic pie rather than increasing the size of the pie (Sawani, 2013). Public administration had become a tool dominated by, and subordinate to, the wishes of populist national and regional leaders.

Post-Gaddafi transitional public administration

When the Gaddafi regime fell in late 2011, the transitional authority faced the challenge of governing a country that had long lacked an efficient system of public administration. What remained was a weak and corrupt system, while the eight-month-long civil war paved the way for the advancement of the periphery at the expense of the center. This is related to a contradiction that Libya shares with other Arab nations in both their modern Western model of the nation state, liberal and bureaucratic-Westphalian sense, and the Khaldunian and Sultanic Patriarchal, traditional Arab-Islamic model. Both the monarchy and the Gaddafi regime attempted to resolve this by relying on the more traditional roots of the Libyan state but both failed to transcend the contradiction. Therefore, it is only to be expected that the old, traditional, local roots of the state resurface at every possible opportunity. This is particularly so whenever there is a weak state or authority, employing different, interacting elements of society (especially identities at a subsumed level to the national, all-encompassing identity), and the economy, which further expose the state and its fragility.

Looking back at the last decade of Gaddafi rule, much of the public administration that exists in Libya today is, in some sense, a continuation of it, though under a different guise. This is particularly the case with the structural and geographic distribution of public administration; planning; economic liberalization aimed at reducing state intervention in the economic sphere; and public finance management. According to one former minister of planning, the essential objective of the first post-Gaddafi government was to restore law and order in those spheres, which was presumed only to be feasible by revitalizing public administration by returning to implementing previous laws and regulations.[2] This was bound to continue as long as conflict continued. All the while, the public sector remained burdened with new employees, becoming the employer of 85 percent of the active work force.[3]

Transitional national governance system

The National Transitional Council (NTC), on August 3, 2011, proclaimed the Transitional Constitutional Declaration in which a number of the articles detail the structures and functions of national and local governments and their relationship. Articles 17–29 specify the operation of the interim government, while Article 30 provides a roadmap for the transition (Sawani, 2012). The governance system comprises the Council of Ministers as the superior executive body, and the House of Representatives (HoR) as the unicameral legislature.[4]

Post-2011 leaders, in particular, failed to play a positive role in leading the country to become a modern state. On December 17, 2015, Libyans signed the Libyan Political Agreement (LPA), sponsored by United Nations Support Mission Libya (UNSMIL) (aka the Skhirat Agreement). Accordingly, Libya now has an internationally recognized Government of National Accord (GNA) led by a Presidential Council (PC) as well as the elected HoR, and a Higher Council of State (HCS) (essentially a revival which includes most members of the defunct 2012 Islamist dominated GNC, while other members are still active and competing for power, resources, and legitimacy under the banner of the defunct congress). However, none of these actually represent the whole nation and, in that struggle, prior to and resulting from LPA, lies the apparent failure to resolve the conflict and achieve the desired peace which would contribute to the needs of state-building.

The UN Security Council endorsed the LPA, and the HoR accepted it in principle but rejected its amalgamation within the Transitional Constitutional Declaration, which would have made it binding. This brought the whole agreement to a standstill. Even though the HoR accepted the PC, the HCS remains unacceptable to many actors because it echoed the interests of Islamists and excluded some regions and tribes. Since April 2019, the country has been engulfed in another cycle of civil war with a military confrontation between the GNA and Libyan National Army (LNA) forces with an increased foreign involvement. The current situation is of political division and continued violence. The recent UNSMIL mediation led to a fragile ceasefire and the convening of a Libyan Political Dialogue Forum (LPDF) that held meetings in Tunisia aimed at restructuring the LPA. Despite inherent deficiencies in the UNSMIL approach, there are hopes that the country may eventually have a unified government that can arrange for fresh elections in December 2021.

The overall legal framework remains incomplete, and the division of labor between the levels of governance remains ambiguous to say the least and generally lacking. The mandates of Libya's executive bodies were not revised following the passing of Local Governance Law, LGL, in 2012 by the GNC (Law 59). Most services and functions remain the responsibility of central executive bodies and their regional branches. This is particularly true in the case of spending budget allocations related to the third chapter of the national budget, which finances developmental projects, including local economic development. Municipalities are not sufficiently empowered enough to take the initiative in their respective areas, and when they do as Law 59 stipulates, they face challenges resulting from overlapping mandates/duties with executive bodies.[5]

Therefore, the national governance structure remains unclear at a time when the country suffers from the ongoing violence and the dwindling resources. This has adversely affected public administration, almost reducing it to rubble. Libya's finances are in a huge disarray with fiscal deficits, mounting public debt, and sharply eroding foreign reserves. Public administration has been unable to perform its functions; salaries have not been paid for months and, when they are, people cannot get cash at the banks. This makes Libya a fragile state, one that is close to becoming a failed state.[6]

Local councils: From rebels to administrators

One consequence of the 2011 revolt was that self-appointed local councils and militias assumed local functions and took almost any course of action independently. Local councils were established clandestinely during the revolt—mostly run by rebels—and many of these councils reflected Islamist and tribal activism (Sawani, 2012, pp. 16–17). Such bodies, as well as the self-appointed *Shura*—wise and elders' councils—and other entities, have been dominating the local scene, resisting central government policies when, for whatever reason, it did not suit them.

These *de facto* councils became part of the provisional authority, the NTC (Evans & Barakat, 2015). The Transitional Constitutional Declaration provides some safeguards for local governance, but lacks any clear provisions to protect it against the central authority's propensity to encroach on the role of local government. So, while Article 18 of the Declaration paved the way for elected local councils and municipalities, it did not provide any basis for the establishment of any intermediate level of governance at the provincial or governorate level that would connect local with central government. Rather, the LGL, Law 59/2012, adopted in 2012 by the now defunct General National Congress, assigned the Ministry of Local Governance (MoLG) the task of acting as a guide to local councils. Despite experience showing an unbalanced and problematic relationship between the two governmental levels, local councils are obliged to listen and adhere to what that ministry sees fit, or otherwise risk being replaced and/or deprived of the ministry's funding, which is their sole source of revenue (Mneinah, 2013).

As Pack and Barak Barfi (2012, p. 7) note, "Libya has shifted from a dictatorship back to its more traditional power structure, with a weak center having difficulty making inroads with a rebellious periphery." This may be explained by the recurrence of a phenomenon that Libya has been experiencing ever since it achieved statehood in 1951. The eight-month revolt—civil war—only strengthened a historical model wherein the periphery challenges the center's authority. This is also related, partially at least, to the undeniable residual effect that Gaddafi's politico-administrative model has had on Libyans' perceptions of local governance.

The LGL, set forth a four-tier system of public administration at the national, regional, local, and semi-administrative levels known as the economic regions. The municipal council members are elected directly by the local population and those elected members elect a mayor from among themselves, but their choice has to be approved by the minister of local governance. Local councils are self-appointed bodies that sprang up during and after 2011 and were bestowed legitimacy by the Transitional Council and later the GNC. They came into existence first clandestinely and then by the initiatives of local leaders. Then, they became part of local governance and received recognition by virtue of government decrees and budgets.

Each municipality has a municipal council and a municipal technocrat administration. Each municipality has a number of branches (depending on size and area) and is also divided into a number of wards or *mahallat, wards, or localities,* which constitute the lowest jurisdiction responsible for interacting with the people. Each ward has its own head, a *Mukhtar* of the locality, appointed based on merit by the governor upon the nomination of the relevant mayor. Both the municipal branches and the *Mukhtars* do not have executive authority but are part of the general municipal administration. Municipal councils are also supposed to establish a *Shura* consultative council of local notables. The *Shura* council's role is advisory as far as matters related to local governance and development are concerned. *Shura* councils are basically political and tribal formation that are self-appointed and are essentially the creation of Islamists and their allies in almost all areas. However, they are now limited to west and south Libya and no longer exist in the east. The GNC, seeking control and alliance building, also appointed many of these councils during the political crisis, which actually gives them no sound legal grounds. In most cases, the military councils act independently but they are affiliated with the *Shura* councils and coordinate with them in Islamist-held areas.

As the LGL stipulates,[7] municipalities are tasked with a number of functions that include:

- urban planning and management (this includes the issuing of permits for construction);
- local economic development;
- creation and oversight of local facilities delivering public social and administrative services;
- civil registration;
- issuing of permits for businesses;
- Public health and environment monitoring.

However, local councils and municipalities are obliged to listen and adhere to what the MoLG sees fit or otherwise risk being replaced and/or deprived of funding as the MoLG is their source of revenue. Though the law prescribes that councils are directly elected (Article 26) by local citizens, its decisions at regional and local levels are subject to official approval by the minister. Moreover, all elected local officials are answerable to the national minister (Articles 16 and 18) in each sector, who holds the power to veto their decisions.

Not all local municipal councils were elected because of the political crisis and some who were elected were replaced by appointees in the east (specifically in *Barqa*). Some councils in west and south were not elected either for tribal/political reasons or because they are controlled by forces (mainly Islamists) who do not want elections for fear of losing control or because their population and leaders, such as in areas like Bani Waleed, have no taste for the post-2011 order. Reminiscent of the 2011 uprisings, many areas still have self-appointed military councils that have more power and influence than municipalities. The military councils are independent and make their will effective by employing force, especially in major cities like Tripoli, Misrata, Zawia, Sabratha, Ghariyan, and Zintan. Many municipal councils are facing the problem of controlling armed formations, while the legitimacy of these local councils, the capabilities of its members, their political orientation, and their performance have come into doubt and their term has come to an end. There have been calls to dissolve the self-appointed local councils and those elected councils whose terms have expired and to initiate elections to select new councils. Recently, the Central Local Elections Committee organized local elections for some municipalities, whereas all elected have gone beyond their four-year terms and fresh elections are long overdue.

Public administration and the local governance (administration) law no. 54/2012

Legally speaking, there is a kind of principal-agent relationship between the municipalities or local councils and the central government. The minister of local governance acts on behalf of the government in consolidating such a relationship and enjoys the power to approve or nullify decisions adopted by them. However, and given the current division and crisis, the local councils are almost completely independent and only revert to a (central) government to obtain any possible funding. They have been active in establishing their independence including in relations with foreign governments. One development has been the recent direct contact and work with the European Union (EU) and some member states at the expense of the national government. This further weakens the already fragile national authority and hampers the country's unification process. This is particularly true of west and south, but not in *Barqa* in the east, where the HoR and its government, empowered by the LNA, have limited the scope or margin of movement for municipal councils and many of them are now run by appointees who are subordinate to the military governor.

Nevertheless, councils and municipalities all over the country have been able to interact and coordinate activities and this has increased more recently either with the active role of the PC or the projects run by foreign actors, EU, USA, or UN agencies. In July 2017, about 46 local bodies mainly supportive of GNA, including those controlled by Islamists, set up a coordinating body. Also, the local bodies in the Nafusa mountain region have set up a coordinating body. Lately, a Higher Council for Local Governance, as prescribed in LGL, was set up.

The law allows for the financing of the local councils and municipalities from the national budget. Recent years have seen the dwindling of funding from the centers due to the crisis. Municipalities have suffered greatly as a result, thus becoming almost unable to provide the services. However, the situation has improved recently with the GNA and HoR government, who began providing much needed finance to municipalities. Nevertheless, central funding has been anything but sufficient and municipalities have asked for special provisions allowing them to levy local taxes and raise revenues. The HoR government in the east has not taken any steps in this regard but the GNA has in the last few months allowed councils and municipalities to raise local revenue and levy taxes. However, municipalities are only likely to generate limited income as long as the political impasse and the economic stagnation are in place.

This, in addition to the absence of any system of vertical separation of powers, renders the current system similar to what had been in place during Gaddafi rule, when all substantial matters and decisions rested with the central authority in the capital Tripoli, thus increasing the sense of marginalization at the regional and local levels. In fact, what the law created resembled a Gaddafi-styled popular administration that holds no real authority. The local level effectively remains under the purview of the central government at both the Council of Ministers' level and at the different levels of sector ministries and specialized authorities. All matters and decisions at the local level appear to be at the unlimited liberty of the MoLG to accept, approve, or nullify, as well as deprive of appropriate funding.

Furthermore, the performance of municipalities is severely restricted since there remain real issues with the formulation of intergovernmental relations. The chaotic situation is evidently arising from lack of clear-cut procedures, as well as interference and conflict between official bodies and a lack of transparency and widespread corruption. There exists no clear division of labor, as the municipalities are almost entirely dependent on the financial allocations provided in the national budget. Rifts and civil war made municipalities unable to get appropriate funding or became underfunded. With no proper taxation system in place at all levels, municipalities face enormous challenges without any sufficient resources. Meanwhile, irregular budget allocations are spent, almost completely, on salaries of an oversized civil service and on running costs.

The proclamation of local governance legislation put forward a four-tier system of public administration: national, regional, and local, as well as in economic regions (at the semi-administrative level) (Evans & Barakat, 2015). This law, however, has not determined the number, locations, or boundaries of any of these units, preferring to give the central government's Council of Ministers the power and right to determine the number of governorates and municipalities and their geographical scope.

The next level as set by the LGL is that of the governorates. However, this level never saw the light of day. The law does not determine the number, the locations, or the boundaries of any of these units but gives the central government Council of Ministers the power and right to determine how many governorates and municipalities and their geographical scope. The different governments seemed content with the politics of buying regional and local support, and as stipulated in Article 4 of the LGL, reacted by creating more municipalities, renaming and/or merging and modifying existing ones in the hope that this will loosen the current crisis. The total number of municipalities therefore reached 104, 22 of them in *Barqa* in addition to some 16 councils.

There remain tensions over boundaries of the municipalities and there are calls for creating even more municipalities while others reject what they consider the fragmentation of some cities like Tripoli, Misrata, and Zawia into a larger number of municipalities. The electoral districts for local governance are divided regionally along similar lines as the national electoral districts for general elections and they cover Libya's major regions, which are now 13. However, each national district is divided internally into local districts represented in municipal division. These are too many and there is no available map to demarcate them. However, the elections for each municipality are run as one electoral district, amounting to about 120 districts nationwide. Each municipality is considered one electoral district that may have as many wards as needed in accordance with logistical requirements or tribal considerations.

The regional-level initiative never saw light of day, and the Council of Ministers has modified, on many occasions, the number and boundaries of municipalities in order to adapt to regional and tribal concerns and demands. The central government seemed content with the politics of buying regional and local support. As permitted under Article 4 of the 2012 LGL, the central government has created more municipalities, renaming and/or merging and modifying existing ones, all in the hope that this will tackle the current crisis. This indicates that law actually established principal–agent relationship between the municipalities and the central government. The minister of local governance acts on behalf of the government in consolidating such a model and enjoys the power to approve or nullify decisions adopted by municipalities (Böckenförde & Megerisi, 2016).

All post-Gaddafi governments have lacked any clear-cut policy and objectives, so they rely on addressing concerns and providing resources and creating local bodies in response to local pressures. The UNDP (2014, p. 4) has recently concluded:

> At central level, the MoLG is not able to pursue policy formulation nor to provide comprehensive guidance and capacity development support to the newly elected MCs [municipal councils]. At local level, many of the incoming municipal councilors and staff seem inexperienced with the management of local affairs. On the other hand, a large share of the local civil servants (on the central government payroll) has remained but is reluctant to any type of change. This difficult situation in terms of human capacities does limit the possibility for municipalities to assume greater roles, as given by the new law, but also to respond aptly to the crisis impacts. In particular, municipalities struggle to conduct multi-sectorial needs assessment and integrated planning and to involve significantly civil society and wider population in such exercises. Municipalities also suffer from limited experience and means for public outreach and strategic communications.

More recently, however, the GNA in an attempt to buy more support issued executive orders allowing the municipalities to have the right to spend their own local revenue in addition to the extra amount allocated to them in state budget. They will have the right to collect local revenue and not hand it over to Ministry of Finance (MoF) as before. Despite the fact that only few municipalities have the potential to generate local income, they would be able to spend whatever they collect on service provision and other local municipal expenditure including projects in the fields of local economic development. They would be able to spend but the funds have to be managed in accordance with the law and with the approval of a financial controller who is part of MoF. They would also able to move funds allocated for projects to other areas of expenditure with approval from MoLG. The new permission given to municipalities theoretically widens their mandate and ability to spend their own revenues including funds provided by the GNA. However, in reality, they are bound by the same law 59/2012, which gives the upper hand to MoLG.

Municipalities are facing serious challenges inhibiting their capacity to take action and are actually unable to secure the funds required to perform the functions of development and service delivery. The Libyan system of local government has been inherently flawed since its inception. In addition to being constantly underfunded, local municipal councils are unable to provide basic services to the people and this inability has been made worse since the country moved from one conflict to another, particularly since 2014, leading to the deterioration of its infrastructures amid fragile security. The study identifies two more fundamental weaknesses that characterize local municipal councils: lack of communication and the lack of collaboration with the public (Elmagbri & Cohen, 2017).

This is likely to remain the situation given the ongoing conflict, which has almost eroded the ability of the central authority to act and infiltrate the country. This has enabled the periphery to flourish at the center's expense. Yet, local government remains weak and in much need of further consolidation. According to UNDP (2015, p. 4), "the overall structure and functionality of the local governance system reflects the absence of a nationally adopted vision and policy framework that would define the nature, mission, mandates and functions of Libya's system of local governance. The system remains centralized—but with a central government that is, with every day passing, less capable of fulfilling its command, control and support roles."

The challenges of a transition amidst continuous conflict

With the fall of the Gaddafi regime, Libya entered a transitional phase. It had its first elections in more than five decades. The country is yet to have a constitution that determines its political system. This is likely to take a long time, given current political schisms and military tensions. The transition has ultimately transformed itself into a bloody civil war. With this, hopes for, and attempts at, creating a vibrant private sector have evaporated; unemployment especially among the youth has rocketed; and all the people's hopes remain in limbo.

In the post-Gaddafi years, the country's institutions were hijacked and appropriated for the sake of partisan or tribal and regional interests and objectives, thus creating more cause for the conflict's continuation. Many new institutions were actually built around existing actors or to answer to the interests and demands of particular factions. Institutions became reflective of the conflict and the deepening divide between different parties, thus entrenching the struggle rather than reconciling the needs of the perpetrators of the conflict with the need for state-building.

The debate about the relationship between the central and the peripheral modes of government has been intense and part of a wider debate about the form and nature of the future Libyan state and its political system of government. Therefore, the issue of federalism sprang up right after the establishment of the first transitional authority—NTC—but its negative manifestations were visible as early as summer 2011, well before Gaddafi regime fell. Leaders in the spring of 2012 uprising were making strong demands for greater decentralization by calling for the establishing a federal council for Libya's eastern *Barqa* region (Halm, 2013, pp. 35–38).

Public administration reform

In the last decade of Gaddafi's rule, the size of civil service, the level of corruption, and the inefficiency of public administration all increased considerably. Several policies were designed with help from international organizations as well as well-established private consultancies. These were geared toward the reform of the civil service—its size, recruitment, efficiency, and performance. However, such attempts went in vain. Meanwhile, demand for civil services continued to increase in size and budget (Sawani, 2013, pp. 106–117).

What is revealing is that, because of the conflict and civil war, post-Gaddafi transitional governments have ignored most of the administrative reform initiatives and policies adopted or partially implemented prior to 2011. Governments preferred to return to more centralization and rigid practices, even though that ran counter to all claims of democratization and betrayed the aspirations of the people who revolted against the Gaddafi regime. There are still no adequate and functional controls on public administration, and the central government continues expanding their powers. Therefore, the post-Gaddafi era has seen two competing phenomena taking place simultaneously: the expansion of public administration and civil servants employed, and the contraction of governance space left for local authorities.

The constitution drafting process and the future governance system

The Constitution Drafting Authority (CDA), elected in 2014, was expected to come up with a definitive constitution. It exceeded its time mandate, having continued for years with interruptions and delays beyond all expectations. After much controversy, the CDA was able to vote on a draft constitution in July 2017 and adopted it by a majority. It was then submitted to the HoR for a referendum. The draft constitution deals in detail with the governance system and the structure of local authorities and their roles, but does not mention the civil service nor does it provide guidance for public administration (except for Article 17, which requires merit-based appointments to public office). In addition to rifts within the authority itself, previous drafts echoed the ongoing conflict and disparate approaches. Debate about federalism has overshadowed its preparatory work and has impinged sharply on local governance and led to the paralyzing of the constitution-drafting authority, which experienced mounting disagreements among its members (Stephen, 2016).

CDA was able to adopt the draft constitution after a long and intensive debate among its members, reflecting the wider variety of views among different elites and public opinion. The debate focused on the most appropriate form of state structure and administration that is still running at all levels, and on semantics (Pickard, 2013). The debate centered round dichotomies of federal versus unitary forms of state, unicameral versus bicameral legislatures, and the election and authority of the head of state. Obviously, such debates have proved unproductive, even damaging, and offer no prospect of dealing with the real issues confronting Libya, thus distracting attention away from alternative approaches (Sawani & Pack, 2013). This reflects the effects of the interplay of different political, tribal, ideological, and regional dynamics. It also indicates the degree to which any important state-building and governance matter is rooted in the political experience, culture, and history of Libya. It underlines the devastating impact of the authoritarian rule of the Gaddafi era, marked by a strong disdain of institutions that disguised autocracy in sham democratic structures.

Decentralization governance model in the 2017 constitutional draft

The draft constitutional provisions on local government advance a system based on the principle of expanded decentralization, committing the state to support it within the framework of a unitary state. Local governance would include local, municipal, and provincial levels of government. This local three-tier governance structure foresees greater devolution within a decentralized multi-level governance (including financial and legislative functions, and the ability of elected municipal councils and regional governments to raise their own revenue).[8] The proposed structure provides for an extensive or enlarged degree of decentralization in which local authorities would be the providers of services and would be self-managed. However, Article 150 implicitly dispels concerns that this proposal would threaten or pose any risk to national unity or violate the constitution and laws. Article 149 stipulates that all local government units should be subject to subsequent oversight at the central level to ensure the legitimacy of their work.

Article 144 of the draft constitution details the hierarchy of the political system and straightforwardly divides the country into a number of governorates or provinces (*muhafazaat*) in addition to municipalities. The rationale behind doing so was to preserve national security and strike a balance between the size of population, area, geographical linkage, social justice and harmony, economic considerations, historical factors, developmental objectives, and the efficiency and effectiveness of every area or governorate and its public administration. The text of this essential article is clearly in favor of the administrative and financial independence of the regions. The draft constitution (Article 153) establishes a body for inter-governance coordination called the Consultative Council of Local Governance that includes governors and aims at strengthening cooperation and conflict resolution, and advises the central authorities on legislation proposals and budget and other issues with a potential effect on local governance.

Articles 145, 147–152 open the door for the further expanding of the functions and duties of local bodies. They further award them the power to issue regulations in accordance with the constitution and national laws. Their domain of functions and duties includes all that relates to public amenities and service provisions in the sectors of education, health, social affairs, economic affairs, tourism, urban planning, environment, civil affairs, and municipal police. The central executive powers have the right to devolve any of its functions and have the authority to contract these to local authorities and duly compensate them. This further consolidates local governance units while implying independent yet interlinked and interdependent levels of authority.

The financial independence outlined in Articles 145, 148, and 150 of the draft constitution provides grounds for a broader financial decentralization. It gives the governorates and municipalities the right to attain financial resources from the national budget, so as to enable them perform their functions. The financial decentralization offered in these articles is unprecedented in Libya's local government history. It allows local authorities to invest, receive grants or wills, and acquire loans and any other possible sources of income. It indicates that competition and solidarity should be maintained among councils, as well as a liberal approach as it opens unlimited possibilities for local authorities to seek financial resources.

According to Article 148, the state guarantees maintaining of the financial balance among the local government units in a manner that ensures harmony. Therefore, no local authority can assume any function or competence such as executing projects unless it has available appropriate financial resources in its budget provisions. Article 151, which allows for the setting up of partnerships between governorates and municipalities to achieve integration, only consolidates this approach. It also indicates that local governance units have the right to set up joint economic zones that serve their interests. This extensive broad decentralization model even allows locals to enter into foreign partnerships (supervised by the central authority) to help achieve development.

Such a far-reaching model of decentralization is almost unlimited, except for the general provision that it cannot contradict national laws. According to Article 150, the central executive authority has no right to interfere in the work of local governance units unless they exceed or undertake what is beyond their functions and role. This also applies to limiting the interference of central authorities to follow up and afterward control the activities of local units. This applies to cases of local governments becoming unable to perform their functions or their refusal to be accountable to norms, policies, and national plans, as well as inflicting harm to public interests or those of other local governments.

The draft constitution also envisages the establishment of an Advisory Council for Local Government, its members made up of all governors. Article 152 assigns this council the duties of providing recommendations on draft laws related to planning, budget, local finance, and any other laws related to local governance. The council may also propose relevant draft laws. Its main role, however, remains that of strengthening coordination and cooperation among local government units and with the executive authorities. It also has a conflict resolution role. Both competing Libyan governments have attempted to employ local government tools and mechanisms to cement their support and constituency. Both governments have also devolved many functions to municipalities and sought assistance from international actors to achieve this goal.

In September 2019, a Libyan Local Government Forum was held in Tunis with help from United States Agency for International Development (USAID), the World Bank, and the German state cooperation agency (GIZ) and was attended by local officials from across Libya. The objective was to help streamline the work of local entities and improve their financial management and service delivery. The participants highlighted the importance of developing a strategic roadmap to support decentralization. In fact, many foreign actors, including NGOs, have been involved in supporting municipalities at the expense of the central governments on the assumption that improving their service delivery capacities is far more important than conflict resolution. However, such objectives remain abstract as long as the political divide and civil war continue threatening Libya's unity and social cohesion. Both government interventions and the aggressive international support in favor of municipalities may bring in yet more challenges for the Libyan state and its stability. This is particularly the case since further empowering local entities through foreign support bestows upon them legitimacy from the outside, which actually weakens an already weak-fragile center thus posing more challenges to the country's transition from conflict.

Civil service: Continuity despite change

Despite all political and structural changes and uncertainties, the civil service remains subject to Act 55 of 1976. It outlines the organization and governance of public administration, including recruitment, salary scale, promotion, and discipline. However, this act has not been reformed in the past four decades.

Overall, the pre-2011 legal framework for public administration remains almost intact. Central specialized authorities and sector ministries remain the essential components of public administration. A major issue has been how government's policies, or the lack thereof, have been reactive rather than proactive. All post-Gaddafi governments lacked any clear-cut policies and objectives and relied on answering concerns and providing resources and creating local bodies to respond to local pressures. This is likely to remain the case given the ongoing conflict, which almost eroded the ability of the central authority to act, in return enabling the periphery to flourish at its expense.

Good governance: A continuing challenge

The absence of the state and its institutions, exacerbated by the increase in the number of armed militias that hijacked the state's institutions and harnessed them for partisan or tribal and regional interests, led to the creation of more reason for conflict. Many new arrangements and institutions were established to serve existing actors, or to respond to the interests and demands of particular agendas. At the same time, institutions have become a manifestation of conflict, reflecting deepening division and the further entrenchment of the conflict. Rushing to an early electoral process in 2012 before the realization of an agreement on a unified vision for the desired state caused more social polarization both horizontally and vertically. This, in addition to the neglect of the requirements of effective and successful conflict resolution, meant that economic recovery and state-building became remote possibilities (ACBF, 2004, p. 4).

The UN-led LPA has not been able to tackle division and conflict since it lacks a clear consensus on important issues, and ironically, the GNA has not even been able to escape its internal division. Power-sharing arrangements of the LPA have not achieved the desirable outcome as developments so far have only confirmed the inability of the bodies, resulting from the *Skhirat* Agreement, to unite, gain legitimacy, work together, and act in a coherent and uniform manner. The result has been more division, chaos, and civil war, leading Libya to witness its bloodiest phase since General Haftar's rise to power in 2014, and culminating with the LNA launching an offensive to capture Tripoli on April 4, 2019.

GNA has been exploiting the support and legitimacy it received from the UN, but apparently failing to be truly representative of all parties. The GNA in Tripoli and its rival in Bayda have constructed façade bodies and organizations. This is similar to what took place in Somalia where the regime sought to justify external interventions through a technique to copycat organizations associated with the Weberian state, while, in reality, such organizations were used to channel funds to elites. While foreign intervention intensifies, both sides and other actors seek to increase the profile of local actors through projects that proclaim the objective of local capacity building. As the Somali experience indicates, such steps and interventions only tuned out to be an extra burden and did not lead to the desired objectives (Clausen, 2016, pp. 301–302).

Libya's oil wealth promises the population a "soft option" in seeking employment in government. But the government cannot provide enough real jobs. Thus "hidden employment" overburdens the public sector and starves the private sector of manpower. The political and economic costs created by this imbalance are mounting. Public administration has to be transformed into a professional merit-based system. A new Civil Service Act is urgently needed to replace the outdated law that has been in practice for the last six decades. The new legislation should create a civil service that is an organ of the state, one that responsible before the public. The law, the democratic government, and its employees should be politically neutral.

Another necessary mechanism to achieve the objectives is to create an independent and neutral Civil Service Commission (CSC). Such badly needed body will be tasked with effecting the desired reform and restructuring at all levels of public administration while maintaining a merit-based and professional civil service. Its role could be consolidated and given priority with the establishment of a high profile inter-ministerial committee subordinate to the prime minister or a minister in charge of the civil service (UNDP, 2015).

These challenges have helped create an atmosphere of irresponsibility and a lack of accountability. The following problems result in:

- an erosion of the average citizens' trusts in the government and consequent skepticism, even cynicism, about democracy and the merits of the uprising and the political change it brought about in 2011;
- a lack of truth-telling by ordinary citizens who also do not raise the alarm against corruption and illegal practices, officials, and experts for fear of reprisal from competing actors and the militias, who have been enjoying impunity;
- corrupt behavior in authorities, and resulting criminal activities.

Good governance or lack thereof, has remained a persistent challenge for Libya which has not adopted any policy to realize such a goal. No legal provisions exist that indicate government concern with governance related issues and practices, despite Gaddafi-era reform and the ensuing transition in the post-2011 uprisings. Currently, there is no official government policy or any reporting on governance. All material available are those published by foreign sources, including UN agencies and programs like UNDP, WB, IMF or academic research papers and journalism. The post-Gaddafi governments have not paid any attention to good governance despite strong recommendations from UN agencies and some foreign governments. Good governance remains outside government occupation and nothing that resembles a strategy or some of its features exist (Libyan Organization of Policies & Strategies, 2016).

Human resources: Recruitment, grades, salaries, training, and capacity building

The 1976 legislation provides no mechanism for recruitment into the civil service. Employment is through executive appointment—not based on merit—reflecting political, regional, tribal, and personal relations. The dominant rentier culture considers civil service jobs to be a right, especially for graduates and school-leavers. Appointment can take place at both regional and national levels, making the government bureaucracy a safety net. The civil service has become a major employer, a trend that has intensified after 2011, with hundreds of thousands added to the government payroll every year. Female employees make up a considerable portion of civil servants, especially in the education and health sectors where they are a majority. In 2015, the Audit Bureau claimed that there are currently 1.5 million public administration employees in Libya and this has risen to 1.6 million employees in 2017. Unofficial estimates reveal that the number of people receiving state paid salaries has actually reached 2.5 million, including an estimated 500,000 ghost or "phantom" workers or duplicates on the public administration payroll (Libyan Audit Bureau, 2015, 2017).

Throughout Libya's modern history, most recruitment into the public sector was often based on nepotism instead of the qualifications of the applicant. Since 2011, the country continues to struggle with nepotism in recruitments, and public officials keep nurturing their own personal networks instead of ensuring a well-functioning public administration that aims at realizing the public good. Nepotism in recruitments not only excludes potential qualified staff from employment opportunities in the public sector but also creates a culture where public officials owe loyalty to the person or tribe that has helped them secure employment (Transparency International, 2015)

Transparency International reports that though the current legal framework provides sufficient measures and guidelines on appointments, promotions, and how to prevent political interference and conflicting interests, "rules are only rarely enforced efficiently and as a result, external interference, especially in relation to appointments and promotions of civil servants, often take place" (Transparency International, 2014). A direct effect has been that public sector's recruitment process becoming almost fully unregulated, resulting in vast overemployment as well as employees holding duplicate positions in the public sector (Libyan Audit Bureau, 2017). This has also led to a public sector being staffed with under-qualified individuals, thus crippling a sector with already poor capacities and an increasing neglect of regulations, wasting badly needed resources, and leading to bad management and widespread corruption. This, in turn, further damages what remains of an integral system and increases peoples' frustrations and lack of trust in the state, thereby causing the value of institutions retreat in the public eye in favor of militias and other non-state actors that have come to fill this vacuum.

Despite recent decrees by the Government of National Unity raising salaries for employees at many sectors, civil service salaries are essentially determined according to a law (Law 15 of 1981, as amended), which sets out a hierarchy of 13 grades with matching salaries, which increase annually by a small margin, based on years of experience and qualifications. This law also establishes a system of annual reports to evaluate the employees' performance so as to determine their promotion accordingly. Employees are, however, almost universally promoted, making these reports a mere formality (UNDESA, 2004a, 2004c). All civil service employees enjoy social security and a state pension. The system has in place incentives for hard work and devotion awards for excellence and training. However, these have been subject to favoritism, and the annual performance reports are seldom taken into consideration.[9]

Civil service training and capacity building was, for a long time, exclusively done by the National Administrative Institute. Although there has been no official evaluation of the quality of its contribution, the private sector has been permitted to set up private training facilities offering demand-driven executive and technical training to civil servants.[10] The transitional authorities have also neglected earlier plans to set up a state-run school of business and government. Training schemes in foreign countries have not affected the civil service positively, given the political stalemate in the country since 2013. Previous cooperation with some British universities, including the London School of Economic and Political Science, has been frozen or abandoned. Capacity building has not received the required attention throughout the transition.

However, many foreign countries and organizations provided help to Libyan authorities in this regard, but the results have been rather moderate and their success rather difficult to evaluate. Between 2012 and 2019, the European Commission lent Libya direct support through working with the ministry of planning to provide public administration capacity building. Similar assistance was provided by the UNDP and the German government through German Foundation for International Cooperation (GIZ), Italian Agency for Development Cooperation (AICS), the USAID, the Association of Dutch Municipalities (VNG), and Expertise France (EF). However, these schemes were eventually limited and either confined to one department at the ministry or did not materialize. Most of the activities were ad hoc trainings in select line ministries that focused on formulating requests for technical assistance and strengthening capacity to adopt a robust donor coordination mechanism and did not go beyond that. Foreign assistance has also been behind many similar trainings on governance and capacity-building initiatives.

Noticeable among these has been a three-year program, the "Libya Local Governance and Stabilization program." Funded by the EU and the Dutch Government, the program has the overall objective of strengthening and empowering local governance in Libya, especially the management of select municipal councils, service delivery by local government, and the participation and interaction of civil society in council's affairs and conflict prevention. In 2019, a similar program, the "Recovery, Stability and Socio-economic Development of Libya program," was set up and was funded by the EU, through the Emergency Trust Fund for Africa, North Africa Window. The initiative was geared toward supporting the capacities of local public authorities and administrations in providing basic and social services while improving timely and quality access to these services, in particular for the most vulnerable people.

Public budgeting and finance

During the Gaddafi era, a number of weaknesses in budget planning, preparation, and execution were identified by the World Bank and the International Monetary Fund. These have still to be tackled. "The new government has not yet had an opportunity to address these weaknesses, which have been compounded in practice by the damage and upheaval associated with the revolution" (World Bank & IMF, 2013, p. 37). Six key weaknesses were identified:

1 Budget formulation remains fragmented and mostly driven by a mechanical and incremental approach, especially for current spending.
2 Although the capital projects component of the development budget (Chapter 3) is prepared and authorized on a three-year basis, capital budget spending is not guided/constrained by an overall ceiling as determined by a Medium-Term Fiscal Framework (MTFF) in line with government's fiscal policy objectives, nor are projects always selected on grounds of developmental priority.
3 The preparation of development budgets follows two separate and uncoordinated processes, with institutional separation both at the central and at line ministries/agencies levels.

4 There are a number of issues in budget presentation, classification, and coverage. The budget classification does not follow internationally accepted standards and the distinction between "current" and "capital" allocations is blurred.
5 The coverage of the budget circular is limited to wages and goods and services (chapters I and II) and does not provide guidance on macroeconomic parameters such as GDP growth and inflation, which need to be taken into account in ministries' budget proposals. The budget circular does not provide ceilings for budget preparation by line ministries/agencies.
6 The budget is yet to become an effective policy tool. The linkage between the government's policy priorities and budgetary allocations remains weak and is not articulated in a budget policy/strategy paper. No distinction is also made between ongoing and new policies and initiatives.

In terms of Libya's public finances, the lack of security and widening space of conflict has dealt a heavy blow to the country's public revenue as oil production and exportation has almost stopped. This has had serious impacts on the national budget, with large fiscal deficits reaching an all-time high. It has had a destructive effect on the economy, as the balance of payment's current account deficit has also reached a record high. The effect on the standard of living has also been visible. With no proper taxation system in place, governments at all levels are, without sufficient resources, facing enormous challenges. Irregular budget allocations are spent, almost completely, on the salaries and running costs of an oversized civil service.

The draft constitution of 2017 foresaw the authorization elected municipal councils and regional governments to raise their own revenue, and this would on top of all else oblige the central government to allocate a prescribed share of the national revenue to local government bodies.

Public-sector ethics and integrity system

Corruption

Libya has been characterized as a country with high corruption rates, including the civil service sector as all sectors, including public procurement and oil, have significant corruption rates while bribery and favoritism remain common practices. Nine years since the collapse of the former regime, there has been an escalation of and rapid spread of bribery, corruption, and mismanagement. The root causes of these problems are numerous, but poor public resources management is a key deficiency (Wijaya & Shariha, 2016). Some attempts were made during the Gaddafi era to combat corruption, which somewhat improved the country's rankings in corruption indexes, but the trend has since been reversed. According to the latest report of World Lists, Libya is eighth among the top-ten most corrupt countries of the world.[11] The squandering and embezzlement of public funds for personal, partisan, and regional gains have only increased in recent years; Libya is the 172nd least corrupt nation out of 180 countries (Transparency International, 2018) and scored 17 points out of 100, according to the 2021 Corruption Perceptions Index reported by Transparency International (Trading Economics, 2021, https://tradingeconomics.com/libya/corruption-index).

As corruption has continued almost unchecked, it has hindered an already weak, inefficient, and divided public administration. Corruption also runs through local government. A majority of financial resources disappear in every budget allocation. The current conflict situation also accelerates the incidence and magnitude of corruption. The penal code, and other specialized legal frameworks, all deal with corruption by prohibiting favoritism, nepotism, bribery, theft, and misuse by employees of their responsibilities in order to enrich themselves or their relatives.

This spread of corruption may be explained by the fact that 80 percent of the country's GDP and, of course 99 percent of state revenue, are drawn from oil and gas exports. The revenue from these exports is received and deposited in a transitional account at the state-owned Libyan Foreign Bank and then transferred to the country's Central Bank that controls state funds and dispenses them. There are no laws that demand the transparency of the bank to disclose the use of state funds with their constituents. The legal system lacks most prerequisites for combating corruption in addition to lacking an enforcement mechanism, though some are found, for example, in the penal code and the Law on Economic Crimes and the Law on Abuse of Position or Occupation (Macaraniag, 2019).

There also exists a number of institutions and independent bodies tasked with combating corruption, including the public audit office—the authority responsible for administrative control—and a national authority responsible for promoting transparency and combating corruption, but their inefficiencies and partisan political orientations limit their impact on corruption.

The institutional framework that governs corruption prevention also remains weak and fragile. On December 14, 2014, the General National Congress adopted Law No. 11 of 2014 to establish the National Anti-Corruption Commission. However, despite its formal existence and allocation of state budget, this body is ridden with corruption at worst and dysfunctional at best. It has been subject to political and regional disagreements regarding its administration.

The conflict makes corruption even wider, causing impunity to be the name of the game. This is particularly the case with militias and security bodies that are legally and practically protected from investigation, exacerbating corruption and impunity. Law No. 38 of 2012, which grants militias a pardon and immunity form persecution for human rights violations or other criminal and illegal acts, including corruption, is a case in point. According to a report assessing the Libyan integrity system:

"There are hardly any anti-corruption activities in these institutions and the few initiatives taken have not been sufficient to significantly combat corruption and inform about the devastating effects corruption has on the economy and the country as a whole. The internal institutional governance is also poor, especially in terms of integrity mechanisms. A low level of integrity in the public sector is fundamental for the entire Libyan integrity system. The relatively new-founded National Anti-Corruption Commission has so far not been able to fulfil its mandate. The lack of proper qualified staff hampers development opportunities and ability of CSOs to fulfil their role as watchdogs."[12]

Transparency and accountability

Public administration still suffers from the effects of lacking any proper mechanism for transparency and accountability. After the fall of the Gaddafi regime, it appears as though the transitional authorities and the rebels-turned-officials were happy with the continuation of unaccountability. For the rebels who took charge of the country, their first order of business was self-enrichment. The lack of the rule of law, the ongoing conflict and insecurity, and an inefficient judiciary have all contributed to wider corruption in the post-Gaddafi era. The negative impact of these shortcomings has been multiplied by a culture of impunity (Wijaya & Shariha, 2016). The latest anti-corruption report released by GAN's Risk & Compliance Portal indicates that the Libyan regulatory system "lacks transparency and the and the legal and policy frameworks are difficult to navigate" (Gan Integrity Report, 2019).

The spread of corruption and lack of accountability led the UN Secretary-General's Special Representative in Libya (UNSGSR), Ghassan Salame, to openly criticize the situation. He pointed out that the extent of looting in Libya was incalculable and could not be assessed, highlighting the need for greater transparency. Astonished at the scale of corruption, the UNSGSR declared: "In Libya, everyday there is a new millionaire and the middles class shrinks more and more day in and day out" ([The] Libya Observer, March 19, 2019). Salame openly accused the political leaders in Libya of corruption beyond expression. He indicated that the worst is their exploitation of their posts to take money and employ it abroad to their own benefit, and not in their country ([The] Libya Observer, March 19, 2019).

Lack of transparency and accountability amid political struggle meant Libya was making foreign investments, leading to unprecedented plunder of Libyan state funds in foreign countries. Reports reveal that this has also been possible thanks to cooperation between corrupt officials and specialized networks. The Islamists played an important role in this, and they created the rumor that these investments and assets were Gaddafi's personal funds, even though they are registered in the name of the Libyan state and its institutions.

Role of civil society

Civil society in Libya is a rather new phenomenon that has for long suffered from the domination of the state over four decades of authoritarian rule. Gaddafi considered civil society a part of his own design for direct democracy and thus incorporated it into the formal governance system. As Mogherbi (1995) indicates, civil society, professional associations, and trade unions were part of the formal system in what resembled state corporatism that had no room for an independent civil society and led to the criminalization of political parties. Civil society had no governance space of its own in which it could play a role (Mogherbi, 1995). Civil society organizations (CSOs) mushroomed in post-Gaddafi Libya benefiting from the euphoria that followed the downfall of the regime as well as the holding of the country's first free elections. Their activities became wide ranging and included all fields that had hitherto been prohibited by the previous regime, including political and human rights and minority issues.

Civil society reflected a wide range of issues from gender, charity, and rights, to political activism. Islamist groups have figured prominently in civil society, as have regional and tribal practices of civil society, while the entire scene reflected divisions and competition (Bertelsmann Stiftung, BTI [Bertelsmann Stiftung's Transformation Index], 2016). Despite the fact that a number of laws opened the doors for the development of independent CSOs, their role and participation remained unclear, and the transitional constitution and the LGL neglected them altogether (Sawani, 2012). However, the latest CDA draft of 2017 (Article 41) enshrines the independence of CSOs and obliges authorities to guarantee their freedom. The draft ensures the legal protection of CSOs against government intrusion into their freedom by making a court ruling a must before any action is to be taken against them or before an order for their dissolution.[13]

Most of Libyan CSOs are actually inexperienced, lack any proper understanding of the role civil society should be playing, and are in many cases instruments for opportunism, money and social/political standing or prestige. A great part of CSOs is established and dominated by individuals while governance within is not democratic or even clear. Some CSOs do actually represent families or relatives and friends who employ it for different purposes. In many cases, the establishment of an organization demonstrates an attitude of wishing to go with the trend. Most do not actually have offices and rely on contacts and at best social media while most of their web pages are defunct or have not been updated for ages.

Cooperation among CSOs is quite rare and any exchanges are a result of contesting with one another. Seldom do CSOs reveal their governance structures, their management, and their finances. This may be partially at least explained by the fact that CSOs have been essentially dominated either by individuals or Islamists who use it as fronts for ideological and political purposes and this particularly true of those established during the political crisis.[14]

Gender equality: Secularism, patriarchy, and Sharia

During the Gaddafi era, Libya adopted many gender-sensitive legislations, policies, and practical steps reflecting "positive discrimination" that promoted the involvement of women in civil service and public life. Women were legally equal to men and laws left no room for discrimination against women and stressed the principle of equal opportunity. Women assumed ministerial and other senior positions, including in the army, security services, and the judiciary (Mahmoud, 2006).

Females are attracted to civil service employment, as their workload and some cultural factors allow them an easy entrance and lesser responsibilities. The secular and gender equality-based policies of the Gaddafi regime were fundamentally what enlarged women's share in civil service. Al-Hadad (2015, p. 68) has concluded, "Libya tends to have [workplace equal opportunities] policies; however, they tend to be too general and do not specify or utilize exact and well-defined terminology... [they leave] great room for discrimination and corrupt interpretation within legislation and regulations by government and delegated bodies."

The draft constitution of 2017 does, however, enshrine more gender equality rights. It awards women equal political and civil rights and prohibits any form of discrimination against women, making it a criminal act to withhold or deprive any citizen from their rights based on gender. It enshrines equal opportunity in all aspects and before the law, making its realization the duty of the state. Article 57 obliges state authorities to take all necessary measures to protect women, promote their social welfare, and combat cultural prejudices and traditions that degrade women and discriminate against them. Any contradictory future law would be unconstitutional. Article 270 prescribes a female quota of 25 percent in the membership of the two legislative chambers and local councils. This quota must remain in place for 12 years after the adoption of the constitution.[15]

However, gender issues related to women rights, employment, and equal opportunity, as well as in the workplace, remain in flux and reflect the pre-2011 situation. Currently, Libya has laws or policies that tend to be too general and do not specify or utilize exact and well-defined terminology. Great room for discrimination does exist. Examples of a reversal trend are numerous. In particular, reference could be made to the removal of the previous restrictions on polygamy, the Grand Mufti's fatwa against the UN Report on Violence Against Women considering it against Islamic values requesting the government not to adhere to its provisions, and the limited number of ministerial and senior positions awarded to women. This further demonstrates how Salafist tendencies have employed Sharia to curtail women's rights and empowerment. Although women gained their voice during the uprising, obstacles to their greater political participation and long-term, sustainable gender equality set by the new government, may prevent their voices from being heard in post-Gaddafi Libya. Leading women activists indicate that despite the transitional authorities' pledges to empower women, actual policies and laws lack a gender-sensitive approach to counter new kinds of political violence and exclusion.

Many fatwas have been issued after 2011 and they all move in a direction that restores rigid Sharia law and its interpretations. Some sheikhs and the Mufti continuously issue fatwas restricting the rights of women. They propagate their reactionary views in talk shows and in Friday mosque sermons. This has led to imposing an "Islamic" dress code, banning the import of cosmetic products, shutting down women beauty and hair salons, and forbidding women from traveling unaccompanied by their husbands, fathers or brothers or those who they, according to Sharia, should not marry. Segregation at schools, including primary schools, or at universities has been imposed in many regions. A fatwa from March 2013 by Libya's grand mufti stipulating that women can attend a university only if it is gender-segregated caused an uproar. An earlier call by the cleric had gone even further, calling for gender segregation in all public institutions, universities, and hospitals. The March 2013 fatwa also called on female students to dress according to Islamic traditions, which include covering the hair, to lessen the dangers of "mixing" between the genders.

One example that relates to Gaddafi-era provisions is the rights of women to become judges. The Islamists brought a case regarding this before the Supreme Court, asking the court to consider the employment of women as judges against Sharia and to nullify it. Though the case has not been ruled on yet, activists feel that in practice women's appointment into the judiciary has been already restricted. Women were discouraged from joining the army and the police sectors while the only two female academies established during Gaddafi were shut down. There remain some women who work in the police and the army but with limited numbers and duties such as guarding women prisoners and interrogating women suspects. At airports, there are women working in immigration and customs and deal with women travelers. Society's reaction is not easy to measure but there are many voices that speak about women losing rights. The intense debate over the role of Sharia in law is an indication of some Libyan's fear of more extremism and hardline reactionary policies against women.

Much of what women may be able to gain or, rather, be deprived of, is closely connected to the fact that the deeply patriarchal Libyan social order considers women to be inferior to men. It also depends on the outcome of an ongoing struggle to control Libya, between Salafist and extremist Islamists on the one hand, and their liberal or moderate Islamist rivals on the other. The post-Gaddafi order is still in transition, but some steps taken by the authorities may well herald a reversal of the progress made during the Gaddafi era toward gender equality in law. Referring to Spellman-Poots (2011), Jurasz (2013) and Langhi (2013a, 2013b) observe "the ways in which the new Libyan state chooses to appropriate or obliterate the remnants of Gaddafi's gender regime also remain to be seen."

However, the issue is sensitive and is closely connected to Libyan culture, which is patriarch in nature and not gender-sensitive. Libyan society still rejects the idea of gender equality—even women themselves tend to hold conservative views about what they can and cannot do. After years of zero accountability, individuals, paramilitaries, and militias are imposing "self-justice" according to their own standards and beliefs. Married women do have a better social standing than single or divorced women. Single women are always seen and looked at as in need of guidance, guardianship and should not live on their own. Divorced women are even less empowered as they are considered less worthy of independence and should be protected and controlled, otherwise their honor may be in jeopardy. Married women are the responsibility of their husbands while the single or the divorced are a potential risk to the reputation of their families and, thus, must be restricted. Globally, the labor force participation rate of women is 52 percent.

Libya's Gaddafi-era legal framework consisted of laws and key international declarations that ensured equality between women and men. Traditionally, women worked in sectors such as education, and were encouraged and supported to work in these areas by policies in place. Gaddafi-era policies since the early 1980s have focused on establishing female institutes for teachers and nurses while the government made elementary education almost a domain for female teachers only. Ninety-three percent of women work in the state/government sectors.

Currently, women still occupy most jobs in education while positions they hold in health sector and government civil service are also high. They are also active in sectors such as agriculture and their role in the private sector is increasing with businesswomen setting up their own businesses. According to the World Bank, women make up 24.6 percent of the national work force, which is about 50 percent of the total population.[16] There are no recent data available, but according to some studies, the labor force participation rate among young women aged 15–24 is 19 percent, while the corresponding percentage for young men is 53 percent. For women aged 15 years and above, the labor force participation rate is 25 percent (compared to 79 percent for men).[17]

No real regional differences are worth mentioning except that in rural areas, women's employment is almost limited to education. Remuneration is governed by the same legal provisions and these do not impose any disparity based on gender. Law number 12 issued in 2010 dictates that employment is the right of all male and female citizens. It also outlines that women should not be forced to work in areas that contradicts their "nature." It categorically rejects discrimination in work and pay and other related areas like compensation, leaves, social security, and pensions, and favors women's early retirement over men. It also allows special provisions for pregnant and nursing mothers. It forbids sacking women while pregnant or nursing, giving pregnant women three months of paid vacation as per Social Security Law. These rights were consolidated by Law number 20/1991, which is called the Law for the Consolidation of Freedom.

Gaddafi-era laws and policies encouraged women's political participation and in many instances in contradiction to existing interpretations of Sharia. Women organizations were set up to help "liberate" them along with special popular congresses for women to participate in his style of direct democracy. Many women occupied leading positions. At some time, it was obligatory that each leading government or legislative position, locally, regionally and nationally, had positions open for women.

However, the post-Gaddafi transition has not so far brought in any significant change. The NTC had 150 members, only two of whom were women (4 percent) while its executive only had one female member among 15 total memberships. The 2012 parliamentary election, however, saw voters elect 33 women to the 200-member General National Congress. The electoral law included a gender parity provision requiring each party to place their female candidates in an alternating pattern with male candidates on their lists to ensure that women were elected. But the first transitional government of 2012 had 26 ministers and tens of deputies of which only two ministers and six deputies were women. The subsequent 2013 government had 31 members with only two females. As of 2017, the HoR has only 30 female deputies out of total 188 (15.96 percent).[18] Most of them are not active and seldom appear in debates. The same applies to the HCS which includes some female members who are basically members of the Muslim Brotherhood.

Libyan women have become more involved in civil society after the fall of the Gaddafi regime. They are most active in organizations that focus on women advocacy and humanitarian and social activities and issues. The conflict in Libya poses important challenges to women's meaningful exercise of their rights and engagement in the transition and the advancement of gender equality in the country, including the ability to create inclusive governance institutions. The most significant obstacle to women's full exercise of human rights, political participation, and share of decision-making roles is currently the unchecked militarization and violent extremism plaguing Libya today, which have perpetuated armed conflict and war crimes.[19]

E-government in Libya: Much to be desired

A review of UN reports suggests that Libya still lags behind in the field of ICT in general and e-governance in particular (UNDESA, 2004b, 2004d, 2010, 2014). It is in the lower margin of countries with a rather low online service performance relative to income, with a near-bottom rank on the service index that measures the value and role of online service utility and its impact on the provision of services and on business environment (UNDESA, 2014). It also falls behind in terms of e-governance readiness even compared to other countries in the MENA region (Asogwa, 2011). The poor state of the IT sector and its late adoption of new technology hindered the development of any worthwhile e-services with the exception of a number of limited services as publishing national examinations results, National Identification Number queries, and some limited SMS-based services in the banking sector or point of sale (POS) transactions.

Though the first National Information System (NATIS) was adopted in the mid-1970s putting the country ahead of the region in paying attention to information technology (IT), the Libyan government's official website first came online only in 2008, when, along with economic reforms, Libya acquired the necessary new technologies. A state internet provider was established, enabling the country to improve marginally its global ranking in 2008 (UNDESA, 2014). In 2010, Libya took the initiative with a new project—E-Libya—aimed at turning the country into an IT literate and information-based society. Just before the popular uprisings against Gaddafi regime erupted in early 2011, internet services and social media use increased dramatically (Mohamed, 2017).

According to Forti et al. (2014, p. 323), "The Libyan government has 70 percent of its national ministries online, with provision of information about services." This development was well placed within a broader vision of Libya's future and had the aim of increasing its competitiveness, but fell well short of a full-fledged internet-based government engagement with the citizens. Although the government included an ITC component in its National Inclusive Economic and Social Strategy that sought to increase citizens' role in the policy process, government ministries' websites remain underdeveloped. The Information and Telecommunication Authority contracted a multinational company in 2013 to execute the project in a five-year plan that should move the country into transitioning fully to e-services in 2018. The project included e-government, open government (access to information), e-commerce, and e-education, but it has stalled because of current insecurities.[20] However, this ambitious goal remains remote as the country descended into chaos and political division that escalated into another cycle of civil war in 2019–2020.

Though much of the recessive conditions during Gaddafi era could by understood in light of the ultra-concern the regime had with security, the end of the authoritarian regime seems to have had a limited impact on the situation. The post-Gaddafi period has so far not witnessed any real ICT development in any field, so Libya remains essentially behind the rest of countries in the MENA region or in those of the Middle Income Group as identified by the UNDP. Users struggle with terribly slow internet speed and are only able to interact with the government via e-mails (Forti et al., 2014). The latest available data suggest, however, that Libyan internet-users have increased in number, to an all-time high of some 1.3 million (some 20 percent of the total population) and are, more importantly, growing at annual rate of 9 percent (Al-Kilani & Kobziev, 2015). According to the ICT readiness index, Libya ranks as the lowest forth country (from 144 countries) when it comes to the availability of new technology, according to the 2015 Global Competitiveness Report. In the area of internet usage by citizens and broadband subscriptions, Libya also fared very low, coming in at 108th and 106th, respectively.

Forti et al. (2014) argue that government of Libya must continue to improve its e-government services in order to be able to conduct online government transactions. ICT infrastructure is available but it is not designed with the objective of e-governance in mind. All government departments and authorities and other public institutions funded by the central government, as well as local bodies, have been acquiring hardware and employ a significant number of IT and computer specialists. Most central and municipal authorities have some kind of web presence, but this falls shorter than required and attempting to use it for services is cumbersome. The governmental websites particularly at the local level' "fall short in terms of their quality and achieving their potential as viable outreach tools …. it opens to a beautifully edited, colourful homepage with a host of broken links and virtually empty comment sections."[21]

However, such developments do not really spring from the belief in the merits of e-governance. Government officials still think that all it takes is a website (Sweisi, 2010). As Al-Kilani and Kobziev (2015, p. 817) observe, "most of the ICT infrastructure in Libya is designed to be used within the organization and is not centred on citizen services." And as Basu (2004) commented, "[g]overnments departments in Libya are using different ICT tools which make it difficult to centralize the services from various departments and avail to citizens through e-government platform." Recent studies indicate that Libyan government websites have significant usability problems and most of these are rated as major and catastrophic. Karaim and Inal (2019, p. 207) conducted an analysis of these websites and concluded that they violate heuristic criteria, including "visibility of system status, user control and freedom, user help recognize. Diagnosis and recover from errors." Moreover, all Libyan government websites failed the "A Checker" tool that measures the accessibility and had major problems regarding search functionality (Karaim & Inal, 2019).

Libyan public administration: Challenges and opportunities

Libya is currently dominated by militias and its resources are squandered by, a multitude of non-state actors. Dysfunctionality became the order of the day with critical lack of control over public spending which led to further corruption and squandering of public funds at unprecedented level. This has had the effect of bringing the state to near collapse. The most substantial power currently lies outside the formal system. This has only helped to create an atmosphere of irresponsibility, corruption, lack of accountability, and to waste much needed resources for reconstruction and development. Graft and rent-seeking by politicians and officials at all levels has reduced the ability of citizens to hold the government to account, aided, and abetted by successor governments over many decades not seeing the need to tax the population to keep functioning. Therefore, any future government must be concerned with diversifying the economy to avoid oil dependency, with creating a more pluralistic and entrepreneurial private sector and fostering a culture of accountability.

The future government needs to take measures to grow civil society and a free media. So, it is necessary to educate and motivate citizens to play an active part in their country's governance and take more responsibility for their individual circumstances. A strong central government would have the ability to develop and implement coherent national strategies for reform and development; to ensure the proper distribution of national income and resources (especially of oil) based on need and national priorities; and to promote national identity (and consequently social cohesion) above regional or tribal affiliations.

UNESCWA (2013, p. 20) has described Libya as a "unique model where the central government will, at some stage in the future, have to negotiate with various tribes, towns and cities, their local councils and militias to convince them to restore some of the governance functions and mandates of the central government." However, negotiating with contending non-state actors—particularly militias—has proved to be more than a conundrum for all post-Gaddafi governments. Especially convincing them of the merits of this objective is not entirely dependent on central government's ability to negotiate but rather importantly on the willingness of these actors to forsake the stakes levied on them by their foreign backers.

The turbulent political environment and an ongoing struggle poses two fundamental challenges most evident in transitional phases. According to Böckenförde and Megerisi (2016, p. 8), "Groups are advocating models of decentralization on the premise that now is the right time to do so, as this opportunity might not be available in the future." The obvious rationale is that a weak central government is also a weak negotiator. Such attitudes are indicative of expediency and political opportunism. This was evidently clear when regional and local groups calling for federalism in the eastern part of Libya interfered with the work of the CDA and attempted to force the adoption of their model by its members.

Another serious challenge relates to the evolving and changing attitudes of public opinion. Implementing wider decentralization could lead to national integration becoming an elusive target, as it would strengthen the already stronger local, regional, and tribal identities. The ambitious model suggested in the contested draft constitution of 2017 ignores that localism and regionalism are now at their highest, but this is likely to change, given the evolving nature of transition. It is therefore most important that the draft constitution, when eventually put to referendum, includes some precautionary measures to cater for such dynamics. There is a need for building nationwide consensus around fiscal decentralization to promote national development. The debate about regionalism that has been disruptive to the constitutional process needs to be reconsidered, not as a political choice but as one tied to national development priorities (Democracy Reporting International, 2013).

Any proposal must introduce bottom-up initiatives that help establish appropriate links between the state and the citizenry and ensure social and political inclusion. As far as development is concerned, bottom-up approaches are strategically positioned so that a participatory model of planning and a democratic economic model that rectifies the imbalances in the distribution of resources regionally and by sector are guaranteed. This would be instrumental to fostering a self-sustaining and locally driven governance system that could trigger and reinforce development. This would also be instrumental in effecting a well-functioning local government or decentralized system. In the immediate future, there is a need to establish credible institutions and for these to be awarded rights that help make the state and the central government's capacity stronger. The country needs to have an inclusive debate over formulating a national vision for decentralization and local governance to be enshrined in legislation and the final constitution.

A major hindrance to the democratic transition has been the exclusionary policies and practices put in place since 2012. Public administration has suffered as a result of banning civil servants who occupied top or medium level positions during the previous regime. Hundreds of thousands of state employees were banned under the pretext of lustration of public administration from Gaddafi era officials as prescribed in the 2013 Administrative and Political Isolation Law, thus depriving the civil service from their indispensable expertise. As state audit reports indicate, hiring public personnel has been nothing but a corrupt and political process of opportunism, unguided by any development policy and devoid of effecting institutional strength, capacity building and efficiency.

Libya clearly lacks a well-developed public administration system despite the fact its public workforce as a percentage of the total workforce is largest in the world. Given the role played by local councils and an array of militias, regional, and tribal actors in public administration, the current government organization remains unclear. Transitional authorities, once the security situation improves, need to think about the best strategy for public administration reform. Public institutions must be committed to inclusion and leverage on champions who play a role in promoting dialogue and inclusion.

Authorities should also focus on capacity building, on a comprehensive review and reform of Gaddafi era civil service legislation, and on placing greater emphasis on evaluation, monitoring, and accountability, for which tools need to be developed. There is a dire need to strengthen civil society as a prerequisite for having a much needed vibrant and active citizen-centered society and government with efficient local governance. As comparative studies indicate, such changes and developments are important measures for transforming a corrupt, inefficient, and command-and-control bureaucracy into an efficient, neutral, and apolitical civil service (Lust et al., 2015).

The UN released in March 2013 its Lessons Learnt Review on the UN's role in supporting core government functions in the aftermath of conflict, emphasizing the importance of state-building. The report identified core government tasks in post-conflict contexts and highlighted the need for core government structures to accomplish them. Therefore, the focus on functions rather than state-building has not led to any success in the Libyan case despite the adoption of the entire UN system, including UNSMIL, of this approach. Without institutions, the function-based approach, as current reality attests, has not been worthwhile or constructive. Because of the country's history, marked by a continuous weakness in state-building and the role played by Gaddafi in hindering its development for four decades and given the crisis that followed the downfall of his regime which has further weakened the state, any plan or government that ignores these facts will enter into an uncalculated risk-taking process.

Given the harsh realities of the post-2011 conflict, weak governments replaced the state and acted in a manner that reflected a bias against major sectors of society and existing state institutions. Therefore, with a fragile governance system "working" in a context dominated by militias, nepotism, tribalism, and lack of effective and exclusionary political process, Libya went even further down institutional failures. Therefore, it is paramount that the state-building process moves ahead and right away so that Libya may have a unified government that could regain trust and help regain and re-establish legitimacy to the state.

Notes

1 Substantially revised and updated from Youssef Mohammad Sawani (2018). Public administration in Libya: Continuity and change. *International Journal of Public Administration*, 41(10), 807–819. Reprinted by permission of the publisher Taylor & Francis Ltd., http://www.tandfonline.com
2 Issa Tuwegiar, ex-minister of planning in 2012, telephone interview, July 12, 2016.
3 The Declaration text can be accessed at https://www.constituteproject.org/constitution/Libya_2011.pdf
4 See http://www.libya-analysis.com/ for frequent reports on the current situation.
5 Faraj Sayah, ex-minister for capacity building, telephone interview, July 30, 2016.
6 Faraj Sayah, ex-minister for capacity building, telephone interview, July 30, 2016.
7 Local Governance Law, https://security-legislation.ly/node/31807
8 The latest draft constitution is available at https://www.temehu.com/CDA/final-libyan-draft-constitution-29-july-2017.pdf
9 Faraj Sayah, ex-minister for capacity building, telephone interview, July 30, 2016.
10 Faraj Sayah, ex-minister for capacity building, telephone interview, July 30, 2016.
11 See http://www.wonderslist.com/world-10-most-corrupt-countries/
12 Transparency International, National Integrity System Assessments Libya 2014, http://files.transparency.org/content/download/1972/12900/file/2014_NIS_Libya_ENG.pdf
13 2017 Draft Constitution, https://www.temehu.com/CDA/final-libyan-draft-constitution-29-july-2017.pdf
14 Commission of Civil Society in Libya, Annual Report, https://bit.ly/2Miyy1B
15 2017 Draft Constitution, https://www.temehu.com/CDA/final-libyan-draft-constitution-29-july-2017.pdf
16 https://data.worldbank.org/indicator/SL.TLF.TOTL.FE.ZS?locations=LY
17 Statistics are available from the World bank and ILO at https://data.worldbank.org/indicator/SL.TLF.ACTI.MA.ZS?locations=LY
18 The Inter-Parliamentary Union, Women in National Parliaments, http://archive.ipu.org/wmn-e/classif.htm
19 Commission of Civil Society in Libya, Annual Report, https://bit.ly/2Miyy1B
20 See http://workspace.unpan.org/sites/internet/Documents/UNPAN048745.pdf (in Arabic).
21 https://www.libyaherald.com/2017/09/01/op-ed-an-uncertain-future-for-libyan-local-governance/

References

African Capacity Building Foundation (ACBF). (2004). *Reconstruction and capacity building in post-conflict countries in Africa: A summary of lessons of experience from Mozambique, Rwanda, Sierra Leone & Uganda* (Occasional Papers No. 3). ACBF. Retrieved November 20, 2019, https://www.africaportal.org/documents/17212/OP_3.pdf

Al-Hadad, N. F. (2015). *Working women and their rights in the workplace: International human rights and its impact on Libyan law*. Routledge.

Al-Kilani, M., & Kobziev, V. (2015). Study of implementing e-government in Libya using technology–organization–environment (TOE) model. *Journal of Environmental Science, Computer Science and Engineering & Technology*, 4(4), 816–826.

Asogwa, B. E. (2011). The state of e-government readiness in Africa: A comparative web assessment of selected African countries. *Journal of Internet and Information Systems*, 2(3), 43–57.

Basu, S. (2004). E-government and developing countries: An overview. *International Review of Law Computers & Technology*, *18*(1), 109–132. http://workspace.unpan.org/sites/Internet/Documents/UNPAN93468.Pdf

Bertelsmann Stiftung (BTI). (2016). *Libya country report*. Bertelsmann Stiftung. https://www.bti-project.org/fileadmin/files/BTI/Downloads/Reports/2016/pdf/BTI_2016_Libya.pdf

Böckenförde, M., & Megerisi, T. (2016). *Decentralization in Libya*. Democracy Reporting International. http://democracy-reporting.org/newdri/wp-content/uploads/2016/03/dri-ly-rpt_en_decentralisation_in_libya.pdf

Centre for Administrative Innovation in the Euro-Mediterranean Region (CAIMED). (1990). *Administrative reform in the Mediterranean region: Comparative summary*. CAIMED. http://unpan1.un.org/intradoc/groups/public/documents/caimed/unpan019395.pdf

Clausen, M.-L.. (2016). *State-building in fragile states: Strategies of embedment* [PhD thesis]. Retrieved October 24, 2019, http://politica.dk/fileadmin/politica/Dokumenter/ph.d.-afhandlinger/maria-louise_clausen.pdf

Crisis Group. (2011, June 6). https://www.crisisgroup.org. Retrieved August 14, 2018, from https://www.crisisgroup.org/middle-east-north-africa/north-africa/libya/popular-protest-north-africa-and-middle-east-v-making-sense-libya

Democracy Reporting International. (2013). *Decentralization in Libya*. Retrieved March 6, 2018, from https://democracy-reporting.org/dri_publications/report-decentralisation-in-libya/

El-Fathal, O., Palmer, M., & Chackerian, R. (Eds.). (1977). *Political development and bureaucracy in Libya*. Lexington.

Elmagbri, M., & Cohen, J. (2017). Op-Ed: An uncertain future for Libyan local governance. *Libya Herald*. Retrieved February 11, 2018, from https://www.libyaherald.com/2017/09/01/op-ed-an-uncertain-future-for-libyan-local-governance/

Evans, M., & Barakat, S. (2015). *Defining the challenge, making the change: A study of public administration reform in Arab transitions*. UNDP. http://www.undp-aciac.org/publications/ac/2015/f_UNDP_PAR-TransitionPA.pdf

Forti, Y., Bechkoum, K., Turner, S., & Ajit, S. (2014). The adoption of e-government in Arab countries: The case of Libya. In A. Ionas (Ed.), *Proceedings of the 14th European conference on e-government: ECEG 2014* (pp. 319–327). Academic Conferences and Publishing International.

Gan Integrity Report. (2019). Retrieved March 8, 2020, from https://www.ganintegrity.com/portal/country-profiles/libya/

Halm, U. (2013). Libya in transition: The fragile and insecure relation between the local, the national and the regional. In L. R. Anderson (Ed.), *How the local matters: Democratization in Libya, Pakistan, Yemen and Palestine (DIIS report 2013:01)* (pp. 26–45). Danish Institute for International Studies.

Jurasz, O. (2013). Women of the revolution: The future of women's rights in post-Gaddafi Libya. In C. Panara & G. Wilson (Eds.), *The Arab spring: New patterns for democracy and international law* (pp. 123–144). Martinus Nijhoff.

Karaim, N. A., & Inal, Y. (2019). Usability and accessibility evaluation of Libyan government websites. *Universal Access in the Information Society*, *18*, 207–216. https://doi.org/10.1007/s10209-017-0575-3

Langhi, Z. (2013a). *Women in public life after the revolution–A participatory experience in Libya–Women's battle for the elections*. Right to Nonviolence. Retrieved March 8, from http://www.righttononviolence.org/wp-content/uploads/2013/05/20130308_Langhi_LWPP_Electoral-Law.pdf

Langhi, Z. (2013b). Gender and state-building in Libya: Towards a politics of inclusion. *Journal of North African Studies*, *19*(2), 200–210. https://doi.org/10.1080/13629387.2014.881736

Libyan Audit Bureau. (2015). Report 2015. Official, Bureau, Libyan Audit, Tripoli: Libyan Audit Bureau. Retrieved May 12, 2017, from https://bit.ly/2KRPvdq

Libyan Audit Bureau. (2017). Report 2017. Official, Bureau, Libyan Audit, Tripoli: Libyan Audit Bureau. http://audit.gov.ly/home/pdf/LABR-2017.pdf

Libyan Organization of Policies & Strategies. (2016, March 8). http://loopsresearch.org/ Retrieved April 10, 2018, from http://loopsresearch.org/media/images/photofewkt1kfra.pdf

Lust, E., Rohne, R., & Wichmann, J. (2015). *The political economy of public administration: A study of the Arab transitions*. UN Development Program. http://voluntasadvisory.com/wp-content/uploads/2015/12/UNDP_JMW_PAR_PoliticalEconomy.pdf

Macaraniag, L. (2019). *10 facts about corruption in Libya*. https://borgenproject.org/10-facts-about-corruption-in-libya/

Mahmoud, A. S. (2006). *The development of Libyan women movement in Libyan society: From empowerment to activation* (A documenting study) (in Arabic). The Libya Human and Political Development Forum. Retrieved July 19, 2016, from http://www.mafhoum.com/press9/281S30.htm

Mattes, H. (2008). Formal and informal authority in Libya since 1969. In D. Vandewalle (Ed.), *Libya since 1969: Qadhafi's revolution revisited* (pp. 55–81). Palgrave Macmillan.

Metz, H. C. (Ed.). (1987). *Libya: A country study* (4th ed.). Library of Congress.

Mneinah, A. I. (2013). A reading into law (59) for local administration system. In K. Mohamed & A. Bahroun (Eds.), *Administrative organization in Libya* (pp. 75–86). Centre for Political, Economic and Social Research.

Mogherbi, M. Z. (1995). *Civil society and democratization in Libya* (in Arabic). Ibn Khaldoun Center for Development Studies.

Mohamed, A. H. (2017). *E-government as a tool for stability and socio-economic development in post-conflict Libya*. https://core.ac.uk/download/pdf/231827561.pdf

Obeidi, A. (2001). *Political culture in Libya*. Curzon.

Pack, J., & Barak Barfi, B. (2012). *In war's wake: The struggle for post-Gadhafi Libya* (Policy focus #118). The Washington Institute for Near East Policy. https://www.temehu.com/NTC/the-struggle-for-post-gaddafi-libya.pdf

Pickard, D. (2013). *Decentralization in Libya*. Atlantic Council. http://www.atlanticcouncil.org/blogs/menasource/decentralization-in-libya

Sawani, Y. (2012). Post-Qadhafi Libya: Interactive dynamics and the political future. *Contemporary Arab Affairs*, *5*(1), 1–26. https://doi.org/10.1080/17550912.2012.650007

Sawani, Y. (2013). *Revolution and challenges of state-building* (in Arabic). Centre for Arab Unity Studies.

Sawani, Y., & Pack, J. (2013). Libyan constitutionality and sovereignty post-Qadhafi: The Islamist, regionalist, and Amazigh challenges. *Journal of North African Studies*, *18*(4), 523–543. https://doi.org/10.1080/13629387.2013.838056

Shalgam, A. (2012). *Persons around Gaddafi*. Ferjani and Madarek Publishers.

Spellman-Poots, K. (2011). Women in New Libya: Challenges ahead. *Open Democracy*. https://www.opendemocracy.net/5050/kathryn-spellman-poots/women-in-new-libya-challenges-ahead

Stephen, C. (2016). Libya's draft constitution—Overview. *Libya Herald*, Retrieved July 21, from https://www.libyaherald.com/2016/07/21/libyas-draft-constitution-overview/

Sweisi, N. (2010). *E-government services an exploration of the main factors that contribute to successful implementation in Libya*. [PhD thesis, School of Computing, and University of Portsmouth]. http://eprints.port.ac.uk/1667/1/thesis-15-09-2010-2007.pdf

[The] Libya Observer. (2019, March 19). Remarks by UNSGSR Ghassan Salame. https://www.libyaobserver.ly/news/un-envoy-says-10-countries-are-intervening-libya-and-arms-supply-continues-despite-embargo

Trading Economics. (2021). https://tradingeconomics.com/libya/corruption-rank

Transparency International. (2018). *Corruption Perceptions Index 2017*. Retrieved August 8, 2018, from https://www.transparency.org/country/LBY

Transparency International. (2014). *Conflicts of interest in public sector recruitments in Libya* [Working paper]. Retrieved August 8, 2018, from https://www.transparency.org/files/content/publication/Conflicts_of_Interest_in_Public_Sector_Recruitments_in_Libya_Jan15_Workking_Paper.pdf

Transparency International. (2015). *Conflicts of interest in public sector recruitment in Libya* [Working paper]. https://www.transparency.org/files/content/publication/Conflicts_of_Interest_in_Public_Sector_Recruitments_in_Libya_Jan15_Workking_Paper.pdf

UNDP. (2015). *Rapid diagnostic on the situation of local governance and local development in Libya*. https://www.undp.org/content/dam/libya/docs/UNDP%20Libya%20Rapid%20Diagnostic%20of%20Local%20Governance%20-%20Synthesis%20Report%20(Final%20Version).pdf

United Nations Department of Economic and Social Affairs (UNDESA). (2004a). *Libyan Arab Jamahiriya public administration*. Country profile 2004. UNDESA. http://unpan1.un.org/intradoc/groups/public/documents/UN/UNPAN023273.pdf

United Nations Department of Economics and Social Affairs (UNDESA). (2004b). *Global e-government readiness report 2004: Toward access for opportunity*. UNDESA. https://publicadministration.un.org/egovkb/portals/egovkb/Documents/un/2004-Survey/Complete-Survey.pdf

United Nations Department of Economics and Social Affairs (UNDESA). (2004c). *Global e-government report 2005 from e-government to e-inclusion*. UNDESA. https://publicadministration.un.org/egovkb/Portals/egovkb/Documents/un/2005-Survey/Complete-survey.pdf

United Nations Department of Economics and Social Affairs (UNDESA). (2004d). *United Nations e-government survey 2008 from e-government to connected governance*. UNDESA. https://publicadministration.un.org/egovkb/portals/egovkb/documents/un/2008-survey/unpan028607.pdf

United Nations Department of Economics and Social Affairs (UNDESA). (2010). *United Nations e-government survey: Leveraging e-government at a time of financial and eco-nomic crisis*. UNDESA. https://publicadministration.un.org/egovkb/portals/egovkb/documents/un/2010-survey/complete-survey.pdf

United Nations Development Program (UNDP). (2014). *Country: Libya program inception plan*. UNDP. http://www.ly.undp.org/content/dam/libya/docs/Resilience%20Recovery%20.pdf

United Nations Economic and Social Commission for Western Asia (UNESCWA). (2013). *Institutional development and transition decentralization in the course of political transformation*. UNESCWA.

United Nations, Department of Economics and Social Affairs (UNDESA). (2014). *United Nations e-government survey: E-government for the future we want.* UNDESA. https://publicadministration.un.org/egovkb/portals/egovkb/documents/un/2014-survey/e-gov_complete_survey-2014.pdf

Wijaya, A. F., & Shariha, J. E. M. (2016). Comparison between corruption in Libya during Gaddafi's rule and corruption in Libya post-Gaddafi. *IOSR Journal of Business and Management, 18*(5), 19–25. http://www.iosrjournals.org/iosr-jbm/papers/Vol18-issue5/Version-3/D1805031925.pdf

World Bank & International Monetary Fund (World Bank & IMF). (2013). *Libya public financial management reform priorities in the new environment.* IMF. https://www.imf.org/external/pubs/ft/scr/2013/cr1336.pdf

INDEX

Note: Page references in *italics* denote figures, in **bold** tables and with "n" endnotes.

Abboud, Ibrahim 123
Aberbach, J. D. 68
accountability: Libya 159–160; Morocco 87, 89, 95–96; public financial 119; in public-sector projects 11; zero 163
administrative freedom 90
administrative performance (Jordan) 73–74
administrative reform failure: Jordan 69–73; nepotism 72–73; reforming public budgeting 69–72
advanced regionalization 89–91
African Development Bank 88, 92, 110
Afro-Arab Cooperation 125
agile government 6
Alaouite dynasty 85
"al-Aylula" policies 127
Al Bashir, Omar 129–130
Al-Hadad, N. F. 161
Al-Kilani, M. 166
Al Maktoum, Sheikh Mohammed Bin Rashed 8, 10, 13
AlSayegh, A. 15
Antoun, R. 36, 53
Arab Anti-Corruption and Integrity Network 53
Arab NGO Network for Development (ANND) 40
Arab Spring 62

Arab uprisings 83, 89
Association of Dutch Municipalities (VNG) 156

Bahçeli, Devlet 21
Banking Control Commission (Lebanon) 40
Bank of Lebanon 40
Barak Barfi, B. 142
Bashir, I. E. 44, 45–46
Basu, S. 166
Bertelsmann Transformation Index (BTI) 97
bifurcated system 83
Bilbao, J. R. 87
Biygautane, M. 92
Blacksburg Manifesto 31
Böckenförde, M. 167
Bou Jaoude, R. 52
"The Breadbasket Strategy" 125
Bretton Wood institutions 97
Brinkerhoff, D. W. 85, 99
Buckley, R. P. 100
budget/budgeting: praxis in Lebanon 47–48; reforms and developments in Lebanon 49
Budget Department (Jordan) 71–72

Index

bureaucracy 27; public, in Turkey 20; Republic of Lebanon 36, 44, 52; Weberian model of bureaucracy 3, 4
Bureau of Accounting and Audit (Jordan) 71–72

capitalism 31, 98
Carroll, Katherine 66
Carthage agreement 112
Carthage plan 120
Central Intelligence Agency 35
centralization 31, 148; of decision-making 89; excessive 34, 37; of public management 73
Chamber of Deputies 41, 47–48
Chinese CNPC 128
Christensen, T. 68
citizen-centric strategies: managerial reforms 10–11; UAE 10–11
civic culture, Jordan 66
civil service: continuity despite change 152; gender and diversity 46–47; legal basis 44; Libya 152; recruitment and promotion 45–46; remuneration 46; Republic of Lebanon 44–47; structure and processes 44–45; training 46
Civil Service Board (Lebanon) 44, 45
Civil Service Bureau (Jordan) 72–73, 76
civil service employment 128, 161
civil society 106, 111, 118, 127, 156; Gaddafi on 160; Libya 160–161; and Libyan women 164
civil society organizations (CSOs) 160–161
civil society reforms and developments: civil service (Lebanon) 47; NGOs (Lebanon) 39
collaborative governance 11
confessionalism 35
Constitution Drafting Authority (CDA) 149
corruption: in Jordan 66, 74–75; in Lebanon 52; Libya 157–159; pervasive 94; state-led 129–131; systemic 95
Corruption Perceptions Index 158
COVID-19 pandemic 31, 132
crony capitalism 98

Daadaoui, M. 86
DAC OECD evaluation criteria 116
Daoud, C. Y. 42

decentralization: and advanced regionalization 89–91; governance model in constitutional draft 149–152; in Libya 135–138, 149–152; in the MENA region 90; in Morocco 89–91; in Sudan 127; top-down 138
Demirel, Süleyman 21
democratic transition: economic reforms challenges during 105–120; institutional reforms challenges during 105–120
demographics: Jordan 64; Lebanon 35
Department of Personnel Administration (Lebanon) 45
developing countries: bureaucracies 91; bureaucratic efficiency 4; pervasive corruption 94; public sector reforms 87, 99; socio-economic development 65; Weberian impersonal bureaucracy 4
digital-era governance (DEG) model 5
digital governance: Dubai Data Law 12–13; social media 13; United Arab Emirates 12–13; *see also* governance
digital government model 5
digitalization: changes 5; incentives for 93; of public services 93–94
digital transformation 93–94
diversity: civil service (Lebanon) 46–47; and gender 46–47; of trajectories of reform 5
Doha Agreement 43
dualism 91, 98; institutional 85–86, 90
Dubai Data Law 12–13
Dubai Government Excellence Program (DGEP) 9–10
Dubai Quality Award (DQA) 8
Dubai Quality Group 8
Dubai Roads and Transport Authority (RTA) 11
Dunleavy, P. 5

École Nationale d'Administration (ENA) 46
economic reforms: challenges during democratic transition 105–120; reform project cycle *110*, 110–113; structural 113, 119
economy: dismantling state control over 126–128; neoliberal rentier 128–129
e-government (Lebanon) 50–51; e-participation 50–51; readiness 50; reforms and developments 51
e-government in Libya 165–167

Elamin, N. 129
Electricite du Liban 49
El Gezira and El Managil Scheme Producers Association 131
El Junaid Sugar Producers Authority 131
El Maaraj Peace and Development Organization 130
El Massnaoui, K. 92
El Nour Islamic Complex 130
El Rahad Agricultural Producers Association 131
employment: civil service 45–46, 128, 161; hidden 153; in Lebanon 45; private sector 11; tourism and real estate 114; of women 162, 164
e-participation 50–51
Erdoğan, Recep Tayyip 21–22, 29
ethics: Code of Conduct for Public Servants 52; Lebanon's public administration 51–53; public-sector 35, 157–159; reforms and developments 52–53; transformation 94–96
European Commission 155
European Foundation for Quality Management (EFQM) 9
European sovereign debt crisis 7
European Union (EU) 46, 88, 92, 96, 144; Emergency Trust Fund for Africa 156
evaluation phase, of public policies 118
executive branch, Lebanon 42
exogenous modernization 128
Expertise France (EF) 156

Fadlelmawla, Hasan 130
Falk, Richard 65
Farazmand, A. 7, 67
Federal National Council 6
Fitzgerald, S. M. 100
Flashes of Thought: Inspired by a Dialogue at the Government Summit 2013 (Al Maktoum) 8
foreign direct investment, in United Arab Emirates 7
foreign financial aid 65, 75
Forti, Y. 165, 166
Free Officers Organization 125
French Revolution 100
Fukuyama, F. 100

Gaddafi, Muammar 134; *The Green Book* 136; *Jamahiriya* governance system 135–137
Gaebler, T. 30
Gausse, F. G. 98
gender: civil service (Lebanon) 46–47; and civil society 160; and diversity 46–47; segregation 162; *see also* women
gender equality: and patriarchy 161–165; rights 161; and secularism 161–165; and Sharia 161–165
General National Congress (Libya) 142, 158, 164
Georges-Picot, Francois 62
German Foundation for International Cooperation (GIZ) 151, 156
German Technical Cooperation (GTZ) 69
Ghosn, F. 37
Global Corruption Barometer 95
global financial crisis (2008-2009) 7
global governance 83, 85
globalization: Jordan 66–68; United Arab Emirates 7
Goldsmith, A. A. 85, 99
governance: collaborative 11; in context 85–86; digital 12–13; global 83–85; Libya 152–154; local reality 84–85; and public administration reform in Morocco 83–101; societal 35–36
governance structures (Lebanon): executive branch 42; judicial branch 42–43; legal reforms and developments 43–44; legislative branch 41; municipal government 43; national government 41; regional government 43
Government of National Accord (GNA) 140–141, 144, 147, 152–153
Gözler, K. 22
Greater Nile Petroleum Operating Company (GNPOC) 128
The Green Book 136

Haftar, Khalifa 153
Hariri, Rafik 40
Harnisch, A. 90, 91
Hassan II, King of Morocco 87, 90
Hemeida, Mamoun 131
Hennebert, P. 93
hidden employment 153
Higher Council for Privatization 40–41
Houdret, A. 90, 91

Human Development Index (HDI) 65
human resources: capacity building 154–156; grades/salaries,training 154–156; recruitment 154–156

Idrisid dynasty 85
INA Canada 120
Inal, Y. 166
Indian GNC 128
Industrial Oil Producers Authority 131
information and communication technology (ICT) 5, 12, 50; impact on public service delivery 14
INJAZ (e-information management system) 118
institutional development 74
institutional dualism 85–86, 90
institutional reforms: and democratic transition 105–120; in Tunisia 105–120
Interim Action Program 125
International Criminal Court 129
international financial institutions (IFIs) 108
International Monetary Fund (IMF) 49, 65, 78, 88, 97, 154, 156
International Standard Organization 8
Islam 86
Italian Agency for Development Cooperation (AICS) 156

Jamahiriya governance system 135–137
January 4, 2020 charter for Dubai 11–12
Joffe, G. 85
Jones, C. W. 7
Jordan: administrative reform failure 69–73; changing context of governance 64–68; corruption and civic culture 66; demographic change 64; globalization 66–68; obstacles to reform 73–75; overview 62–64; political system in 63; public administration and development 62–79; socio-economic development 65–66
The Jordan Times 72
judicial branch, Lebanon 42–43
Jurasz, O. 163
Justice and Development Party (Turkey) 21

Karaim, N. A. 166
Khartoum International Airport Company 130
Khoury, A. 37
Kisirwani, M. 52
Kobziev, V. 166
Kraemer, K. 30

Langhi, Z. 163
Law for the Consolidation of Freedom (Libya) 164
Law for the Privatization of the Public Sector (Sudan) 126
Law for the Release of State Control over the Public Sector (Sudan) 126
Law on Abuse of Position or Occupation (Libya) 158
Law on Associations 38, 39
Law on Economic Crimes (Libya) 158
Lebanese Civil War 34, 36, 37
Lebanon War (2006) 40
legislative branch, Lebanon 41
Libya: authoritarianism, dynamics of 137–138; civil service 152; Civil Service Act 153; Civil Service Commission (CSC) 153; civil society 160–161; constitution drafting process 149; corruption 157–159; decentralization governance model 149–152; e-government in Libya 165–167; future governance system 149; gender equality 161–165; General National Congress 142, 158, 164; good governance 152–154; Government of National Accord (GNA) 140; hidden employment 153; human resources 154–156; Law for the Consolidation of Freedom 164; Law on Abuse of Position or Occupation 158; Law on Economic Crimes 158; local councils 141–144; local governance 137–138; Local Governance Law 141–142; local governance (administration) law no. 54/2012 144–147; National Administrative Institute 155; National Transitional Council (NTC) 140; overview 134–135; patriarchy 161–165; post-Gaddafi public administration 139–140; public administration 135–147, 167–169; public budgeting and finance 156–157; public-sector ethics and integrity system 157–159;

rebels and administrators 141–144; secularism 161–165; Sharia 161–165; structures of local government 138–139; transitional national governance system 140–141; transition amidst continuous conflict 147–148; transparency and accountability 159–160
"Libya Local Governance and Stabilization program" 156
Libyan Foreign Bank 158
Libyan Local Government Forum 151
Libyan National Army (LNA) 141
Libyan Political Agreement (LPA) 140–141
Libyan Political Dialogue Forum (LPDF) 141

Maana, Salah 130
Maghraoui, A. M. 97, 99
Makhzen 86, 90–91
Malaysian Petronas 128
managerial reforms: citizen-centric strategies 10–11; collaborative governance 11; fourth-generation model of government excellence 9–10, *10*; January 4, 2020 charter for Dubai 11–12; public-private partnerships 11; service quality and excellence 8–9; United Arab Emirates 8–12
managerial transformation 91–93
Mansour, M. W. 42
marketization, and Lebanon 39–40
market reforms and developments 40–41
"Maroc Digital 2020" 94
Maronite Christian 42
Megerisi, T. 167
Middle East and North Africa (MENA) region 87, 92
Minister of Finance (Jordan) 70–71
Ministry of Finance (Lebanon) 39, 49
Ministry of Possibilities (UAE) 11
Ministry of Telecommunication (Lebanon) 48
modernization: exogenous 128; and good governance 85; public administration reforms 87–89; public sector 88
Mogherbi, M. Z. 160
Mohamed VI, King of Morocco 87
Mohammed Bin Rashid Government Excellence Award 9
Mohammed Bin Salman 129

Morachiella, E. 52
moralization of public administration 94–96
Moroccan Court of Accounts (MCA) 95
Morocco: advanced regionalization 89–91; Central Instance for Corruption Prevention 95; decentralization 89–91; Development Policy Loans 97; digitalization of public services 93–94; digital transformation 93–94; Economic and Social Reform Program 87; ethical transformation 94–96; governance 84–85; governance in context 85–86; independence 86; managerial transformation 91–93; moralization of public administration 94–96; National Authority for Integrity and the Prevention and Fighting of Corruption 95; National Plan for the Reform of the Administration 89; organizational transformation 89–91; public administration reforms 87–89; rationalization of public administration 91–93; rhetoric and reality 96–99
Mudawana 86
Muhafazah 43
Muhafiz 43
Municipal Act of 1977 43
municipal government, Lebanon 43
Muslim Brotherhood 164

National Anti-Corruption Commission (Libya) 158–159
National Congress Party (Sudan) 129–130
National Information System (NATIS) 165
Nationalist Movement Party (MHP) 21
National Pension and Social Security Fund (*Caisse Nationale de Retraite et de Prévoyance Sociale*, CNRPS) 115
National School of Administration (Lebanon) 46
needs-based holism 5
neo-liberal market ideology 3
neoliberal rentier economy 128–129
nepotism 72–73
new public management (NPM) 3, 4–5, 91–92, 97, 109

Nimery, Jaafar 123–124
nongovernmental organizations (NGOs): domestic and international 38; Lebanon 38

Office of the Minister of State for Administrative Reform (OMSAR) 36, 37, 46–47, 50–51, 54
Official Gazette 41
Ombudsman Law 38–39
organizational transformation 89–91
Organization for Economic Co-operation and Development (OECD) 84, 88, 96, 99
Organization of the Petroleum Exporting Countries (OPEC) 125
Osborne, D. 30
Ottoman Empire 38
Özal, Turgut 21

Pack, J. 142
Pal, L. A. 84
Pan-Arab Strategy 125
Pan-Islamic Solidarity 125
Parliamentary Bureau 41
patriarchy 161–165
Perry, J. 30
pervasive corruption 94
positive deviance theory 5
predator economics 65
presidency government system (PGS) 22
Presidential Decree Number 3 28
Presidential Decree Number 13 28
prismatic society 86
privatization: Lebanon 39–40; program in Sudan 126–128
problem-driven iterative adaptation (PDIA) 5
Prophet Mohamed 85
Public Accounting Law of 1963 49
public administration reforms 148; concepts and models 4–6; in Libya 148; and modernization 87–89; in Morocco 83–101; in non-Western world 3; positive deviance theory 5; results and policy implications 13–15; theory and practice of 3–16; in United Arab Emirates (UAE) 8–16
public budgeting: budgeting praxis 47–48; public finance 48–49; reform failure in Jordan 69–72; Republic of Lebanon 47–49; *see also* budget/budgeting
public budgeting and finance 156–157
public bureaucracy 4; in Turkey 20; *see also* bureaucracy
public employee alienation 28
public finance (Lebanon) 48–49
public management 62, 77; centralization of 73; performance-based 76; professionalizing 67, 77
Public Management: Public and Private Perspectives (Perry and Kraemer) 30
public-private partnerships (PPPs): Lebanon 40–41; managerial reforms 11
public sector: accountability 38; ethics 35; ethics and integrity system 157–159; January 4, 2020 charter for Dubai 11; reforms, developing countries 87, 99; Republic of Lebanon 36–37; vacancies 45; *see also* public administration reforms
public services: digitalization of 93–94; improvement of 85, 88

Qada' 43, 44
Qa'immaquam 43
Quality Management System (QMS) 8

Rached, Cynthia Abi 40
Rahman, M. H. 10
rationalization of public administration 91–93
reality and rhetoric 96–99
"Recovery, Stability and Socio-economic Development of Libya program" 156
recruitment *see* employment
reforms *see specific reforms*
regional government, Lebanon 43
regionalization, advanced 89–91
regulatory structures, Lebanon 40
reintegration, DEG model 5
Reinventing Government: How the Entrepreneurial Spirit Is Transforming the Public Sector (Osborne and Gaebler) 30
remuneration: civil service (Lebanon) 46; Lebanese government 46
Republic of Lebanon: bureaucratic system 36; civil service 44–47; e-government 50–51; ethics in public administration 51–53; governance structures 41–44; marketplace 39–41;

public administration in 34–54; public budgeting 47–49; public-sector size and scope 36–37; Public Sector Staff Regulations 51; societal governance 35–36; socio-economic background 35; state and civil society 38–39
rhetoric and reality 96–99
Riggs, F. W. 86
Robinson, M. 91, 99
Rosenau, J. N. 83

Safa, O. 38
Salame, Ghassan 159
Salem, F. 12–13
Sarker, A. E. 10
secularism 161–165
shabiyyat 137–138
Sharia 161–165
Sheikh Khalifa Excellence Award (SKEA) 9
Shura councils 135, 141–143
Skhirat Agreement 152
social media: digital governance and UAE 13; and Gaddafi regime 165; and NGOs 39; unregulated 77
social security reform: example of 115–116; Tunisia 115–116
societal governance: and public administration 35–36; Republic of Lebanon 35–36
socio-economic dynamics: Jordan 65–66; United Arab Emirates 6–7
solution- and leaderdriven change (SLDC) 5
Spellman-Poots, K. 163
state: and civil society 38–39; -led corruption 129–131; and marketplace 39–41
state-owned enterprises (SOEs) 107, 127
"State Personnel Presidency" (SPP) case 29
structural adjustment programs 65
Sudan: crisis of contemporary Sudan 131–132; erosion of public administration in 123–132; historical notes on unmaking of 124–126; Law for the Privatization of the Public Sector 126; Law for the Release of State Control over the Public Sector 126; neoliberal rentier economy 128–129; privatization program (2007) 126–128; state control over economy 126–128; state-led corruption 129–131
Sudan Airports Holding Company 130
Sudan Anti-Corruption Committee 131
Sudanese Workers' Trade Union Federation 127
Sudapet 128
Sykes, Sir Mark 62
Sykes-Picot Agreement 62–63
Syrian Civil War 35
systemic corruption 95

"The Technical Committee for the Release of Public Sector Entities" (TCRPSE) 126
Telecommunications Law 40
Teti, A. 98
Third World debt crisis (1980) 65
transformation: digital 93–94; ethical 94–96; managerial 91–93; organizational 89–91
Transitional Constitutional Declaration 140, 141–142
transparency: of government decisions 78; importance of promoting 120; Libya 159–160; and OMSAR 54
Transparency International 52, 154, 158; Corruption Perceptions Index 95
Tunisia: action plan, developing 120; coordinating reforms 114; coordination process 119–120; executive orders issuance 112–113; governmental leadership and reforms 113–114; government's agenda 112; lack of consensus 112; literature review 108–110; National Capacity Development Program 119; national review and evaluation systems 116–120, *117*; political and economic context 107–108; reform project cycle *110*, 110–113; reform vision 119; sequencing reform priorities 114–115; social security reform 115–116; weak technical capabilities of ministry 111–112
Turkey: amendment of constitution 20–26; parliamentary system 21; presidency government system (PGS) 22; public bureaucracy in 20
Turkey Wealth Fund 25
Turkish Grand Assembly 24, 26
Turkish Presidency: attached institutions of *25*; organizational layout of *23*
Turkish public administration 20–31; and amendment of constitution 20–26,

32n3; analyzing reconstruction 29–31; overload problem 27–28; overview 20; potential complications for 27–29; task overlapping 28; transformation 20–26; work alienation 28–29

Union Oasis Project 11

United Arab Emirates (UAE): context of government in 6–7; digital governance 12–13; Ease of Doing Business global rank 13–14; Federal National Council 6; foreign direct investment 7; globalization 7; governance indicators in **14**; managerial reforms 8–12; public administration reforms in 8–16; socio-economic dynamics 6–7; Supreme Council of Rulers 6

United Nations (UN) 37; Development Program 46; International Children's Emergency Fund 47; Report on Violence Against Women 162; Security Council 140

United Nations Department of Economic and Social Affairs (UNDESA) 50

United Nations Development Program (UNDP) 65, 88, 96, 146–147, 154, 156, 166

United Nations Economic and Social Commission for West Asia (UNESCWA) 136, 167

United Nations Educational, Scientific and Cultural Organization (UNESCO) 88

United Nations Support Mission Libya (UNSMIL) (Skhirat Agreement) 140, 141, 169

United States Agency for International Development (USAID) 151, 156

UN Women 88

Voluntary Retirement Program (VRP) 92

Weberian model of bureaucracy 3, 4
Wilson, Woodrow 34
women: and civil society 164; employment of 162, 164; Jordan municipal councils 63; Lebanese labor work force 47; Lebanon electoral reform 44; in Libya 161–165
work alienation 28–29
World Bank 13, 35, 46, 49, 65, 84, 87, 92, 96–97, 110, 151, 154, 156, 163; Country Partnership Framework (CPF) 88; Country Partnership Strategy for Morocco 89
World Development Report 109

Yom, S. L. 98

Zaki, L. 90

Printed in the United States
by Baker & Taylor Publisher Services